WHAT IS ART?

WHAT IS RELIGION?

INTRODUCTION

In answer to the question, "What is Art?" Count Tolstoï analyzes and tests the various definitions of Art given by other writers. He shows up with merciless severity what he considers the fallacy in the popular delusion that the fetish of Art pardons bestiality, obscenity, and whatever conduces to stimulating the passions. The work is strongly controversial, and attacks unsparingly many current conceptions, as, for instance, that "Art is the manifestation of some mysterious idea of God," or "the expression of man's emotions by external signs," or the production of pleasing objects.

Tolstoï believes that Art has a loftier function. He proceeds elaborately to argue in favor of a universal activity, a union among men so that they may have the same noble feelings, and may progress together toward individual and general well-being. "Art for art's sake" is meaningless to him.

It is interesting to notice that the most original and independent of the French critics has recently taken practically the same ground in a lecture, in which he asserts that it is the critic's business to test Art and Literature, and that Art has a most intimate relation with morality.

The discussion of "What is Religion?" will be found to bear more than a literary or ethical interest, when the late disagreement between Tolstoï and the Russian Church is recalled to mind. Here he sets forth the tenets of his own broad creed. He defines Religion as "the establishment by man of such a relation to the Infinite Life around him, as, while connecting his life with this Infinitude and directing his conduct, is also in agreement with his reason and with human knowledge."

INTRODUCTION

Upon this basis of a religion founded upon reason he stands flatly, although such position has often been found shifting sands. "Reason was termed the source of error," he says again, "and the Gospel was interpreted not as common sense demands, but as those who composed the Church desired." Nevertheless, in view of his present beliefs, which question many of the fundamental truths of the Bible, one does not see how his Church could avoid refusing him the sacrament; for he follows Voltaire at more than one point, while yet adhering to the "true religion, that is, a true relation to the source of all, — God."

Of scarcely less import, though a much shorter article, is the succeeding paper "On Religious Tolerance." Here he sounds the note of the prophet — and the iconoclast. Then come a score of essays and letters, not one of which is without its interest. Nearly all of them are of theological trend. We cannot give the bent of his mind better than by quoting once more from the author, where he takes issue with Coleridge and says: "I began by loving my Orthodox faith more than my peace; then I loved Christianity more than my Church; and now I love the Truth more than anything in the world. And until now the Truth coincides for me with Christianity as I understand it; and I profess this Christianity, and in that measure in which I do profess it I peacefully and joyously live and peacefully and joyously am approaching death."

The various translations are in each case authorized. Mr. Aylmer Maude, translator of "What is Art?" has had the benefit of the author's suggestions in regard to certain points. The other essays were translated by V. Tchertkoff and A. C. Fifield.

CONTENTS

WHAT IS ART?

CHAPTER I

Time and labor spent on art — Lives stunted in its service — Morality sacrificed to and anger justified by art — The rehearsal of an opera described

CHAPTER II

Does art compensate for so much evil ? — What is art ? — Confusion of opinions — Is it " that which produces beauty " ? — The word "beauty" in Russian — Chaos in æsthetics

CHAPTER III

Summary of various æsthetic theories and definitions, from Baumgarten to to-day

CHAPTER IV

Definitions of art founded on beauty — Taste not definable — A clear definition needed to enable us to recognize works of art

CHAPTER V

Definitions not founded on beauty — Tolstoï's definition — The extent and necessity of art — How people in the past have distinguished good from bad in art

CONTENTS

CONTENTS

CONTENTS

WHAT IS RELIGION?

WHAT IS ART?

TRANSLATOR'S PREFACE

THE fundamental thought expressed in this book leads inevitably to conclusions so new, so unexpected, and so contrary to what is usually maintained in literary and artistic circles, that although it is clearly and emphatically expressed (and this I hope has not been lost in translation), most readers who wish to possess themselves of it will have to read the work carefully, and to digest it slowly.

Especially the introductory Chapters II., III., IV., and V., need careful perusal by any who, having adopted one or other of the current theories on beauty and art, may find it difficult to abandon a preconceived view, and to clear their minds for a fair appreciation of what is new to them.

The first four chapters raise the problem, and tell us briefly what has been said by previous writers. Chapter III. gives (in highly condensed form) the substance of the teaching of some sixty philosophers on this subject, and since many of them were extremely confused, the chapter cannot, in the nature of things, be easy reading.

I should like to remark, in passing, that though Tolstoï in this chapter (presumably for convenience of verification) refers chiefly to the compilations of Schasler, Kralik, and Knight, he has gone behind these authorities to the primary sources. To give a single instance: in the paragraph on Darwin, the foot-note refers us to Knight, but the remark that the origin of the art of music may be traced back to the call of the males to the females in the animal world will be found in Darwin, but will not be found in Knight.

In Chapter V. we come to Tolstoï's definition of art,

which definition should be kept well in mind while read- ' ing the rest of the book.

No doubt most of those to whom it is an end in itself, who live by it, or make it their chief occupation, will read this book (or leave it unread) and go on in their former way, much as Pharaoh, of old, hardened his heart, and did not sympathize with what Moses had to say on the labor question. But for those of us who have felt that art is too valuable a matter to be lost out of our lives, and who, in their quest for social justice, have met the reproach that they were sacrificing the pleasures and advantages of art, this book is of inestimable value, in that it solves a perplexed question of far-reaching importance to practical life.

To this class of readers neither the masterly elucidation of the former theories contained in the opening chapters, nor the explanation of how it has come about that such great importance is attached to the activity we call art (Chapters VI. and VII.), nor the explanation and illustrations of the perversion that art has undergone, nor even the elucidation of the terrible evils this perversion is producing (XVII.), will equal in significance the remaining chapters of the book. These show us what to look for in art, how to distinguish it from counterfeits (XV., XVI., and XVIII.), treat of the true art of the future (XIX.), and explain how science and art are linked together in man's life, are directed by his perception of the meaning of life, and inevitably react on all he thinks and feels.

THE AUTHOR'S PREFACE

THIS book of mine, "What is Art?" appears now for the first time in its true form. More than one edition has already been issued in Russia, but in each case it has been so mutilated by the "Censor," that I request all who are interested in my views on art only to judge of them by the work in its present shape. The causes which led to the publication of the book — with my name attached to it — in a mutilated form were the following : In accordance with a decision I arrived at long ago, — not to submit my writings to the "Censorship" (which I consider to be an immoral and irrational institution), but to print them only in the shape in which they were written, — I intended not to attempt to print this work in Russia. However, my good acquaintance, Professor Grote, editor of a Moscow psychological magazine, having heard of the contents of my work, asked me to print it in his magazine, and promised me that he would get the book through the "Censor's" office unmutilated if I would but agree to a few very unimportant alterations, merely toning down certain expressions. I was weak enough to agree to this, and it has resulted in a book appearing under my name, from which not only have some essential thoughts been excluded, but into which the thoughts of other men — even thoughts utterly opposed to my own convictions — have been introduced.

The thing occurred in this way. First, Grote softened my expressions, and in some cases weakened them. For instance, he replaced the words : *always* by *sometimes*, *all* by *some*, *Church* religion by *Roman Catholic* religion, "*Mother of God*" by *Madonna*, *patriotism* by *pseudo-patriotism*, *palaces* by *palatii*,[1] etc., and I did not consider

---

[1] Tolstoï's remarks on Church religion were re-worded so as to seem to relate only to the Western Church, and his disapproval of luxurious life was made to apply, not, say, to Queen Victoria or Nicholas II., but to the Cæsars or the Pharaohs. —TR.

it necessary to protest. But when the book was already in type, the Censor required that whole sentences should be altered, and that instead of what I said about the evil of landed property, a remark should be substituted on the evils of a landless proletariate.[1] I agreed to this also, and to some further alterations. It seemed not worth while to upset the whole affair for the sake of one sentence, and when one alteration had been agreed to it seemed not worth while to protest against a second and a third. So, little by little, expressions crept into the book which altered the sense and attributed things to me that I could not have wished to say. So that by the time the book was printed it had been deprived of some part of its integrity and sincerity. But there was consolation in the thought that the book, even in this form, if it contains something that is good, would be of use to Russian readers whom it would otherwise not have reached. Things, however, turned out otherwise. *Nous comptions sans notre hôte.* After the legal term of four days had already elapsed, the book was seized, and, on instructions received from Petersburg, it was handed over to the " Spiritual Censor." Then Grote declined all further participation in the affair, and the " Spiritual Censor " proceeded to do what he would with the book. The " Spiritual Censorship " is one of the most ignorant, venal, stupid, and despotic institutions in Russia. Books which disagree in any way with the recognized state religion of Russia, if once it gets hold of them, are almost always totally suppressed and burnt; which is what happened to all my religious works when attempts were made to print them in Russia. Probably a similar fate would have overtaken this work also, had not the editors

---

[1] The Russian peasant is usually a member of a village commune, and has therefore a right to a share in the land belonging to the village. Tolstoï disapproves of the order of society which allows less land for the support of a village full of people than is sometimes owned by a single landed proprietor. The " Censor " will not allow disapproval of this state of things to be expressed, but is prepared to admit that the laws and customs, say, of England — where a yet more extreme form of landed property exists, and the men who actually labor on the land usually possess none of it — deserve criticism. — Tr.

of the magazine employed all means to save it. The re
sult of their efforts was that the " Spiritual Censor," a
priest who probably understands art and is interested in
art as much as I understand or am interested in church
services, but who gets a good salary for destroying whatever is likely to displease his superiors, struck out all that
seemed to him to endanger his position, and substituted
his thoughts for mine wherever he considered it necessary to do so. For instance, where I speak of Christ
going to the Cross for the sake of the truth He professed,
the " Censor " substituted a statement that Christ died
for mankind, *i.e.* he attributed to me an assertion of the
dogma of the Redemption, which I consider to be one of
the most untrue and harmful of Church dogmas. After
correcting the book in this way, the " Spiritual Censor "
allowed it to be printed.

To protest in Russia is impossible — no newspaper
would publish such a protest; and to withdraw my book
from the magazine, and place the editor in an awkward
position with the public, was also not possible.

So the matter has remained. A book has appeared
under my name containing thoughts attributed to me
which are not mine.

I was persuaded to give my article to a Russian magazine in order that my thoughts, which may be useful,
should become the possession of Russian readers ; and
the result has been that my name is affixed to a work
from which it might be assumed that I quite arbitrarily
assert things contrary to the general opinion, without
adducing my reasons ; that I only consider false patriotism bad, but patriotism in general a very good feeling ;
that I merely deny the absurdities of the Roman Catholic
Church and disbelieve in the Madonna, but that I believe
in the Orthodox Eastern faith and in the " Mother of
God " ; that I consider all the writings collected in the
Bible to be holy books, and see the chief importance
of Christ's life in the Redemption of mankind by His
death.

I have narrated all this in such detail because it strikingly illustrates the indubitable truth that all compromise

with institutions of which your conscience disapproves,
— compromises which are usually made for the sake of
the general good, — instead of producing the good you
expected, inevitably lead you, not only to acknowledge
the institution you disapprove of, but also to participate
in the evil that institution produces.

I am glad to be able by this statement at least to do
something to correct the error into which I was led by
my compromise.

I have also to mention that besides reinstating the
parts excluded by the Censor from the Russian editions,
other corrections and additions of importance have been
made in this edition.

29th March, 1898.

WHAT IS ART?

CHAPTER I

TAKE up any one of our ordinary newspapers, and you will find a part devoted to the theater and music. In almost every number you will find a description of some art exhibition, or of some particular picture, and you will always find reviews of new works of art that have appeared, of volumes of poems, of short stories, or of novels.

Promptly, and in detail, as soon as it has occurred, an account is published of how such and such an actress or actor played this or that rôle in such and such a drama, comedy, or opera ; and of the merits of the performance, as well as of the contents of the new drama, comedy, or opera, with its defects and merits. With as much care and detail, or even more, we are told how such and such an artist has sung a certain piece, or has played it on the piano or violin, and what were the merits and defects of the piece and of the performance. In every large town there is sure to be at least one, if not more than one, exhibition of new pictures, the merits and defects of which are discussed in the utmost detail by critics and connoisseurs.

New novels and poems, in separate volumes or in the magazines, appear almost every day, and the newspapers consider it their duty to give their readers detailed accounts of these artistic productions.

For the support of art in Russia (where for the education of the people only a hundredth part is spent of what would be required to give every one the opportunity of instruction) the government grants millions of roubles in subsidies to academies, conservatoires, and theaters. In

France twenty million francs are assigned for art, and similar grants are made in Germany and England.

In every large town enormous buildings are erected for museums, academies, conservatoires, dramatic schools, and for performances and concerts. Hundreds of thousands of workmen — carpenters, masons, painters, joiners, paperhangers, tailors, hairdressers, jewelers, molders, type-setters — spend their whole lives in hard labor to satisfy the demands of art, so that hardly any other department of human activity, except the military, consumes so much energy as this.

Not only is enormous labor spent on this activity, but in it, as in war, the very lives of men are sacrificed. Hundreds of thousands of people devote their lives from childhood to learning to twirl their legs rapidly (dancers), or to touch notes and strings very rapidly (musicians), or to draw with paint and represent what they see (artists), or to turn every phrase inside out and find a rhyme to every word. And these people, often very kind and clever, and capable of all sorts of useful labor, grow savage over their specialized and stupefying occupations, and become one-sided and self-complacent specialists, dull to all the serious phenomena of life, and skilful only at rapidly twisting their legs, their tongues, or their fingers.

But even this stunting of human life is not the worst. I remember being once at the rehearsal of one of the most ordinary of the new operas which are produced at all the opera houses of Europe and America.

I arrived when the first act had already commenced. To reach the auditorium I had to pass through the stage entrance. By dark entrances and passages, I was led through the vaults of an enormous building, past immense machines for changing the scenery and for illuminating; and there in the gloom and dust I saw workmen busily engaged. One of these men, pale, haggard, in a dirty blouse, with dirty, work-worn hands and cramped fingers, evidently tired and out of humor, went past me, angrily scolding another man. Ascending by a dark stair, I came out on the boards behind the scenes. Amid

various poles and rings and scattered scenery, decorations and curtains, stood and moved dozens, if not hundreds, of painted and dressed-up men, in costumes fitting
tight to their thighs and calves, and also women, as usual,
as nearly nude as might be. These were all singers, or
members of the chorus, or ballet-dancers, awaiting their
turns. My guide led me across the stage and, by means
of a bridge of boards across the orchestra (in which perhaps a hundred musicians of all kinds, from kettledrum
to flute and harp, were seated), to the dark pit-stalls.

On an elevation, between two lamps with reflectors,
and in an arm-chair placed before a music-stand, sat the
director of the musical part, *bâton* in hand, managing
the orchestra and singers, and, in general, the production
of the whole opera.

The performance had already commenced, and on the
stage a procession of Indians who had brought home a
bride was being presented. Besides men and women in
costume, two other men in ordinary clothes bustled and
ran about on the stage; one was the director of the dramatic part, and the other, who stepped about in soft
shoes and ran from place to place with unusual agility,
was the dancing-master, whose salary per month ex-
ceeded what ten laborers earn in a year.

These three directors arranged the singing, the orchestra, and the procession. The procession, as usual,
was enacted by couples, with tinfoil halberds on their
shoulders. They all came from one place, and walked
round and round again, and then stopped. The procession took a long time to arrange: first the Indians with
halberds came on too late; then too soon; then at the
right time, but crowded together at the exit; then they
did not crowd, but arranged themselves badly at the sides
of the stage; and each time the whole performance was
stopped and recommenced from the beginning. The
procession was introduced by a recitative, delivered by
a man dressed up like some variety of Turk, who, opening his mouth in a curious way, sang, " Home I bring
the bri-i-ide." He sings and waves his arm (which is of
course bare) from under his mantle. The procession com-

mences, but here the French horn, in the accompaniment
of the recitative, does something wrong; and the director,
with a shudder as if some catastrophe had occurred, raps
with his stick on the stand. All is stopped, and the director, turning to the orchestra, attacks the French horn,
scolding him in the rudest terms, as cabmen abuse each
other, for taking the wrong note. And again the whole
thing recommences. The Indians with their halberds
again come on, treading softly in their extraordinary
boots; again the singer sings, "Home I bring the
bri-i-ide." But here the pairs get too close together.
More raps with the stick, more scolding, and a recom-
mencement. Again, "Home I bring the bri-i-ide," again
the same gesticulation with the bare arm from under the
mantle, and again the couples, treading softly with halberds on their shoulders, some with sad and serious faces,
some talking and smiling, arrange themselves in a circle
and begin to sing. All seems to be going well, but again
the stick raps, and the director, in a distressed and angry voice, begins to scold the men and women of the
chorus. It appears that when singing they had omitted
to raise their hands from time to time in sign of anima-
tion. "Are you all dead, or what? Cows that you are!
Are you corpses, that you can't move?" Again they
recommence, "Home I bring the bri-i-ide," and again,
with sorrowful faces, the chorus-women sing, first one
and then another of them raising their hands. But two
chorus-girls speak to each other, — again a more vehe-
ment rapping with the stick. "Have you come here to
talk? Can't you gossip at home? You there in red
breeches, come nearer. Look toward me! Recommence!" Again, "Home I bring the bri-i-ide." And
so it goes on for one, two, three hours. The whole of
such a rehearsal lasts six hours on end. Raps with the
stick, repetitions, placings, corrections of the singers, of
the orchestra, of the procession, of the dancers, — all
seasoned with angry scolding. I heard the words,
"asses," "fools," "idiots," "swine," addressed to the
musicians and singers at least forty times in the course
of one hour. And the unhappy individual to whom the

abuse is addressed, — flautist, horn-blower, or singer, — physically and mentally demoralized, does not reply, and does what is demanded of him. Twenty times is repeated the one phrase, " Home I bring the bri-i-ide," and twenty times the striding about in yellow shoes with a halberd over the shoulder. The conductor knows that these people are so demoralized that they are no longer fit for anything but to blow trumpets and walk about with halberds and in yellow shoes, and that they are also accustomed to dainty, easy living, so that they will put up with anything rather than lose their luxurious life. He therefore gives free vent to his churlishness, especially as he has seen the same thing done in Paris and Vienna, and knows that this is the way the best conductors behave, and that it is a musical tradition of great artists to be so carried away by the great business of their art that they cannot pause to consider the feelings of other artists.

It would be difficult to find a more repulsive sight. I have seen one workman abuse another for not supporting the weight piled upon him when goods were being unloaded, or, at hay-stacking, the village elder scold a peasant for not making the rick right, and the man submitted in silence. And, however unpleasant it was to witness the scene, the unpleasantness was lessened by the consciousness that the business in hand was needful and important, and that the fault for which the head man scolded the laborer was one which might spoil a needful undertaking.

But what was being done here? For what, and for whom? Very likely the conductor was tired out, like the workman I passed in the vaults; it was even evident that he was; but who made him tire himself? And for what was he tiring himself? The opera he was rehearsing was one of the most ordinary of operas for people who are accustomed to them, but also one of the most gigantic absurdities that could possibly be devised. An Indian king wants to marry; they bring him a bride; he disguises himself as a minstrel; the bride falls in love with the minstrel and is in de

spair, but afterwards discovers that the minstrel is the
king, and every one is highly delighted.

That there never were, or could be, such Indians,
and that they were not only unlike Indians, but that
what they were doing was unlike anything on earth
except other operas, was beyond all manner of doubt;
that people do not converse in such a way as recitative, and do not place themselves at fixed distances,
in a quartet, waving their arms to express their
emotions; that nowhere, except in theaters, do people
walk about in such a manner, in pairs, with tinfoil
halberds and in slippers; that no one ever gets angry
in such a way, or is affected in such a way, or laughs
in such a way, or cries in such a way; and that no one
on earth can be moved by such performances; all this
is beyond the possibility of doubt.

Instinctively the question presents itself: For whom
is this being done? Whom *can* it please? If there
are, occasionally, good melodies in the opera, to which
it is pleasant to listen, they could have been sung
simply, without these stupid costumes and all the processions and recitatives and hand-wavings.

The ballet, in which half-naked women make voluptuous movements, twisting themselves into various sen-
sual wreathings, is simply a lewd performance.

So one is quite at a loss as to whom these things
are done for. The man of culture is heartily sick of
them, while to a real working-man they are utterly incomprehensible. If any one can be pleased by these
things (which is doubtful), it can only be some young
footman or depraved artisan, who has contracted the
spirit of the upper classes but is not yet satiated with
their amusements, and wishes to show his breeding.

And all this nasty folly is prepared, not simply, nor
with kindly merriment, but with anger and brutal
cruelty.

It is said that it is all done for the sake of art, and
that art is a very important thing. But is it true that
art is so important that such sacrifices should be made
for its sake? This question is especially urgent, be-

cause art, for the sake of which the labor of millions, the lives of men, and, above all, love between man and man, are being sacrificed, — this very art is becoming something more and more vague and uncertain to human perception.

Criticism, in which the lovers of art used to find support for their opinions, has latterly become so self-contradictory, that, if we exclude from the domain of art all that to which the critics of various schools themselves deny the title, there is scarcely any art left.

The artists of various sects, like the theologians of the various sects, mutually exclude and destroy themselves. Listen to the artists of the schools of our times, and you will find, in all branches, each set of artists disowning others. In poetry the old romanticists deny the parnassiens and the decadents; the parnassiens disown the romanticists and the decadents; the decadents disown all their predecessors and the symbolists; the symbolists disown all their predecessors and *les mages;* and *les mages* disown all, all their predecessors. Among novelists we have naturalists, psychologists, and "nature-ists," all rejecting each other. And it is the same in dramatic art, in painting, and in music. So that art, which demands such tremendous labor-sacrifices from the people, which stunts human lives and transgresses against human love, is not only *not* a thing clearly and firmly defined, but is understood in such contradictory ways by its own devotees that it is difficult to say what is meant by art, and especially what is good, useful art, — art for the sake of which we might condone such sacrifices as are being offered at its shrine.

CHAPTER II

For the production of every ballet, circus, opera, operetta, exhibition, picture, concert, or printed book, the intense and unwilling labor of thousands and thousands of people is needed at what is often harmful and humiliating work. It were well if artists made all they require for themselves, but, as it is, they all need the help of workmen, not only to produce art, but also for their own usually luxurious maintenance. And, one way or other, they get it; either through payments from rich people, or through subsidies given by government (in Russia, for instance, in grants of millions of roubles to theaters, conservatoires, and academies). This money is collected from the people, some of whom have to sell their only cow to pay the tax, and who never get those æsthetic pleasures which art gives.

It was all very well for a Greek or Roman artist, or even for a Russian artist of the first half of our century (when there were still slaves, and it was considered right that there should be), with a quiet mind to make people serve him and his art; but in our day, when in all men there is at least some dim perception of the equal rights of all, it is impossible to constrain people to labor unwillingly for art, without first deciding the question whether it is true that art is so good and so important an affair as to redeem this evil.

If not, we have the terrible probability to consider, that while fearful sacrifices of the labor and lives of men, and of morality itself, are being made to art, that same art may be not only useless but even harmful.

And therefore it is necessary for a society in which works of art arise and are supported, to find out whether all that professes to be art is really art; whether (as is presupposed in our society) all that which is art is good; and whether it is important and worth those sacrifices which it necessitates. It is still more necessary for every conscientious artist to know this, that he may be sure that all he does has a valid meaning; that it is not merely an infatuation of the small circle of people among whom he lives which excites in him the false assurance that he is doing a good work; and that what he takes from others for the support of his often very luxurious life, will be compensated for by those productions at which he works. And that is why answers to the above questions are especially important in our time.

What is this art, which is considered so important and necessary for humanity that for its sake these sacrifices of labor, of human life, and even of goodness may be made? "What is art? What a question! Art is architecture, sculpture, painting, music, and poetry in all its forms," usually replies the ordinary man, the art amateur, or even the artist himself, imagining the matter about which he is talking to be perfectly clear, and uniformly understood by everybody. But in architecture, one inquires further, are there not simple buildings which are not objects of art, and buildings with artistic pretensions which are unsuccessful and ugly and therefore cannot be considered as works of art? Wherein lies the characteristic sign of a work of art?

It is the same in sculpture, in music, and in poetry. Art, in all its forms, is bounded on one side by the practically useful, and on the other by unsuccessful attempts at art. How is art to be marked off from each of these? The ordinary educated man of our circle, and even the artist who has not occupied himself especially with æsthetics, will not hesitate at this question either. He thinks the solution has been found long ago, and is well known to every one.

"Art is such activity as produces beauty," says such a man.

If art consists in that, then is a ballet or an operetta art? you inquire.

"Yes," says the ordinary man, though with some hesitation, "a good ballet or a graceful operetta is also art, in so far as it manifests beauty."

But without even asking the ordinary man what differentiates the "good" ballet and the "graceful" operetta from their opposites (a question he would have much difficulty in answering), if you ask him whether the activity of costumiers and hairdressers, who ornament the figures and faces of the women for the ballet and the operetta, is art; or the activity of Worth, the dressmaker; of scent-makers and men cooks, — then he will, in most cases, deny that their activity belongs to the sphere of art. But in this the ordinary man makes a mistake, just because he is an ordinary man and not a specialist, and because he has not occupied himself with æsthetic questions. Had he looked into these matters, he would have seen in the great Renan's book, "Marc Aurele," a dissertation showing that the tailor's work is art, and that those who do not see in the adornment of woman an affair of the highest art are very small-minded and dull. "*C'est le grand art,*" says Renan. Moreover, he would have known that in many æsthetic systems — for instance, in the æsthetics of the learned Professor Kralik, "Weltschönheit, Versuch einer allgemeinen Æsthetik, von Richard Kralik," and in "Les Problèmes de l'Esthétique Contemporaine," by Guyau — the arts of costume, of taste, and of touch are included.

"*Es Folgt nun ein Fünfblatt von Künsten, die der subjectiven Sinnlichkeit entkeimen*" (There results then a pentafoliate of arts, growing out of the subjective perceptions), says Kralik (p. 175). "*Sie sind die ästhetische Behandlung der fünf Sinne.*" (They are the æsthetic treatment of the five senses.)

These five arts are the following : —

Die Kunst des Geschmacksinns — The art of the sense of taste (p. 175).

Die Kunst des Geruchsinns — The art of the sense of smell (p. 177).

Die Kunst des Tastsinns — The art of the sense of touch (p. 180).

Die Kunst des Gehörsinns — The art of the sense of hearing (p. 182).

Die Kunst des Gesichtsinns — The art of the sense of sight (p. 184).

Of the first of these — *die Kunst des Geschmacksinns* — he says : "*Man hält zwar gewöhnlich nur zwei oder höchstens drei Sinne für würdig, den Stoff künstlerischer Behandlung abzugeben, aber ich glaube nur mit bedingtem Recht. Ich will kein allzugrosses Gewicht darauf legen, dass der gemeine Sprachgebrauch manch andere Künste, wie zum Beispiel die Kochkunst kennt.*" [1]

[1] Only two, or at most three, senses are generally held worthy to supply matter for artistic treatment, but I think this opinion is only con-

And further : " *Und es ist doch gewiss eine ästhetische Leistung, wenn es der Kochkunst gelingt aus einem thierischen Kadaver einen Gegenstand des Geschmacks in jedem Sinne zu machen. Der Grundsatz der Kunst des Geschmacksinns (die weiter ist als die sogenannte Kochkunst) ist also dieser: Es soll alles Geniessbare als Sinnbild einer Idee behandelt werden und in jedesmaligem Einklang zur auszudrückenden Idee.*" [1]

This author, like Renan, acknowledges a *Kostümkunst* (Art of Costume) (p. 200), etc.

Such is also the opinion of the French writer, Guyau, who is highly esteemed by some authors of our day. In his book, " Les Problèmes de l'Esthétique Contemporaine," he speaks seriously of touch, taste, and smell as giving, or being capable of giving, æsthetic impressions : " *Si la couleur manque au toucher, il nous fournit en revanche une notion que l'œil seul ne peut nous donner, et qui a une valeur esthétique considérable, celle du* doux, *du* soyeux, *du* poli. *Ce qui caractérise la beauté du velours, c'est sa douceur au toucher non moins que son brillant. Dans l'idée que nous nous faisons de la beauté d'une femme, le velouté de sa peau entre comme élément essentiel.*"

" *Chacun de nous probablement avec un peu d'attention se rappellera des jouissances du goût, qui ont été de véritables jouissances esthétiques.*" [2] And he recounts how a glass of milk drunk by him in the mountains gave him æsthetic enjoyment.

---

ditionally correct. I will not lay too much stress on the fact that our common speech recognizes many other arts, as, for instance, the art of cookery.

[1] And yet it is certainly an æsthetic achievement when the art of cooking succeeds in making of an animal's corpse an object in all respects tasteful. The principle of the Art of Taste (which goes beyond the so-called Art of Cookery) is therefore this : All that is eatable should be treated as the symbol of some Idea, and always in harmony with the Idea to be expressed.

[2] If the sense of touch lacks color, it gives us, on the other hand, a notion which the eye alone cannot afford, and one of considerable æsthetic value, namely, that of *softness, silkiness, polish.* The beauty of velvet is characterized not less by its softness to the touch than by its luster. In the idea we form of a woman's beauty, the softness of her skin enters as an essential element.

Each of us, probably, with a little attention, can recall pleasures of taste which have been real æsthetic pleasures.

So it turns out that the conception of art, as consisting in making beauty manifest, is not at all so simple as it seemed, especially now, when in this conception of beauty are included our sensations of touch and taste and smell, as they are by the latest æsthetic writers.

But the ordinary man either does not know, or does not wish to know, all this, and is firmly convinced that all questions about art may be simply and clearly solved by acknowledging beauty to be the subject-matter of art. To him it seems clear and comprehensible that art consists in manifesting beauty, and that a reference to beauty will serve to explain all questions about art.

But what is this beauty which forms the subject-matter of art? How is it defined? What is it?

As is always the case, the more cloudy and confused the conception conveyed by a word, with the more *aplomb* and self-assurance do people use that word, pretending that what is understood by it is so simple and clear that it is not worth while even to discuss what it actually means.

This is how matters of orthodox religion are usually dealt with, and this is how people now deal with the conception of beauty. It is taken for granted that what is meant by the word beauty is known and understood by every one. And yet not only is this not known, but, after whole mountains of books have been written on the subject by the most learned and profound thinkers during one hundred and fifty years (ever since Baumgarten founded æsthetics in the year 1750), the question, What is beauty? remains to this day quite unsolved, and in each new work on æsthetics it is answered in a new way. One of the last books I read on æsthetics is a not ill-written booklet by Julius Mithalter, called "Rätsel des Schönen" (The Enigma of the Beautiful). And that title precisely expresses the position of the question, What is beauty? After thousands of learned men have discussed it during one hundred and fifty years, the meaning of the word beauty remains an enigma still. The Germans answer the question in their manner, though in a hundred different ways. The physiologist·

æstheticians, especially the Englishmen, Herbert Spencer, Grant Allen, and his school, answer it, each in his own way; the French eclectics, and the followers of Guyau and Taine, also each in his own way; and all these people know all the preceding solutions given by Baumgarten, and Kant, and Schelling, and Schiller, and Fichte, and Winckelmann, and Lessing, and Hegel, and Schopenhauer, and Hartmann, and Schasler, and Cousin, and Lévêque, and others.

What is this strange conception "beauty," which seems so simple to those who talk without thinking, but in defining which all the philosophers of various tendencies and different nationalities can come to no agreement during a century and a half? What is this conception of beauty, on which the dominant doctrine of art rests?

In Russian, by the word *krasota* (beauty) we mean only that which pleases the sight. And though latterly people have begun to speak of "an ugly deed," or of "beautiful music," it is not good Russian.

A Russian of the common folk, not knowing foreign languages, will not understand you if you tell him that a man who has given his last coat to another, or done anything similar, has acted "beautifully," that a man who has cheated another has done an "ugly" action, or that a song is "beautiful."

In Russian a deed may be kind and good, or unkind and bad. Music may be pleasant and good, or unpleasant and bad; but there can be no such thing as "beautiful" or "ugly" music.

Beautiful may relate to a man, a horse, a house, a view, or a movement. Of actions, thoughts, character, or music, if they please us, we may say that they are good, or, if they do not please us, that they are not good. But beautiful can be used only concerning that which pleases the sight. So that the word and conception "good" includes the conception of "beautiful," but the reverse is not the case; the conception "beauty" does not include the conception "good." If we say "good" of an article which we value for its appearance, we thereby say that the article is beautiful ; but if we say it is "beautiful," it does not at all mean that the article is a good one.

Such is the meaning ascribed by the Russian language, and therefore by the sense of the people, to the words and conceptions " good " and " beautiful."

In all the European languages, *i.e.* the languages of those nations among whom the doctrine has spread that beauty is the essential thing in art, the words "beau," "schön," "beautiful," " bello," etc., while keeping their meaning of beautiful in form, have come to also express "goodness," "kindness," *i.e.* have come to act as substitutes for the word "good."

So that it has become quite natural in those languages to use such expressions as "belle ame," "schöne Gedanken," of "beautiful deed." Those languages no longer have a suitable word wherewith expressly to indicate beauty of form, and have to use a combination of words such as "beau par la forme," "beautiful to look at," etc., to convey that idea.

Observation of the divergent meanings which the words "beauty" and "beautiful" have in Russian on the one hand, and in those European languages now permeated by this æsthetic theory on the other hand, shows us that the word "beauty" has, among the latter, acquired a special meaning, namely, that of " good."

What is remarkable, moreover, is that since we Russians have begun more and more to adopt the European view of art, the same evolution has begun to show itself in our language also, and some people speak and write quite confidently, and without causing surprise, of beautiful music and ugly actions, or even thoughts ; whereas forty years ago, when I was young, the expressions "beautiful music" and "ugly actions" were not only unusual, but incomprehensible. Evidently this new meaning given to beauty by European thought begins to be assimilated by Russian society.

And what really is this meaning? What is this " beauty " as it is understood by the European peoples?

In order to answer this question, I must here quote

at least a small selection of those definitions of beauty
most generally adopted in existing æsthetic systems. I
especially beg the reader not to be overcome by dullness,
but to read these extracts through, or, still better, to
read some one of the erudite æsthetic authors. Not to
mention the voluminous German æstheticians, a very
good book for this purpose would be either the German
book by Kralik, the English work by Knight, or the
French one by Lévêque. It is necessary to read one
of the learned æsthetic writers in order to form at first-
hand a conception of the variety in opinion and the
frightful obscurity which reigns in this region of specu-
lation; not, in this important matter, trusting to another's
report.

This, for instance, is what the German æsthetician
Schasler says in the preface to his famous, voluminous,
and detailed work on æsthetics : —

" Hardly in any sphere of philosophic science can we
find such divergent methods of investigation and exposition, amounting even to self-contradiction, as in the
sphere of æsthetics. On the one hand, we have elegant phraseology without any substance, characterized
in great part by most one-sided superficiality ; and on
the other hand, accompanying undeniable profundity
of investigation and richness of subject-matter, we get
a revolting awkwardness of philosophic terminology,
infolding the simplest thoughts in an apparel of abstract science, as though to render them worthy to
enter the consecrated palace of the system; and finally,
between these two methods of investigation and exposition there is a third, forming, as it were, the transition
from one to the other, a method consisting of eclecti-
cism, now flaunting an elegant phraseology, and now
a pedantic erudition. .... A style of exposition that falls
into none of these three defects but it is truly concrete,
and, having important matter, expresses it in clear and
popular philosophic language, can nowhere be found
less frequently than in the domain of æsthetics." [1]

It is only necessary, for instance, to read Schasler's

[1] M. Schasler, " Kritische Geschichte der Æsthetik," 1872, vol. i., p. 13.

own book to convince oneself of the justice of this observation of his.

On the same subject the French writer Véron, in the
preface to his very good work on æsthetics, says: "*Il
n'y a pas de science, qui ait été plus que l'esthétique livrée
aux rêveries des métaphysiciens. Depuis Platon jusqu'
aux doctrines officielles de nos jours, on a fait de l'art je
ne sais quel amalgame de fantaisies quintessenciées, et de
mystères transcendantaux qui trouvent leur expression suprême dans la conception absolue du Beau idéal, prototype
immuable et divin des choses réelles*" ("L'Esthétique,"
1878, p. 5).[1]

If the reader will only be at the pains to peruse the
following extracts, defining beauty, taken from the chief
writers on æsthetics, he may convince himself that this
censure is thoroughly deserved.

I shall not quote the definitions of beauty attributed
to the ancients, — Socrates, Plato, Aristotle, etc., down
to Plotinus, — because, in reality, the ancients had not
that conception of beauty separated from goodness
which forms the basis and aim of æsthetics in our time.
By referring the judgments of the ancients on beauty to
our conception of it, as is usually done in æsthetics, we
give the words of the ancients a meaning which is not
theirs.[2]

CHAPTER III

I BEGIN with the founder of æsthetics, Baumgarten
(1714–1762).

According to Baumgarten,[3] the object of logical

---

[1] There is no science which, more than æsthetics, has been handed over
to the reveries of the metaphysicians. From Plato down to the received
doctrines of our day, people have made of art a strange amalgam of quin-
tessential fancies and transcendental mysteries, which find their supreme
expression in the conception of an absolute ideal Beauty, immutable and
divine prototype of actual things.

[2] See on this matter Benard's admirable book, "L'Esthétique d'Aristote,"
also Walter's "Geschichte der Æsthetik in Altertum."

[3] Schasler, p. 361.

knowledge is Truth, the object of æsthetic (*i.e.* sensuous) knowledge is Beauty.   Beauty is the Perfect (the
Absolute) recognized through the senses; Truth is the
Perfect perceived through reason; Goodness is the Perfect reached by moral will.

Beauty is defined by Baumgarten as a correspondence,
i.e. an order of the parts in their mutual relations to
each other and in their relation to the whole.   The aim
of beauty itself is to please and excite a desire, "*Wohlge-
fallen und Erregung eines Verlangens.*" (A position
precisely the opposite of Kant's definition of the nature
and sign of beauty.)

With reference to the manifestations of beauty, Baumgarten considers that the highest embodiment of beauty
is seen by us in nature, and he therefore thinks that the
highest aim of art is to copy nature. (This position also
is directly contradicted by the conclusions of the latest
æstheticians.)

Passing over the unimportant followers of Baumgarten, — Maier, Eschenburg, and Eberhard, — who only
slightly modified the doctrine of their teacher by dividing the pleasant from the beautiful, I will quote the
definitions given by writers who came immediately after
Baumgarten, and defined beauty quite in another way.
These writers were Sulzer, Mendelssohn, and Moritz.
They, in contradiction to Baumgarten's main position,
recognize as the aim of art, not beauty, but goodness.
Thus Sulzer (1720–1777) says that only that can be considered beautiful which contains goodness.   According
to his theory, the aim of the whole life of humanity is
welfare in social life.   This is attained by the education
of the moral feelings, to which end art should be sub-
servient. Beauty is that which evokes and educates
this feeling.

Beauty is understood almost in the same way by
Mendelssohn (1729–1786). According to him, art is
the carrying forward of the beautiful, obscurely recognized by feeling, till it becomes the true and good. The
aim of art is moral perfection.[1]

[1] Schasler, p. 369.

For the æstheticians of this school, the ideal of beauty is a beautiful soul in a beautiful body. So that these æstheticians completely wipe out Baumgarten's division of the Perfect (the Absolute), into the three forms of Truth, Goodness, and Beauty; and Beauty is again united with the Good and the True.

But this conception is not only not maintained by the later æstheticians, but the æsthetic doctrine of Winckelmann arises, again in complete opposition. This divides the mission of art from the aim of goodness in the sharpest and most positive manner, makes external beauty the aim of art, and even limits it to visible beauty.

According to the celebrated work of Winckelmann (1717–1767), the law and aim of all art is beauty only, beauty quite separated from and independent of goodness. There are three kinds of beauty: (1) beauty of form, (2) beauty of idea, expressing itself in the position of the figure (in plastic art), (3) beauty of expression, attainable only when the two first conditions are present. This beauty of expression is the highest aim of art, and is attained in antique art; modern art should therefore aim at imitating ancient art.[1]

Art is similarly understood by Lessing, Herder, and afterwards by Goethe and by all the distinguished æstheticians of Germany till Kant, from whose day, again, a different conception of art commences.

Native æsthetic theories arose during this period in England, France, Italy, and Holland, and they, though not taken from the German, were equally cloudy and contradictory. And all these writers, just like the German æstheticians, founded their theories on a conception of the Beautiful, understanding beauty in the sense of a something existing absolutely, and more or less intermingled with Goodness or having one and the same root. In England, almost simultaneously with Baumgarten, even a little earlier, Shaftesbury, Hutcheson, Home, Burke, Hogarth, and others, wrote on art.

According to Shaftesbury (1670–1713), "That which is beautiful is harmonious and proportionable, what is

[1] Schasler, pp. 388–390.

harmonious and proportionable is true, and what is at once both beautiful and true is of consequence agreeable and good."[1] Beauty, he taught, is recognized by the mind only. God is fundamental beauty; beauty and goodness proceed from the same fount.

So that, although Shaftesbury regards beauty as being something separate from goodness, they again merge into something inseparable.

According to Hutcheson (1694–1747 — "Inquiry into the Original of our Ideas of Beauty and Virtue"), the aim of art is beauty, the essence of which consists in evoking in us the perception of uniformity amid variety. In the recognition of what is art we are guided by "an internal sense." This internal sense may be in contradiction to the ethical one. So that, according to Hutcheson, beauty does not always correspond with goodness, but separates from it and is sometimes contrary to it.[2]

According to Home, Lord Kames (1696–1782), beauty is that which is pleasant. Therefore beauty is defined by taste alone. The standard of true taste is that the maximum of richness, fullness, strength, and variety of impression should be contained in the narrowest limits. That is the ideal of a perfect work of art.

According to Burke (1729-1797 — "Philosophical Inquiry into the Origin of our Ideas of the Sublime and Beautiful"), the sublime and beautiful, which are the aim of art, have their origin in the promptings of self-preservation and of society. These feelings, examined in their source, are means for the maintenance of the race through the individual. The first (self-preservation) is attained by nourishment, defense, and war; the second (society) by intercourse and propagation. Therefore self-defense, and war, which is bound up with it, is the source of the sublime; sociability, and the sex-instinct, which is bound up with it, is the source of beauty.[3]

---

[1] Knight, "Philosophy of the Beautiful," i., pp. 165, 166.
[2] Schasler, p. 289. Knight, pp. 168, 169.
[3] R. Kralik, " Weltschönheit, Versuch einer allgemeinen Æsthetik," pp. 304–306.

Such were the chief English definitions of art and beauty in the eighteenth century.

During that period, in France, the writers on art were Père André and Batteux, with Diderot, D'Alembert, and, to some extent, Voltaire, following later.

According to Père André ("Essai sur le Beau," 1741), there are three kinds of beauty, — divine beauty, natural beauty, and artificial beauty.[1]

According to Batteux (1713–1780), art consists in imitating the beauty of nature, its aim being enjoyment.[2] Such is also Diderot's definition of art.

The French writers, like the English, consider that it is taste that decides what is beautiful. And the laws of taste are not only not laid down, but it is granted that they cannot be settled. The same view was held by D'Alembert and Voltaire.[3]

According to the Italian æsthetician of that period, Pagano, art consists in uniting the beauties dispersed in nature. The capacity to perceive these beauties is taste, the capacity to bring them into one whole is artistic genius. Beauty commingles with goodness, so that beauty is goodness made visible, and goodness is inner beauty.[4]

According to the opinion of other Italians: Muratori (1672–1750), — "*Riflessioni sopra il buon gusto intorno le science e le arti,*" — and especially Spaletti,[5] — "*Saggio sopra la bellezza*" (1765), — art amounts to an egotistical sensation, founded (as with Burke) on the desire for self-preservation and society.

Among Dutch writers, Hemsterhuis (1720–1790), who had an influence on the German æstheticians and on Goethe, is remarkable. According to him, beauty is that which gives most pleasure, and that gives most pleasure which gives us the greatest number of ideas in the shortest time. Enjoyment of the beautiful, because it gives the greatest quantity of perceptions in the shortest time, is the highest notion to which man can attain.[6]

---

[1] Knight, p. 101.
[3] Knight, pp. 102–104.
[5] Spaletti, Schasler, p. 328.

[2] Schasler, p. 316.
[4] R. Kralik, p. 124.
[6] Schasler, pp. 331–333.

Such were the æsthetic theories outside Germany during the last century. In Germany, after Winckelmann, there again arose a completely new æsthetic theory, that of Kant (1724–1804), which, more than all others, clears up what this conception of beauty, and consequently of art, really amounts to.

The æsthetic teaching of Kant is founded as follows: Man has a knowledge of nature outside him and of himself in nature. In nature, outside himself, he seeks for truth; in himself, he seeks for goodness. The first is an affair of pure reason, the other of practical reason (free will). Besides these two means of perception, there is yet the judging capacity (*Urteilskraft*), which forms judgments without reasonings and produces pleasure without desire (*Urtheil ohne Begriff und Vergnügen ohne Begehren*). This capacity is the basis of æsthetic feeling. Beauty, according to Kant, in its subjective meaning is that which, in general and necessarily, without reasonings and without practical advantage, pleases. In its objective meaning it is the form of a suitable object, in so far as that object is perceived without any conception of its utility.[1]

Beauty is defined in the same way by the followers of Kant, among whom was Schiller (1759–1805). According to Schiller, who wrote much on æsthetics, the aim of art is, as with Kant, beauty, the source of which is pleasure without practical advantage. So that art may be called a game, not in the sense of an unimportant occupation, but in the sense of a manifestation of the beauties of life itself without other aim than that of beauty.[2]

Besides Schiller, the most remarkable of Kant's followers in the sphere of æsthetics was Wilhelm Humboldt, who, though he added nothing to the definition of beauty, explained various forms of it, — the drama, music, the comic, etc.[3]

After Kant, besides the second-rate philosophers, the writers on æsthetics were Fichte, Schelling, Hegel,

---

[1] Schasler, pp. 525–528.   [2] Knight, pp. 61–63.
[3] Schasler, pp. 740–743.

and their followers. Fichte (1762–1814) says that per
ception of the beautiful proceeds from this: the world
— *i.e.* nature — has two sides: it is the sum of our
limitations, and it is the sum of our free idealistic activity. In the first aspect the world is limited, in the
second aspect it is free. In the first aspect every
object is limited, distorted, compressed, confined —
and we see deformity; in the second we perceive its
inner completeness, vitality, regeneration — and we see
beauty. So that the deformity or beauty of an object,
according to Fichte, depends on the point of view of
the observer. Beauty therefore exists, not in the world,
but in the beautiful soul (*schöner Geist*). Art is the
manifestation of this beautiful soul, and its aim is the
education, not only of the mind — that is the business
of the *savant*, not only of the heart — that is the affair
of the moral preacher, but of the whole man. And so
the characteristic of beauty lies, not in anything external,
but in the presence of a beautiful soul in the artist.[1]

Following Fichte, and in the same direction, Fried-
rich Schlegel and Adam Müller also defined beauty.
According to Schlegel (1772–1829), beauty in art is
understood too incompletely, one-sidedly, and disconnectedly. Beauty exists, not only in art, but also in
nature and in love; so that the truly beautiful is expressed by the union of art, nature, and love. There
fore, as inseparably one with æsthetic art, Schlegel
acknowledges moral and philosophic art.[2]

According to Adam Müller (1779–1829), there are
two kinds of beauty: the one, general beauty, which
attracts people as the sun attracts the planet — this is
found chiefly in antique art; and the other, individual
beauty, which results from the observer himself becoming a sun, attracting beauty — this is the beauty
of modern art. A world in which all contradictions
are harmonized is the highest beauty. Every work
of art is a reproduction of this universal harmony.[3]
The highest art is the art of life.[4]

[1] Schasler, pp, 769–771.   [2] Schasler, pp. 786, 787.
[3] Kralik, p. 148.   [4] Kralik, p. 820.

Next after Fichte and his followers came a contemporary of his, the philosopher Schelling (1775–1854),
who has had a great influence on the æsthetic conceptions of our times. According to Schelling's philosophy, art is the production or result of that conception
of things by which the subject becomes its own object,
or the object its own subject. Beauty is the perception of the infinite in the finite. And the chief characteristic of works of art is unconscious infinity. Art is
the uniting of the subjective with the objective, of
nature with reason, of the unconscious with the conscious, and therefore art is the highest means of
knowledge. Beauty is the contemplation of things in
themselves as they exist in the prototype (*In den
Urbildern*). It is not the artist who by his knowledge or skill produces the beautiful, but the idea of
beauty in him itself produces it.[1]

Of Schelling's followers the most noticeable was
Solger (1780–1819 – "Vorlesungen über Æsthetik").
According to him, the idea of beauty is the fundamental
idea of everything. In the world we see only distortions of the fundamental idea, but art, by imagination,
may lift itself to the height of this idea. Art is therefore akin to creation.[2]

According to another follower of Schelling, Krause
(1781–1832), true, positive beauty is the manifestation
of the Idea in an individual form; art is the actualization
of the beauty existing in the sphere of man's free spirit.
The highest stage of art is the art of life, which directs
its activity toward the adornment of life so that it may
be a beautiful abode for a beautiful man.[3]

After Schelling and his followers came the new æsthetic doctrine of Hegel, which is held to this day, consciously by many, but by the majority unconsciously.
This teaching is not only no clearer or better defined
than the preceding ones, but is, if possible, even more
cloudy and mystical.

[1] Schasler, pp. 828, 829, 834–841.
[2] Schasler, p. 891.
[3] Schasler, p. 917.

According to Hegel (1770–1831), God manifests himself in nature and in art in the form of beauty. God expresses himself in two ways: in the object and in the subject, in nature and in spirit. Beauty is the shining of the Idea through matter. Only the soul, and what pertains to it, is truly beautiful; and therefore the beauty of nature is only the reflection of the natural beauty of the spirit — the beautiful has only a spiritual content. But the spiritual must appear in sensuous form. The sensuous manifestation of spirit is only appearance (*schein*), and this appearance is the only reality of the beautiful. Art is thus the production of this appearance of the Idea, and is a means, together with religion and philosophy, of bringing to consciousness and of expressing the deepest problems of humanity and the highest truths of the spirit.

Truth and beauty, according to Hegel, are one and the same thing; the difference being only that truth is the Idea itself as it exists in itself, and is thinkable. The Idea, manifested externally, becomes to the apprehension not only true but beautiful. The beautiful is the manifestation of the Idea.[1]

Following Hegel came his many adherents, Weisse, Arnold Ruge, Rosenkrantz, Theodor Vischer, and others.

According to Weisse (1801–1867), art is the introduction (*Einbildung*) of the absolute spiritual reality of beauty into external, dead, indifferent matter, the perception of which latter, apart from the beauty brought into it, presents the negation of all existence in itself (*Negation alles Fürsichseins*).

In the idea of truth, Weisse explains, lies a contradiction between the subjective and the objective sides of knowledge, in that an individual *I* discerns the Universal. This contradiction can be removed by a conception that should unite into one the universal and the individual, which fall asunder in our conceptions of truth. Such a conception would be reconciled (*aufgehoben*) truth. Beauty is such a reconciled truth.[2]

---

[1] Schasler, pp. 946, 1085, 984, 985, 990.
[2] Schasler, pp. 966, 655, 956,

According to Ruge (1802–1880), a strict follower of Hegel, beauty is the Idea expressing itself. The spirit, contemplating itself, either finds itself expressed completely, and then that full expression of itself is beauty; or incompletely, and then it feels the need to alter this imperfect expression of itself, and becomes creative art.[1]

According to Vischer (1807–1887), beauty is the Idea in the form of a finite phenomenon. The Idea itself is not indivisible, but forms a system of ideas, which may be represented by ascending and descending lines. The higher the idea, the more beauty it contains; but even the lowest contains beauty, because it forms an essential link of the system. The highest form of the Idea is personality, and therefore the highest art is that which has for its subject-matter the highest personality.[2]

Such were the theories of the German æstheticians in the Hegelian direction, but they did not monopolize æsthetic dissertations. In Germany, side by side and simultaneously with the Hegelian theories, there appeared theories of beauty not only independent of Hegel's position (that beauty is the manifestation of the Idea), but directly contrary to this view, denying and ridiculing it. Such was the line taken by Herbart and, more particularly, by Schopenhauer.

According to Herbart (1776–1841), there is not, and cannot be, any such thing as beauty existing in itself. What does exist is only our opinion, and it is necessary to find the base of this opinion (*Ästhetisches Elementarurtheil*). Such bases are connected with our impressions. There are certain relations which we term beautiful; and art consists in finding these relations, which are simultaneous in painting, the plastic art, and architecture, successive and simultaneous in music, and purely successive in poetry. In contradiction to the former æstheticians, Herbart holds that objects are often beautiful which express nothing at all, as, for instance, the rainbow, which is beautiful for its lines and colors, and not for its mythological connection with Iris or Noah's rainbow.[3]

---

[1] Schasler, p. 1017.   [2] Schasler, pp. 1065, 1066.
[3] Schasler, pp. 1097–1100.

Another opponent of Hegel was Schopenhauer, who denied Hegel's whole system, his æsthetics included.

According to Schopenhauer (1788–1860), Will objec-tivizes itself in the world on various planes ; and although the higher the plane on which it is objectivized the more beautiful it is, yet each plane has its own beauty. Re-nunciation of one's individuality and contemplation of one of these planes of manifestation of Will gives us a perception of beauty. All men, says Schopenhauer, possess the capacity to objectivize the Idea on different planes. The genius of the artist has this capacity in a higher degree, and therefore makes a higher beauty manifest.[1]

After these more eminent writers there followed, in Germany, less original and less influential ones, such as Hartmann, Kirkmann, Schnasse, and, to some extent, Helmholtz (as an æsthetician), Bergmann, Jungmann, and an innumerable host of others.

According to Hartmann (1842), beauty lies, not in the external world, nor in "the thing in itself," neither does it reside in the soul of man, but it lies in the "seeming" (*Schein*) produced by the artist. The thing in itself is not beautiful, but is transformed into beauty by the artist.[2]

According to Schnasse (1798–1875), there is no per-fect beauty in the world. In nature there is only an approach toward it. Art gives what nature cannot give. In the energy of the free *ego*, conscious of har-mony not found in nature, beauty is disclosed.[3]

Kirkmann wrote on experimental æsthetics. All as-pects of history in his system are joined by pure chance. Thus, according to Kirkmann (1802–1884), there are six realms of history: The realm of Knowledge, of Wealth, of Morality, of Faith, of Politics, and of Beauty; and activity in the last-named realm is art.[4]

According to Helmholtz (1821), who wrote on beauty as it relates to music, beauty in musical productions is attained only by following unalterable laws. These laws

---

[1] Schasler, pp. 1124, 1107.   [2] Knight, pp. 81, 82.
[3] Knight, p. 83.   [4] Schasler, p. 112L

are not known to the artist; so that beauty is manifested by the artist unconsciously, and cannot be subjected to analysis.[1]

According to Bergmann (1840) ("Ueber das Schöne," 1887), to define beauty objectively is impossible. Beauty is only perceived subjectively, and therefore the problem of æsthetics is to define what pleases whom.[2]

According to Jungmann (d. 1885), firstly, beauty is a suprasensible quality of things; secondly, beauty produces in us pleasure by merely being contemplated; and, thirdly, beauty is the foundation of love.[3]

The æsthetic theories of the chief representatives of France, England, and other nations in recent times have been the following:—

In France, during this period, the prominent writers on æsthetics were Cousin, Jouffroy, Pictet, Ravaisson, Lévêque.

Cousin (1792–1867) was an eclectic, and a follower of the German idealists. According to his theory, beauty always has a moral foundation. He disputes the doctrine that art is imitation and that the beautiful is what pleases. He affirms that beauty may be defined objectively, and that it essentially consists in variety in unity.[4]

After Cousin came Jouffroy (1796–1842), who was a pupil of Cousin's and also a follower of the German æstheticians. According to his definition, beauty is the expression of the invisible by those natural signs which manifest it. The visible world is the garment by means of which we see beauty.[5]

The Swiss writer Pictet repeated Hegel and Plato, supposing beauty to exist in the direct and free manifestation of the divine Idea revealing itself in sense forms.[6]

Lévêque was a follower of Schelling and Hegel. He holds that beauty is something invisible behind nature —a force or spirit revealing itself in ordered energy.[7]

Similar vague opinions about the nature of beauty

[1] Knight, pp. 85, 86. [2] Knight, p. 88.
[3] Knight, p. 88. [4] Knight, p. 112.
[5] Knight, p. 116. [6] Knight, pp. 118, 119.
[7] Knight, pp. 123, 124.

were expressed by the French metaphysician Ravaisson, who considered beauty to be the ultimate aim and purpose of the world. "*La beauté la plus divine et principalement la plus parfaite contient le secret du monde.*"[1] And again, "*Le monde entier est l'œuvre d'une beauté absolue, qui n'est la cause des choses que par l'amour qu'elle met en elles.*"

I purposely abstain from translating these metaphysical expressions, because, however cloudy the Germans may be, the French, once they absorb the theories of the Germans and take to imitating them, far surpass them in uniting heterogeneous conceptions into one expression, and putting forward one meaning or another indiscriminately. For instance, the French philosopher Renouvier, when discussing beauty, says, "*Ne craignons pas de dire qu'une vérité qui ne serait pas belle, ne serait qu'un jeu logique de notre esprit et que la seule vérité solide et digne de ce nom c'est la beauté.*"[2]

Besides the æsthetic idealists who wrote and still write under the influence of German philosophy, the following recent writers have also influenced the comprehension of art and beauty in France: Taine, Guyau, Cherbuliez, Coster, and Véron.

According to Taine (1828–1893), beauty is the manifestation of the essential characteristic of any important idea more completely than it is expressed in reality.[3]

Guyau (1854–1888) taught that beauty is not something exterior to the object itself, — is not, as it were, a parasitic growth on it, — but is itself the very blossoming forth of that on which it appears. Art is the expression of reasonable and conscious life, evoking in us both the deepest consciousness of existence and the highest feelings and loftiest thoughts. Art lifts man from his personal life into the universal life by means, not only of participation in the same ideas and beliefs, but also by means of similarity in feeling.[4]

[1] "La Philosophie en France," p. 232.
[2] "Du Fondement de l'Induction."
[3] "Philosophie de l'Art," vol. i., 1893, p. 47.
[4] Knight, pp. 139–141.

According to Cherbuliez, art is an activity, (1) satisfying our innate love of forms (*apparences*), (2) endowing these forms with ideas, (3) affording pleasure alike to our senses, heart, and reason. Beauty is not inherent in objects, but is an act of our souls. Beauty is an illusion; there is no absolute beauty. But what we consider characteristic and harmonious appears beautiful to us.

Coster held that the ideas of the beautiful, the good, and the true are innate. These ideas illuminate our minds and are identical with God, who is Goodness, Truth, and Beauty. The idea of Beauty includes unity of essence, variety of constitutive elements, and order, which brings unity into the various manifestations of life.[1]

For the sake of completeness, I will further cite some of the very latest writings upon art.

" La Psychologie du Beau et de l'Art, par Mario Pilo " (1895), says that beauty is a product of our physical feelings. The aim of art is pleasure, but this pleasure (for some reason) he considers to be necessarily highly moral.

The "Essai sur l'Art Contemporain, par Fierens Gevaert" (1897), says that art rests on its connection with the past, and on the religious ideal of the present which the artist holds when giving to his work the form of his individuality.

Then again, Sar Peladan's " L'Art Idealiste et Mystique " (1894), says that beauty is one of the manifestations of God. " *Il n'y a pas d'autre Réalité que Dieu, il n'y a pas d'autre Vérité que Dieu, il n'y a pas d'autre Beauté que Dieu* " (p. 33). This book is very fantastic and very illiterate, but is characteristic in the positions it takes up, and noticeable on account of a certain success it is having with the younger generation in France.

All the æsthetics diffused in France up to the present time are similar in kind, but among them Véron's " L'Esthétique " (1878) forms an exception, being reasonable and clear. That work, though it does not give an

[1] Knight, p. 134.

exact definition of art, at least rids æsthetics of the cloudy conception of an absolute beauty.

According to Véron (1825–1889), art is the manifestation of emotion transmitted externally by a combination of lines, forms, colors, or by a succession of movements, sounds, or words subjected to certain rhythms.[1]

In England, during this period, the writers on æsthetics define beauty more and more frequently, not by its own qualities, but by taste; and the discussion about beauty is superseded by a discussion on taste.

After Reid (1704–1796), who acknowledged beauty as being entirely dependent on the spectator, Alison, in his "Essay on the Nature and Principles of Taste" (1790), proved the same thing. From another side this was also asserted by Erasmus Darwin (1731–1802), the grandfather of the celebrated Charles Darwin.

He says that we consider beautiful that which is connected in our conception with what we love. Richard Knight's work, "An Analytical Inquiry into the Principles of Taste," also tends in the same direction.

Most of the English theories of æsthetics are on the same lines. The prominent writers on æsthetics in England during the present century have been Charles Darwin (to some extent), Herbert Spencer, Grant Allen, Ker, and Knight.

According to Charles Darwin (1809–1882 — "Descent of Man," 1871), beauty is a feeling natural not only to man, but also to animals, and consequently to the ancestors of man. Birds adorn their nests and esteem beauty in their mates. Beauty has an influence on marriages. Beauty includes a variety of diverse conceptions. The origin of the art of music is the call of the males to the females.[2]

According to Herbert Spencer (b. 1820), the origin of art is play, a thought previously expressed by Schiller. In the lower animals all the energy of life is expended in life-maintenance and race-maintenance; in man, however, there remains, after these needs are satisfied, some superfluous strength. This excess is used in play,

---

[1] "L'Esthétique," p. 106.   [2] Knight, p. 238.

which passes over into art. Play is an imitation of real activity; so is art. The sources of æsthetic pleasure are threefold: (1) That "which exercises the faculties affected in the most complete ways, with the fewest drawbacks from exercise," (2) "the difference of a stimulus in large amount, which awakens a glow of agreeable feeling," (3) the partial revival of the same, with special combinations.[1]

In Todhunter's "Theory of the Beautiful" (1872), beauty is infinite loveliness, which we apprehend both by reason and by the enthusiasm of love. The recognition of beauty as being such depends on taste; there can be no criterion for it. The only approach to a definition is found in culture. (What culture is, is not defined.) Intrinsically, art — that which affects us through lines, colors, sounds, or words — is not the product of blind forces, but of reasonable ones, working, with mutual helpfulness toward a reasonable aim. Beauty is the reconciliation of contradictions.[2]

Grant Allen is a follower of Spencer, and in his "Physiological Æsthetics" (1877) he says that beauty has a physical origin. Æsthetic pleasures come from the contemplation of the beautiful, but the conception of beauty is obtained by a physiological process. The origin of art is play; when there is a superfluity of physical strength man gives himself to play; when there is a superfluity of receptive power man gives himself to art. The beautiful is that which affords the maximum of stimulation with the minimum of waste. Differences in the estimation of beauty proceed from taste. Taste can be educated. We must have faith in the judgments "of the finest-nurtured and most discriminative" men. These people form the taste of the next generation.[3]

According to Ker's "Essay on the Philosophy of Art" (1883), beauty enables us to make part of the objective world intelligible to ourselves without being troubled by reference to other parts of it, as is inevitable for science. So that art destroys the opposition between the one and

---

[1] Knight, pp. 239, 240.   [2] Knight, pp. 240-243.
[3] Knight, pp. 250-252.

the many, between the law and its manifestation, between the subject and its object, by uniting them. Art is the revelation and vindication of freedom, because it is free from the darkness and incomprehensibility of finite things.[1]

According to Knight's "Philosophy of the Beautiful," Part II. (1893), beauty is (as with Schelling) the union of object and subject, the drawing forth from nature of that which is cognate to man, and the recognition in oneself of that which is common to all nature.

The opinions on beauty and on art here mentioned are far from exhausting what has been written on the subject. And every day fresh writers on æsthetics arise, in whose disquisitions appear the same enchanted confusion and contradictoriness in defining beauty. Some, by inertia, continue the mystical æsthetics of Baumgarten and Hegel with sundry variations; others transfer the question to the region of subjectivity, and seek for the foundation of the beautiful in questions of taste; others — the æstheticians of the very latest formation — seek the origin of beauty in the laws of physiology; and finally, others again investigate the question quite independently of the conception of beauty. Thus Sully, in his "Sensation and Intuition : Studies in Psychology and Æsthetics" (1874), dismisses the conception of beauty altogether, art, by his definition, being the production of some permanent object or passing action fitted to supply active enjoyment to the producer, and a pleasurable impression to a number of spectators or listeners, quite apart from any personal advantage derived from it.[2]

CHAPTER IV

To what do these definitions of beauty amount? Not reckoning the thoroughly inaccurate definitions of beauty which fail to cover the conception of art, and which suppose beauty to consist either in utility, or in adjustment to a purpose, or in symmetry, or in order, or in propor-

[1] Knight, pp. 258, 259.   [2] Knight, p. 243.

tion, or in smoothness, or in harmony of the parts, or in unity amid variety, or in various combinations of these — not reckoning these unsatisfactory attempts at objective definition, all the æsthetic definitions of beauty lead to two fundamental conceptions. The first is that beauty is something having an independent existence (existing in itself), that it is one of the manifestations of the absolutely Perfect, of the Idea, of the Spirit, of Will, or of God; the other is that beauty is a kind of pleasure received by us, not having personal advantage for its object.

The first of these definitions was accepted by Fichte, Schelling, Hegel, Schopenhauer, and the philosophizing Frenchmen, Cousin, Jouffroy, Ravaisson, and others, not to enumerate the second-rate æsthetic philosophers. And this same objective-mystical definition of beauty is held by a majority of the educated people of our day. It is a conception very widely spread, especially among the elder generation.

The second view, that beauty is a certain kind of pleasure received by us, not having personal advantage for its aim, finds favor chiefly among the English æs-thetic writers, and is shared by the other part of our society, principally by the younger generation.

So there are (and it could not be otherwise) only two definitions of beauty: the one objective, mystical, merg-ing this conception into that of the highest perfection, God — a fantastic definition, founded on nothing; the other, on the contrary, a very simple and intelligible subjective one, which considers beauty to be that which pleases (I do not add to the word "pleases" the words "without the aim of advantage," because "pleases" naturally presupposes the absence of the idea of profit).

On the one hand, beauty is viewed as something mystical and very elevated, but unfortunately at the same time very indefinite, and consequently embracing philosophy, religion, and life itself (as in the theories of Schelling and Hegel, and their German and French followers); or, on the other hand (as necessarily fol-lows from the definition of Kant and his adherents) beauty is simply a certain kind of disinterested pleasure received by us. And this conception of beauty, although it seems very clear is, unfortunately, again inexact; for it widens out on the other side, *i.e.* it includes the pleasure derived from drink, from food, from touching a delicate skin, etc., as is acknowledged by Guyau, Kralik, and others.

It is true that, following the development of the æsthetic doctrines on beauty, we may notice that, though at first (in the times when the foundations of the science of æsthetics were being laid) the metaphysical definition of beauty prevailed, yet the nearer we get to our own times the more does an experimental definition (recently assuming a physiological form) come to the front, so that at last we even meet with such æstheticians as Véron and Sully, who try to escape entirely from the conception of beauty. But such æstheticians have very little success, and with the majority of the public, as well as of artists and the learned, a conception of beauty is firmly held which agrees with the definitions contained in most of the æsthetic treatises, *i.e.* which regards beauty either as something mystical or metaphysical, or as a special kind of enjoyment.

What, then, is this conception of beauty, so stubbornly held to by people of our circle and day as furnishing a definition of art ?

In the subjective aspect, we call beauty that which supplies us with a particular kind of pleasure.

In the objective aspect, we call beauty something absolutely perfect, and we acknowledge it to be so only because we receive, from the manifestation of this absolute perfection, a certain kind of pleasure; so that this objective definition is nothing but the subjective conception differently expressed. In reality both conceptions of beauty amount to one and the same thing; namely, the reception by us of a certain kind of pleasure; *i.e.* we call " beauty " that which pleases us without evoking in us desire.

Such being the position of affairs, it would seem only natural that the science of art should decline to content

itself with a definition of art based on beauty (*i.e.* on
that which pleases), and seek a general definition, which
should apply to all artistic productions, and by reference
to which we might decide whether a certain article be-
longed to the realm of art or not. But no such definition is supplied, as the reader may see from those
summaries of the æsthetic theories which I have given,
and as he may discover even more clearly from the original æsthetic works, if he will be at the pains to read
them. All attempts to define absolute beauty in itself
— whether as an imitation of nature, or as suitability to
its object, or as a correspondence of parts, or as symmetry, or as harmony, or as unity in variety, etc. —
either define nothing at all, or define only some traits
of some artistic productions, and are far from including
all that everybody has always held, and still holds, to
be art.

There is no objective definition of beauty. The existing definitions (both the metaphysical and the experimental) amount only to one and the same subjective
definition, which (strange as it seems to say so) is, that
art is that which makes beauty manifest, and beauty is
that which pleases (without exciting desire). Many æstheticians have felt the insufficiency and instability of
such a definition, and, in order to give it a firm basis,
have asked themselves why a thing pleases. And they
have converted the discussion on beauty into a question
concerning taste, as did Hutcheson, Voltaire, Diderot,
and others. But all attempts to define what taste is
must lead to nothing, as the reader may see both from
the history of æsthetics and experimentally. There is
and can be no explanation of why one thing pleases
one man and displeases another, or *vice versa*. So that
the whole existing science of æsthetics fails to do what
we might expect from it, being a mental activity calling
itself a science; namely, it does not define the qualities
and laws of art, or of the beautiful (if that be the content of art), or the nature of taste (if taste decides the
question of art and its merit), and then, on the basis of
such definitions, acknowledge as art those productions

which correspond to these laws, and reject those which do not come under them. But this science of æsthetics consists in first acknowledging a certain set of productions to be art (because they please us), and then framing such a theory of art that all those productions which please a certain circle of people should fit into it. There exists an art canon, according to which certain productions favored by our circle are acknowledged as being art, — Phidias, Sophocles, Homer, Titian, Raphael, Bach, Beethoven, Dante, Shakespear, Goethe, and others, — and the æsthetic laws must be such as to embrace all these productions. In æsthetic literature you will incessantly meet with opinions on the merit and importance of art, founded not on any certain laws by which this or that is held to be good or bad, but merely on the consideration whether this art tallies with the art canon we have drawn up.

The other day I was reading a far from ill-written book by Folgeldt. Discussing the demand for morality in works of art, the author plainly says that we must not demand morality in art. And in proof of this he advances the fact that if we admit such a demand, Shakespear's "Romeo and Juliet," and Goethe's "Wilhelm Meister," would not fit into the definition of good art; but since both these books are included in our canon of art, he concludes that the demand is unjust. And therefore it is necessary to find a definition of art which shall fit the works; and instead of a demand for morality, Folgeldt postulates as the basis of art a demand for the important (*Bedeutungsvolles*).

All the existing æsthetic standards are built on this plan. Instead of giving a definition of true art, and then deciding what is and what is not good art by judging whether a work conforms or does not conform to the definition, a certain class of works, which for some reason please a certain circle of people, is accepted as being art, and a definition of art is then devised to cover all these productions. I recently came upon a remarkable instance of this method in a very good German work, " The History of Art in the Nineteenth Century," by Muther. Describing the pre-Raphaelites, the Decadents and the Symbolists (who are already included in the canon of art), he not only does not venture to blame their tendency, but earnestly endeavors to widen his standard so that it may include them all, they appearing to him to represent a legitimate reaction from the excesses of realism. No matter what insanities appear in art, when once they find acceptance among the upper classes of our society, a theory is quickly invented to explain and sanction them ; just as if there had never been periods in history when certain special circles of people recognized and approved false, deformed, and insensate art which subsequently left no trace and has been utterly forgotten. And to what lengths the insanity and deformity of art may go, especially when, as in our days, it knows that it is considered infallible, may be seen by what is being done in the art of our circle to-day.

So that the theory of art, founded on beauty, expounded by æsthetics, and, in dim outline, professed by the public, is nothing but the setting up as good of that which has pleased and pleases us, *i.e.* pleases a certain class of people.

In order to define any human activity, it is necessary to understand its sense and importance. And, in order to do that, it is primarily necessary to examine that activity in itself, in its dependence on its causes, and in connection with its effects, and not merely in relation to the pleasure we can get from it.

If we say that the aim of any activity is merely our pleasure, and define it solely by that pleasure, our definition will evidently be a false one. But this is precisely what has occurred in the efforts to define art. Now, if we consider the food question, it will not occur to anyone to affirm that the importance of food consists in the pleasure we receive when eating it. Every one understands that the satisfaction of our taste cannot serve as a basis for our definition of the merits of food, and that we have therefore no right to presuppose that the dinners with cayenne pepper, Limburg cheese, alcohol, etc., to which we are accustomed and which please us, form the very best human food.

And in the same way, beauty, or that which pleases us, can in no sense serve as the basis for the definition of art; nor can a series of objects which afford us pleasure serve as the model of what art should be.

To see the aim and purpose of art in the pleasure we get from it, is like assuming (as is done by people of the lowest moral development, *e.g.* by savages) that the purpose and aim of food is the pleasure derived when consuming it.

Just as people who conceive the aim and purpose of food to be pleasure cannot recognize the real meaning of eating, so people who consider the aim of art to be pleasure cannot realize its true meaning and purpose, because they attribute to an activity, the meaning of which lies in its connection with other phenomena of life, the false and exceptional aim of pleasure. People come to understand that the meaning of eating lies in the nourishment of the body only when they cease to consider that the object of that activity is pleasure. And it is the same with regard to art. People will come to understand the meaning of art only when they cease to consider that the aim of that activity is beauty, *i.e.* pleasure. The acknowledgment of beauty (*i.e.* of a certain kind of pleasure received from art) as being the aim of art, not only fails to assist us in finding a definition of what art is, but, on the contrary, by trans- ferring the question into a region quite foreign to art (into metaphysical, psychological, physiological, and even historical discussions as to why such a production pleases one person, and such another displeases or pleases some one else), it renders such definition im- possible. And since discussions as to why one man likes pears and another prefers meat do not help toward finding a definition of what is essential in nourishment, so the solution of questions of taste in art (to which the discussions on art involuntarily come), not only does not help to make clear what this particular human activity which we call art really consists in, but renders such elucidation quite impossible, until we rid ourselves of a conception which justifies every kind of art, at the cost of confusing the whole matter.

To the question, What is this art, to which is offered up the labor of millions, the very lives of men, and even morality itself? we have extracted replies from the existing æsthetics, which all amount to this · that the aim of art is beauty, that beauty is recognized by the enjoyment it gives, and that artistic enjoyment is a good and important thing, because it *is* enjoyment. In a word, that enjoyment is good because it is enjoyment. Thus, what is considered the definition of art is no definition at all, but only a shuffle to justify existing art. Therefore, however strange it may seem to say so, in spite of the mountains of books written about art, no exact definition of art has been constructed. And the reason of this is that the conception of art has been based on the conception of beauty.

CHAPTER V

What is art, if we put aside the conception of beauty, which confuses the whole matter? The latest and most comprehensible definitions of art, apart from the conception of beauty, are the following: (1 *a*) Art is an activity arising even in the animal kingdom, and springing from sexual desire and the propensity to play (Schiller, Darwin, Spencer), and (1 *b*) accompanied by a pleasurable excitement of the nervous system (Grant Allen). This is the physiological-evolutionary definition. (2) Art is the external manifestation, by means of lines, colors, movements, sounds, or words, of emotions felt by man (Véron). This is the experimental definition. According to the very latest definition (Sully), (3) Art is "the production of some permanent object or passing action, which is fitted, not only to supply an active enjoyment to the producer, but to convey a pleasurable impression to a number of spectators or listeners, quite apart from any personal advantage to be derived from it."

Notwithstanding the superiority of these definitions to the metaphysical definitions which depended on the conception of beauty, they are yet far from exact. (1 *a*) The first, the physiological-evolutionary definition, is inexact, because, instead of speaking about the artistic activity itself, which is the real matter in hand, it treats of the derivation of art. The modification of it (1 *b*), based on the physiological effects on the human organism, is inexact, because within the limits of such definition many other human activities can be included, as has occurred in the neo-æsthetic theories, which reckon as art the preparation of handsome clothes, pleasant scents, and even of victuals.

The experimental definition (2), which makes art consist in the expression of emotions, is inexact, because a man may express his emotions by means of lines, colors, sounds, or words, and yet may not act on others by such expression; and then the manifestation of his emotions is not art.

The third definition (that of Sully) is inexact, because in the production of objects or actions affording pleasure to the producer and a pleasant emotion to the spectators or hearers apart from personal advantage may be included the showing of conjuring tricks or gymnastic exercises, and other activities which are not art. And, further, many things, the production of which does not afford pleasure to the producer, and the sensation received from which is unpleasant, such as gloomy, heart-rending scenes in a poetic description or a play, may nevertheless be undoubted works of art.

The inaccuracy of all these definitions arises from the fact that in them all (as also in the metaphysical definitions) the object considered is the pleasure art may give, and not the purpose it may serve in the life of man and of humanity.

In order correctly to define art, it is necessary, first of all, to cease to consider it as a means to pleasure, and to consider it as one of the conditions of human life. Viewing it in this way, we cannot fail to observe that art is one of the means of intercourse between man and man.

Every work of art causes the receiver to enter into a certain kind of relationship both with him who produced, or is producing, the art, and with all those who, simultaneously, previously, or subsequently, receive the same artistic impression.

Speech, transmitting the thoughts and experiences of men, serves as a means of union among them, and art acts in a similar manner. The peculiarity of this latter means of intercourse, distinguishing it from intercourse by means of words, consists in this, that whereas by words a man transmits his thoughts to another, by means of art he transmits his feelings.

The activity of art is based on the fact that a man, receiving through his sense of hearing or sight another man's expression of feeling, is capable of experiencing the emotion which moved the man who expressed it. To take the simplest example: one man laughs, and another, who hears, becomes merry; or a man weeps, and another, who hears, feels sorrow. A man is excited or irritated, and another man, seeing him, comes to a similar state of mind. By his movements, or by the sounds of his voice, a man expresses courage and determination, or sadness and calmness, and this state of mind passes on to others. A man suffers, expressing his sufferings by groans and spasms, and this suffering transmits itself to other people; a man expresses his feeling of admiration, devotion, fear, respect, or love to certain objects, persons, or phenomena, and others are infected by the same feelings of admiration, devotion, fear, respect, or love to the same objects, persons, and phenomena.

And it is on this capacity of man to receive another man's expression of feeling, and experience those feelings himself, that the activity of art is based.

If a man infects another or others, directly, immediately, by his appearance, or by the sounds he gives vent to at the very time he experiences the feeling; if he causes another man to yawn when he himself cannot help yawning, or to laugh or cry when he himself is obliged to laugh or cry, or to suffer when he himself is suffering — that does not amount to art.

Art begins when one person, with the object of join·
ing another or others to himself in one and the same
feeling, expresses that feeling by certain external indi·
cations.   To take the simplest example : a boy, having
experienced, let us say, fear on encountering a wolf, relates that encounter ; and, in order to evoke in others
the feeling he has experienced, describes himself, his
condition before the encounter, the surroundings, the
wood, his own light-heartedness, and then the wolf's
appearance, its movements, the distance between himself and the wolf, etc.   All this, if only the boy, when
telling the story, again experiences the feelings he had
lived through and infects the hearers and compels them
to feel what the narrator had experienced, is art.   If
even the boy had not seen a wolf but had frequently
been afraid of one, and if, wishing to evoke in others
the fear he had felt, he invented an encounter with a
wolf, and recounted it so as to make his hearers share
the feelings he experienced when he feared the wolf,
that also would be art.   And just in the same way it is
art if a man, having experienced either the fear of suffering or the attraction of enjoyment (whether in reality
or in imagination), expresses these feelings on canvas
or in marble so that others are infected by them.   And
it is also art if a man feels or imagines to himself feelings of delight, gladness, sorrow, despair, courage, or
despondency, and the transition from one to another of
these feelings, and expresses these feelings by sounds,
so that the hearers are infected by them, and experience them as they were experienced by the composer.

The feelings with which the artist infects others may
be most various, — very strong or very weak, very important or very insignificant, very bad or very good :
feelings of love for native land, self-devotion and submission to fate or to God expressed in a drama, raptures
of lovers described in a novel, feelings of voluptuousness expressed in a picture, courage expressed in a triumphal march, merriment evoked by a dance, humor
evoked by a funny story, the feeling of quietness transmitted by an evening landscape or by a lullaby, or the

feeling of admiration evoked by a beautiful arabesque
— it is all art.

If only the spectators or auditors are infected by the
feelings which the author has felt, it is art.

*To evoke in oneself a feeling one has once experienced,
and having evoked it in oneself, then, by means of movements, lines, colors, sounds, or forms expressed in words,
so to transmit that feeling that others may experience the
same feeling — this is the activity of art.*

*Art is a human activity, consisting in this, that one
man consciously, by means of certain external signs, hands
on to others feelings he has lived through, and that other
people are infected by these feelings, and also experience
them.*

Art is not, as the metaphysicians say, the manifestation of some mysterious Idea of beauty, or God; it is
not, as the æsthetical physiologists say, a game in which
man lets off his excess of stored-up energy; it is not the
expression of man's emotions by external signs; it is not
the production of pleasing objects; and, above all, it is
not pleasure; but it is a means of union among men,
joining them together in the same feelings, and indispensable for the life and progress toward well-being
of individuals and of humanity.

As, thanks to man's capacity to express thoughts by
words, every man may know all that has been done for
him in the realms of thought by all humanity before his
day, and can, in the present, thanks to this capacity to
understand the thoughts of others, become a sharer in
their activity, and can himself hand on to his contemporaries and descendants the thoughts he has assimilated
from others, as well as those which have arisen within
himself; so, thanks to man's capacity to be infected
with the feelings of others by means of art, all that is
being lived through by his contemporaries is accessible
to him, as well as the feelings experienced by men
thousands of years ago, and he has also the possibility
of transmitting his own feelings to others.

If people lacked this capacity to receive the thoughts
conceived by the men who preceded them, and to pass

on to others their own thoughts, men would be like wild beasts, or like Kaspar Hauser.[1]

And if men lacked this other capacity of being infected by art, people might be almost more savage still, and, above all, more separated from, and more hostile to, one another.

And therefore the activity of art is a most important one, as important as the activity of speech itself, and as generally diffused.

We are accustomed to understand art to be only what we hear and see in theaters, concerts, and exhibitions; together with buildings, statues, poems, novels. .... But all this is but the smallest part of the art by which we communicate with each other in life. All human life is filled with works of art of every kind, — from cradle-song, jest, mimicry, the ornamentation of houses, dress, and utensils, up to church services, buildings, monuments, and triumphal processions. It is all artistic activity. So that by art, in the limited sense of the word, we do not mean all human activity transmitting feelings, but only that part which we for some reason select from it and to which we attach special importance.

This special importance has always been given by all men to that part of this activity which transmits feelings flowing from their religious perception, and this small part of art they have specifically called art, attaching to it the full meaning of the word.

That was how men of old — Socrates, Plato, and Aristotle — looked on art. Thus did the Hebrew prophets and the ancient Christians regard art; thus it was, and still is, understood by the Mahommedans, and thus is it still understood by religious folk among our own peasantry.

Some teachers of mankind — as Plato in his " Republic," and people such as the primitive Christians, the strict

---

[1] "The foundling of Nuremberg," found in the market-place of that town on 26th May, 1828, apparently some sixteen years old. He spoke little, and was almost totally ignorant even of common objects. He subsequently explained that he had been brought up in confinement underground, and visited by only one man, whom he saw but seldom. — TR.

Mahommedans, and the Buddhists — have gone so far as to repudiate all art.

People viewing art in this way (in contradiction to the prevalent view of to-day, which regards any art as good if only it affords pleasure) considered, and consider, that art (as contrasted with speech, which need not be listened to) is so highly dangerous in its power to infect people against their wills, that mankind will lose far less by banishing all art than by tolerating each and every art.

Evidently such people were wrong in repudiating all art, for they denied that which cannot be denied, — one of the indispensable means of communication, without which mankind could not exist. But not less wrong are the people of civilized European society of our class and day, in favoring any art if it but serves beauty, *i.e.* gives people pleasure.

Formerly, people feared lest among the works of art there might chance to be some causing corruption, and they prohibited art altogether. Now, they only fear lest they should be deprived of any enjoyment art can afford, and patronize any art. And I think the last error is much grosser than the first, and that its consequences are far more harmful.

CHAPTER VI

BUT how could it happen that that very art, which in ancient times was merely tolerated (if tolerated at all), should have come, in our times, to be invariably considered a good thing if only it affords pleasure?

It has resulted from the following causes. The estimation of the value of art (*i.e.* of the feelings it transmits) depends on men's perception of the meaning of life; depends on what they consider to be the good and the evil of life. And what is good and what is evil is defined by what are termed religions.

Humanity unceasingly moves forward from a lower, more partial, and obscure understanding of life, to one more general and more lucid. And in this, as in every movement, there are leaders, — those who have under-stood the meaning of life more clearly than others, — and of these advanced men there is always one who has, in his words and by his life, expressed this mean-ing more clearly, accessibly, and strongly than others. This man's expression of the meaning of life, together with those superstitions, traditions, and ceremonies which usually form themselves round the memory of such a man, is what is called a religion. Religions are the exponents of the highest comprehension of life accessible to the best and foremost men at a given time in a given society; a comprehension toward which, inevitably and irresistibly, all the rest of that society must advance. And therefore only religions have always served, and still serve, as bases for the valuation of human sentiments. If feelings bring men nearer the ideal their religion indicates, if they are in harmony with it and do not contradict it, they are good; if they estrange men from it and oppose it, they are bad.

If the religion places the meaning of life in worship-ing one God and fulfilling what is regarded as His will, as was the case among the Jews, then the feelings flowing from love to that God, and to His law, suc-cessfully transmitted through the art of poetry by the prophets, by the psalms, or by the epic of the book of Genesis, is good, high art. All opposing that, as, for instance, the transmission of feelings of devotion to strange gods, or of feelings incompatible with the law of God, would be considered bad art. Or if, as was the case among the Greeks, the religion places the meaning of life in earthly happiness, in beauty and in strength, then art successfully transmitting the joy and energy of life would be considered good art, but art which transmitted feelings of effeminacy or despondency would be bad art. If the meaning of life is seen in the well-being of one's nation, or in honoring one's ancestors and continuing the mode of life led by them, as was the case among the Romans

and the Chinese respectively, then art transmitting
feelings of joy at sacrificing one's personal well-being
for the common weal, or at exalting one's ancestors
and maintaining their traditions, would be considered
good art, but art expressing feelings contrary to this
would be regarded as bad. If the meaning of life is
seen in freeing oneself from the yoke of animalism,
as is the case among the Buddhists, then art successfully transmitting feelings that elevate the soul and
humble the flesh will be good art, and all that transmits feelings strengthening the bodily passions will be
bad art.

In every age, and in every human society, there
exists a religious sense, common to that whole society,
of what is good and what is bad, and it is this religious
conception that decides the value of the feelings transmitted by art. And therefore, among all nations, art
which transmitted feelings considered to be good by
this general religious sense was recognized as being
good and was encouraged; but art which transmitted
feelings considered to be bad by this general religious
conception, was recognized as being bad, and was rejected. All the rest of the immense field of art by
means of which people communicate one with another,
was not esteemed at all, and was only noticed when
it ran counter to the religious conception of its age,
and then merely to be repudiated. Thus it was among
all nations, — Greeks, Jews, Indians, Egyptians, and
Chinese, — and so it was when Christianity appeared.

The Christianity of the first centuries recognized as
productions of good art only legends, lives of saints,
sermons, prayers, and hymn-singing, evoking love of
Christ, emotion at His life, desire to follow His example,
renunciation of worldly life, humility, and the love of
others; all productions transmitting feelings of personal
enjoyment they considered to be bad, and therefore
rejected: for instance, tolerating plastic representations
only when they were symbolical, they rejected all the
pagan sculptures.

· This was so among the Christians of the first cen·

turies, who accepted Christ's teaching, if not quite in its true form, at least not in the perverted, paganized form in which it was accepted subsequently.

But besides this Christianity, from the time of the wholesale conversion of nations by order of the authorities, as in the days of Constantine, Charlemagne, and Vladimir, there appeared another, a Church Christianity, which was nearer to paganism than to Christ's teaching. And this Church Christianity, in accordance with its own teaching, estimated quite otherwise the feelings of people and the productions of art which transmitted those feelings.

This Church Christianity not only did not acknowledge the fundamental and essential positions of true Christianity, — the immediate relationship of each man to the Father, the consequent brotherhood and equality of all men, and the substitution of humility and love in place of every kind of violence, — but, on the contrary, having set up a heavenly hierarchy similar to the pagan mythology, and having introduced the worship of Christ, of the Virgin, of angels, of apostles, of saints, and of martyrs, and not only of these divinities themselves, but also of their images, it made blind faith in the Church and its ordinances the essential point of its teaching.

However foreign this teaching may have been to true Christianity; however degraded, not only in comparison with true Christianity, but even with the life-conception of Romans such as Julian and others, — it was, for all that, to the barbarians who accepted it, a higher doctrine than their former adoration of gods, heroes, and good and bad spirits. And therefore this teaching was a religion to them, and on the basis of that religion the art of the time was assessed. And art transmitting pious adoration of the Virgin, Jesus, the saints and the angels, a blind faith in and submission to the Church, fear of torments and hope of blessedness in a life beyond the grave, was considered good; all art opposed to this was considered bad.

The teaching on the basis of which this art arose

was a perversion of Christ's teaching, but the art which sprang up on this perverted teaching was nevertheless a true art, because it corresponded to the religious view of life held by the people among whom it arose.

The artists of the Middle Ages, vitalized by the same source of feeling — religion — as the mass of the people, and transmitting, in architecture, sculpture, painting, music, poetry or drama, the feelings and states of mind they experienced, were true artists; and their activity, founded on the highest conceptions accessible to their age and common to the entire people, though, for our times a mean art, was, nevertheless a true one, shared by the whole community.

And this was the state of things until, in the upper, rich, more educated classes of European society, doubt arose as to the truth of that understanding of life which was expressed by Church Christianity. When, after the Crusades and the maximum development of papal power and its abuses, people of the rich classes became acquainted with the wisdom of the classics, and saw, on the one hand, the reasonable lucidity of the teaching of the ancient sages, and, on the other hand, the incompatibility of the Church doctrine with the teaching of Christ, they lost all possibility of continuing to believe the Church teaching.

If, in externals, they still kept to the forms of Church teaching, they could no longer believe in it, and held to it only by inertia and for the sake of influencing the masses, who continued to believe blindly in Church doctrine, and whom the upper classes, for their own advantage, considered it necessary to support in those beliefs.

So that a time came when Church Christianity ceased to be the general religious doctrine of all Christian people; some — the masses — continued blindly to believe in it, but the upper classes — those in whose hands lay the power and wealth, and therefore the leisure to produce art and the means to stimulate it — ceased to believe in that teaching.

In respect to religion, the upper circles of the Middle Ages found themselves in the same position in which the educated Romans were before Christianity arose, *i.e.* they no longer believed in the religion of the masses, but had no beliefs to put in place of the worn-out Church doctrine which for them had lost its meaning.

There was only this difference: that whereas for the Romans, who lost faith in their emperor-gods and household-gods, it was impossible to extract anything further from all the complex mythology they had borrowed from all the conquered nations, and it was consequently necessary to find a completely new conception of life, the people of the Middle Ages, when they doubted the truth of the Church teaching, had no need to seek a fresh one. That Christian teaching which they professed in a perverted form as Church doctrine had mapped out the path of human progress so far ahead that they had but to rid themselves of those perversions which hid the teaching announced by Christ, and to adopt its real meaning — if not completely, then at least in some greater degree than that in which the Church had held it. And this was partially done, not only in the reformations of Wyclif, Huss, Luther, and Calvin, but by all that current of non-Church Christianity represented in earlier times by the Paulicians, the Bogomili,[1] and, afterward, by the Waldenses and the other non-Church Christians who were called heretics. But this could be, and was, done chiefly by poor people — who did not rule. A few of the rich and strong, like Francis of Assisi and others, accepted the Christian teaching in its full significance, even though it undermined their privileged positions. But most people of the upper classes (though in the depth of their souls they had lost faith in the Church teaching) could not or would not act thus, because the essence of that Christian view of life, which stood ready to be adopted when once they rejected the Church faith,

---

[1] Eastern sects well known in early Church history, who rejected the Church's rendering of Christ's teaching, and were cruelly persecuted. ⌣ᵕ TR.

was a teaching of the brotherhood (and therefore the equality) of man, and this negatived those privileges on which they lived, in which they had grown up and been educated, and to which they were accustomed. Not, in the depth of their hearts, believing in the Church teaching, — which had outlived its age and had no longer any true meaning for them, — and not being strong enough to accept true Christianity, men of these rich, governing classes — popes, kings, dukes, and all the great ones of the earth — were left without any religion, with but the external forms of one, which they supported as being profitable and even necessary for themselves, since these forms screened a teaching which justified those privileges which they made use of. In reality, these people believed in nothing, just as the Romans of the first centuries of our era believed in nothing. But at the same time these were the people who had the power and the wealth, and these were the people who rewarded art and directed it.

And, let it be noticed, it was just among these people that there grew up an art esteemed, not according to its success in expressing men's religious feelings, but in proportion to its beauty, — in other words, according to the enjoyment it gave.

No longer able to believe in the Church religion, whose falsehood they had detected, and incapable of accepting true Christian teaching, which denounced their whole manner of life, these rich and powerful people, stranded without any religious conception of life, involuntarily returned to that pagan view of things which places life's meaning in personal enjoyment. And then took place among the upper classes what is called the " Renaissance of science and art," and which was really not only a denial of every religion, but also an assertion that religion is unnecessary.

The Church doctrine is so coherent a system that it cannot be altered or corrected without destroying it altogether. As soon as doubt arose with regard to the infallibility of the Pope (and this doubt was then in the minds of all educated people), doubt inevitably followed as to the truth of tradition. But doubt as to the truth of tradition is fatal not only to popery and Catholicism, but also to the whole Church creed, with all its dogmas : the divinity of Christ, the resurrection, and the Trinity ; and it destroys the authority of the Scriptures, since they were considered to be inspired only because the tradition of the Church decided it so.

So that the majority of the highest classes of that age, even the popes and the ecclesiastics, really believed in nothing at all. In the Church doctrine these people did not believe, for they saw its insolvency ; but neither could they follow Francis of Assisi, Keltchitsky,[1] and most of the heretics, in acknowledging the moral, social teaching of Christ, for that teaching undermined their social position. And so these people remained without any religious view of life. And, having none, they could have no standard wherewith to estimate what was good and what was bad art but that of personal enjoyment. And, having acknowledged their criterion of what was good to be pleasure, *i.e.* beauty, these people of the upper classes of European society went back in their comprehension of art to the gross conception of the primitive Greeks which Plato had already condemned. And conformably to this understanding of life, a theory of art was formulated.

CHAPTER VII

From the time that people of the upper classes lost faith in Church Christianity, beauty (*i.e.* the pleasure received from art) became their standard of good and bad art. And, in accordance with that view, an æsthetic theory naturally sprang up among those upper classes justifying such a conception, — a theory according to which the aim of art is to exhibit beauty. The partizans of this æsthetic theory, in confirmation of its truth, af-

---

[1] Keltchitsky, a Bohemian of the fifteenth century, was the author of a remarkable book, "The Net of Faith," directed against Church and State. It is mentioned in Tolstoi's "The Kingdom of God is Within You." — Tr.

firmed that it was no invention of their own, but that it existed in the nature of things, and was recognized even by the ancient Greeks. But this assertion was quite arbitrary, and has no foundation other than the fact that among the ancient Greeks, in consequence of the low grade of their moral ideal (as compared with the Christian), their conception of the good, τὸ ἀγαθόν, was not yet sharply divided from their conception of the beautiful, τὸ καλόν.

That highest perfection of goodness (not only not identical with beauty, but, for the most part, contrasting with it) which was discerned by the Jews even in the times of Isaiah, and fully expressed by Christianity, was quite unknown to the Greeks. They supposed that the beautiful must necessarily also be the good. It is true that their foremost thinkers — Socrates, Plato, Aristotle — felt that goodness may happen not to coincide with beauty. Socrates expressly subordinated beauty to goodness; Plato, to unite the two conceptions, spoke of spiritual beauty; while Aristotle demanded from art that it should have a moral influence on people (κάθαρσις). But, notwithstanding all this, they could not quite dismiss the notion that beauty and goodness coincide.

And consequently, in the language of that period, a compound word (καλο-κἀγαθία, beauty-goodness) came into use to express that notion.

Evidently the Greek sages began to draw near to that perception of goodness which is expressed in Buddhism and in Christianity, and they got entangled in defining the relation between goodness and beauty. Plato's reasonings about beauty and goodness are full of contradictions. And it was just this confusion of ideas that those Europeans of a later age, who had lost all faith, tried to elevate into a law. They tried to prove that this union of beauty and goodness is inherent in the very essence of things; that beauty and goodness must coincide; and that the word and conception καλο-κἀγαθία (which had a meaning for Greeks, but has none at all for Christians) represents the highest ideal of humanity. On this misunderstanding the new science of æsthetics was built up. And, to justify its existence, the teachings of the ancients on art were so twisted as to make it appear that this invented science of æsthetics had existed among the Greeks.

In reality, the reasoning of the ancients on art was quite unlike ours. As Benard, in his book on the æsthetics of Aristotle, quite justly remarks, "*Pour qui veut y regarder de près, la théorie du beau et celle de l'art sont tout à fait séparées dans Aristote, comme elles le sont dans Platon et chez tous leurs successeurs*" ("L'Esthétique d'Aristote et de ses Successeurs," Paris, 1889, p. 28).[1] And indeed the reasoning of the ancients on art not only does not confirm our science of æsthetics, but rather contradicts its doctrine of beauty. But nevertheless all the æsthetic guides, from Schasler to Knight, declare that the science of the beautiful — æsthetic science — was commenced by the ancients, by Socrates, Plato, Aristotle; and was continued, they say, partially by the Epicureans and Stoics: by Seneca and Plutarch, down to Plotinus. But it is supposed that this science, by some unfortunate accident, suddenly vanished in the fourth century, and stayed away for about 1500 years, and only after these 1500 years had passed did it revive in Germany, 1750 A.D., in Baumgarten's doctrine.

After Plotinus, says Schasler, fifteen centuries passed away during which there was not the slightest scientific interest felt for the world of beauty and art. These one and a half thousand years, says he, have been lost to æsthetics, and have contributed nothing toward the erection of the learned edifice of this science.[2]

[1] Any one examining closely may see that the theory of beauty and that of art are quite separated in Aristotle as they are in Plato and in all their successors.

[2] Die Lücke von fünf Jahrhunderten, welche zwischen den Kunst-philosophischen Betrachtungen des Plato und Aristoteles und die des Plotins fällt, kann zwar auffällig erscheinen; dennoch kann man eigentlich nicht sagen, dass in dieser Zwischenzeit überhaupt von ästhetischen Dingen nicht die Rede gewesen; oder dass gar ein völliger Mangel an Zusammenhang zwischen den Kunst-anschauungen des letztgenannten Philosophen und denen der ersteren existire. Freilich wurde die von Aristoteles begründete Wissenschaft in Nichts dadurch gefördert; immerhin aber zeigt sich in jener Zwischenzeit noch ein gewisses Interesse für ästhetische

In reality nothing of the kind happened. The science of æsthetics, the science of the beautiful, neither did nor could vanish, because it never existed. Simply, the Greeks (just like everybody else, always and everywhere) considered art (like everything else) good only when it served goodness (as they understood goodness), and bad when it was in opposition to that goodness. And the Greeks themselves were so little developed morally, that goodness and beauty seemed to them to coincide. On that obsolete Greek view of life was erected the science of æsthetics, invented by men of the eighteenth century, and especially shaped and mounted in Baumgarten's theory. The Greeks (as any one may see who will read Benard's admirable book on Aristotle and his successors and Walter's work on Plato) never had a science of æsthetics.

Æsthetic theories arose about one hundred and fifty years ago among the wealthy classes of the Christian European world, and arose simultaneously among different nations, — German, Italian, Dutch, French, and English. The founder and organizer of it, who gave it a scientific, theoretic form, was Baumgarten.

With a characteristically German, external exactitude, pedantry, and symmetry, he devised and expounded this extraordinary theory. And, notwithstanding its obvious insolidity, nobody else's theory so pleased the cultured crowd, or was accepted so readily and with such an absence of criticism. It so suited the people of the upper classes, that to this day, notwithstanding its entirely fantastic character and the arbitrary nature of its assertions, it is repeated by learned and unlearned as though it were something indubitable and self-evident.

Fragen. Nach Plotin aber, die wenigen, ihm in der Zeit nahestehenden Philosophen, wie Longin, Augustin, u. s. f. kommen, wie wir gesehen, kaum in Betracht und schliessen sich übrigens in ihrer Anschauungsweise an ihn an, — vergehen nicht fünf, sondern *fünfzehn Jahrhunderte*, in denen von irgend einer wissenschaftlichen Interesse für die Welt des Schönen und der Kunst nichts zu spüren ist.

Diese anderthalbtausend Jahre, innerhalb deren der Weltgeist durch die mannigfachsten Kämpfe hindurch zu einer völlig neuen Gestaltung des Lebens sich durcharbeitete, sind für die Aesthetik, hinsichtlich des weiteren Ausbaus dieser Wissenschaft verloren. — MAX SCHASLER.

Habent sua fata libelli pro capite lectoris, and so, or
even more so, theories *habent sua fata* according to the
condition of error in which that society is living, among
whom and for whom the theories are invented. If a
theory justifies the false position in which a certain
part of a society is living, then, however unfounded or
even obviously false the theory may be, it is accepted,
and becomes an article of faith to that section of society.
Such, for instance, was the celebrated and unfounded
theory, expounded by Malthus, of the tendency of that
population of the world to increase in geometrical
progression, but of the means of sustenance to increase
only in arithmetical progression, and of the consequent
over-population of the world; such, also, was the theory
(an outgrowth of the Malthusian) of selection and struggle for existence as the basis of human progress. Such,
again, is Marx's theory, which regards the gradual destruction of small private production by large capitalistic
production, now going on around us, as an inevitable
decree of fate. However unfounded such theories are,
however contrary to all that is known and confessed by
humanity, and however obviously immoral they may be,
they are accepted with credulity, pass uncriticized, and
are preached, perchance for centuries, until the conditions are destroyed which they served to justify, or until
their absurdity has become too evident. To this class
belongs this astonishing theory of the Baumgartenian
Trinity, — Goodness, Beauty, and Truth, — according to
which it appears that the very best that can be done
by the art of nations after 1900 years of Christian teaching, is to choose as the ideal of their life the ideal that
was held by a small, semi-savage, slave-holding people
who lived 2000 years ago, who imitated the nude human
body extremely well, and erected buildings pleasant to
look at. All these incompatibilities pass completely
unnoticed. Learned people write long, cloudy treatises
on beauty as a member of the æsthetic trinity of Beauty,
Truth, and Goodness: *das Schöne, das Wahre, das Gute;*
le Beau, le Vrai, le Bon, are repeated, with capital letters,
by philosophers, æstheticians, and artists, by private in-

dividuals, by novelists, and by *feuilletonistes,* and they all think, when pronouncing these sacrosanct words, that they speak of something quite definite and solid — something on which they can base their opinions. In reality, these words not only have no definite meaning, but they hinder us in attaching any definite meaning to existing art; they are wanted only for the purpose of justifying the false importance we attribute to an art that transmits every kind of feeling, if only those feelings afford us pleasure.

CHAPTER VIII

But if art is a human activity having for its purpose the transmission to others of the highest and best feelings to which men have risen, how could it be that humanity for a certain rather considerable period of its existence (from the time people ceased to believe in Church doctrine down to the present day) should exist without this important activity, and, instead of it, should put up with an insignificant artistic activity only affording pleasure?

In order to answer this question, it is necessary, first of all, to correct the current error people make in attributing to our art the significance of true, universal art. We are so accustomed, not only naïvely to consider the Circassian family the best stock of people, but also the Anglo-Saxon race the best race if we are Englishmen or Americans, or the Teutonic if we are Germans, or the Gallo-Latin if we are French, or the Slavonic if we are Russians, that, when speaking of our own art, we feel fully convinced, not only that our art is true art, but even that it is the best and only true art. But in reality our art is not only not the only art (as the Bible once was held to be the only book), but it is not even the art of the whole of Christendom — only of a small section of that part of humanity. It was correct to speak of a national Jewish, Grecian, or

Egyptian art, and one may speak of a now-existing Chinese, Japanese, or Indian art shared in by a whole people. Such art, common to a whole nation, existed in Russia till Peter the First's time, and existed in the rest of Europe until the thirteenth or fourteenth century ; but since the upper classes of European society, having lost faith in the Church teaching, did not accept real Christianity but remained without any faith, one can no longer speak of an art of the Christian nations in the sense of the whole of art.   Since the upper classes of the Christian nations lost faith in Church Christianity, the art of those upper classes has separated itself from the art of the rest of the people, and there have been two arts, — the art of the people and genteel art.   And therefore the answer to the question, How it could occur that humanity lived for a certain period without real art, replacing it by art which served enjoyment only ? is, that not all humanity, nor even any considerable portion of it, lived without real art, but only the highest classes of European Christian society, and even they only for a comparatively short time, — from the commencement of the Renaissance down to our own day.

And the consequence of this absence of true art showed itself, inevitably, in the corruption of that class which nourished itself on the false art. All the confused, unintelligible theories of art, all the false and contradictory judgments on art, and particularly the self-confident stagnation of our art in its false path, all arise from the assertion, which has come into common use and is accepted as an unquestioned truth, but is yet amazingly and palpably false, the assertion, namely, that the art of our upper classes [1] is the whole of art, the true, the only, the universal art.   And although this assertion (which is precisely similar to the assertion made by religious people of the various Churches who consider that theirs is the only true religion) is quite arbitrary

---

[1] The contrast made is between the classes and the masses ; between those who do not and those who do earn their bread by productive manual labor; the middle classes being taken as an offshoot of the upper classes. — TR.

and obviously unjust, yet it is calmly repeated by all
the people of our circle with full faith in its infallibility.

The art we have is the whole of art, the real, the only
art, and yet two-thirds of the human race (all the peoples
of Asia and Africa) live and die knowing nothing of this
sole and supreme art.   And even in our Christian society hardly one per cent of the people make use of this
art which we speak of as being the *whole* of art; the
remaining ninety-nine per cent live and die, generation
after generation, crushed by toil, and never tasting this
art, which, moreover, is of such a nature that, if they
could get it, they would not understand anything of it.
We, according to the current æsthetic theory, acknowledge art as one of the highest manifestations of the
Idea, God, Beauty, or as the highest spiritual enjoyment;
furthermore, we hold that all people have equal rights,
if not to material, at any rate to spiritual well-being;
and yet ninety-nine per cent of our European population live and die, generation after generation, crushed
by toil, much of which toil is necessary for the production of our art which they never use, and we, nevertheless, calmly assert that the art which we produce is the
real, true, only art — all of art!

To the remark that if our art is the true art every one
should have the benefit of it, the usual reply is that if
not everybody at present makes use of existing art, the
fault lies, not in the art, but in the false organization of
society ; that one can imagine to oneself, in the future,
a state of things in which physical labor will be partly
superseded by machinery, partly lightened by its just
distribution, and that labor for the production of art will
be taken in turns ; that there is no need for some people
always to sit below the stage moving the decorations,
winding up the machinery, working at the piano or
French horn, and setting type and printing books, but
that the people who do all this work might be engaged
only a few hours per day, and in their leisure time might
enjoy all the blessings of art.

That is what the defenders of our exclusive art say.
But I think they do not themselves believe it.   They

cannot help knowing that fine art can arise only on the slavery of the masses of the people, and can continue only as long as that slavery lasts, and they cannot help knowing that only under conditions of intense labor for the workers, can specialists — writers, musicians, dancers, and actors — arrive at that fine degree of perfection to which they do attain, or produce their refined works of art; and only under the same conditions can there be a fine public to esteem such productions. Free the slaves of capital, and it will be impossible to produce such refined art.

But even were we to admit the inadmissible, and say that means may be found by which art (that art which among us is considered to be art) may be accessible to the whole people, another consideration presents itself showing that fashionable art cannot be the whole of art, viz., the fact that it is completely unintelligible to the people. Formerly men wrote poems in Latin, but now their artistic productions are as unintelligible to the common folk as if they were written in Sanscrit. The usual reply to this is, that if the people do not now understand this art of ours, it only proves that they are undeveloped, and that this has been so at each fresh step forward made by art. First it was not understood, but afterward people got accustomed to it.

" It will be the same with our present art; it will be understood when everybody is as well educated as we are — the people of the upper classes — who produce this art," say the defenders of our art. But this assertion is evidently even more unjust than the former; for we know that the majority of the productions of the art of the upper classes, such as various odes, poems, dramas, cantatas, pastorals, pictures, etc., which delighted the people of the upper classes when they were produced, never were afterward either understood or valued by the great masses of mankind, but have remained, what they were at first, a mere pastime for rich people of their time, for whom alone they ever were of any importance. It is also often urged, in proof of the assertion that the people will some day understand our art that some productions of so-called "classical" poetry, music, or painting, which formerly did not please the masses, do — now that they have been offered to them from all sides — begin to please these same masses; but this only shows that the crowd, especially the half-spoilt town crowd, can easily (its taste having been perverted) be accustomed to any sort of art. Moreover, this art is not produced by these masses, nor even chosen by them, but is energetically thrust upon them in those public places in which art is accessible to the people. For the great majority of working-people, our art, besides being inaccessible on account of its costliness, is strange in its very nature, transmitting, as it does, the feelings of people far removed from those conditions of laborious life which are natural to the great body of humanity. That which is enjoyment to a man of the rich classes is incomprehensible, as a pleasure, to a working-man, and evokes in him, either no feeling at all, or only a feeling quite contrary to that which it evokes in an idle and satiated man. Such feelings as form the chief subjects of present-day art — say, for instance, honor,[1] patriotism, and amorousness — evoke in a working-man only bewilderment and contempt, or indignation. So that even if a possibility were given to the laboring classes, in their free time, to see, to read, and to hear all that forms the flower of contemporary art (as is done to some extent, in towns, by means of picture galleries, popular concerts, and libraries), the working-man (to the extent to which he is a laborer, and has not begun to pass into the ranks of those perverted by idleness) would be able to make nothing of our fine art, and if he did understand it, that which he understood would not elevate his soul, but would certainly, in most cases, pervert it. To thoughtful and sincere people there can, therefore, be no doubt that the art of our upper classes never can be the art of the whole people. But if art is an important matter, a spiritual blessing, essential for all men ("like religion," as the

[1] Dueling is still customary among the higher circles in Russia, as in other continental countries. — TR.

devotees of art are fond of saying), then it should be accessible to every one. And if, as in our day, it is not accessible to all men, then one of two things: either art is not the vital matter it is represented to be, or that art which we call art is not the real thing.

The dilemma is inevitable, and therefore clever and immoral people avoid it by denying one side of it, viz., denying that the common people have a right to art. These people simply and boldly speak out (what lies at the heart of the matter), and say that the participators in and utilizers of what, in their esteem, is highly beautiful art, *i.e.* art furnishing the greatest enjoyment, can only be "schöne Geister," "the elect," as the romanticists called them, the "Uebermenschen," as they are called by the followers of Nietzsche; the remaining vulgar herd, incapable of experiencing these pleasures, must serve the exalted pleasures of this superior breed of people. The people who express these views at least do not pretend, and do not try, to combine the incombinable, but frankly admit, what is the case, that our art is an art of the upper classes only. So essentially art has been, and is, understood by every one engaged on it in our society.

CHAPTER IX

THE unbelief of the upper classes of the European world had this effect — that instead of an artistic activity aiming at transmitting the highest feelings to which humanity has attained, — those flowing from religious perception, — we have an activity which aims at affording the greatest enjoyment to a certain class of society. And of all the immense domain of art, that part has been fenced off, and is alone called art, which affords enjoyment to the people of this particular circle.

Apart from the moral effects on European society of such a selection from the whole sphere of art of what did not deserve such a valuation, and the acknowledgment of it as important art, this perversion of art has weakened art itself, and well-nigh destroyed it. The first great result was that art was deprived of the infinite, varied, and profound religious subject-matter proper to it. The second result was that having only a small circle of people in view, it lost its beauty of form and became affected and obscure; and the third and chief result was that it ceased to be either natural or even sincere, and became thoroughly artifical and brain-spun.

The first result — the impoverishment of subject-matter — followed because only that is a true work of art which transmits fresh feelings not before experienced by man. As thought-product is only then real thought-product when it transmits new conceptions and thoughts, and does not merely repeat what was known before, so also an art-product is only then a genuine art-product when it brings a new feeling (however insignificant) into the current of human life. This explains why children and youths are so strongly impressed by those works of art which first transmit to them feelings they had not before experienced.

The same powerful impression is made on people by feelings which are quite new, and have never before been expressed by man. And it is the source from which such feelings flow of which the art of the upper classes has deprived itself by estimating feelings, not in conformity with religious perception, but according to the degree of enjoyment they afford. There is nothing older and more hackneyed than enjoyment, and there is nothing fresher than the feelings springing from the religious consciousness of each age. It could not be otherwise: man's enjoyment has limits established by his nature, but the movement forward of humanity, that which is voiced by religious perception, has no limits. At every forward step taken by humanity — and such steps are taken in consequence of the greater and greater elucidation of religious perception — men experience new and fresh feelings. And therefore only on the basis of religious perception (which shows the highest level of life-comprehension reached by the men of a certain period) can fresh emotion, never before felt

by man, arise. From the religious perception of the
ancient Greeks flowed the really new, important, and
endlessly varied feelings expressed by Homer and the
tragic writers. It was the same among the Jews, who
attained the religious conception of a single God, —
from that perception flowed all those new and important
emotions expressed by the prophets. It was the same
for the poets of the Middle Ages, who if they believed
in a heavenly hierarchy, believed also in the Catholic
commune; and it is the same for a man of to-day who
has grasped the religious conception of true Christianity, — the brotherhood of man.

The variety of fresh feelings flowing from religious
perception is endless, and they are all new; for religious
perception is nothing else than the first indication of
that which is coming into existence, viz., the new relation of man to the world around him. But the feelings
flowing from the desire for enjoyment are, on the contrary, not only limited, but were long ago experienced
and expressed. And therefore the lack of belief of the
upper classes of Europe has left them with an art fed
on the poorest subject-matter.

The impoverishment of the subject-matter of upper-
class art was further increased by the fact that, ceasing
to be religious, it ceased also to be popular, and this again
diminished the range of feelings which it transmitted.
For the range of feelings experienced by the powerful
and the rich, who have no experience of labor for the
support of life, is far poorer, more limited, and more
insignificant than the range of feelings natural to working-people.

People of our circle, æstheticians, usually think and
say just the contrary of this. I remember how Gontchareff, the author, a very clever and educated man, but
a thorough townsman and an æsthetician, said to me
that after Tourgenieff's "Memoirs of a Sportsman" there
was nothing left to write about in peasant life. It was
all used up. The life of working-people seemed to him
so simple that Tourgenieff's peasant stories had used
up all there was to describe. The life of our wealthy

people, with their love-affairs and dissatisfaction with themselves, seemed to him full of inexhaustible subject-matter. One hero kissed his lady on her palm, another on her elbow, and a third somewhere else. One man is discontented through idleness, and another because people don't love him. And Gontchareff thought that in this sphere there is no end of variety. And this opinion — that the life of working-people is poor in subject-matter, but that our life, the life of the idle, is full of interest — is shared by very many people in our society. The life of a laboring man, with its endlessly varied forms of labor, and the dangers connected with this labor on sea and underground; his migrations, the intercourse with his employers, overseers, and companions, and with men of other religions and other nationalities; his struggles with nature and with wild beasts, the associations with domestic animals, the work in the forest, on the steppe, in the field, the garden, the orchard; his intercourse with wife and children, not only as with people near and dear to him, but as with co-workers and helpers in labor, replacing him in time of need; his concern in all economic questions, not as matters of display or discussion, but as problems of life for himself and his family; his pride in self-suppression and service to others, his pleasures of refreshment; and with all these interests permeated by a religious attitude toward these occurrences — all this to us, who have not these interests and possess no religious perception, seems monotonous in comparison with those small enjoyments and insignificant cares of our life, — a life, not of labor nor of production, but of consumption and destruction of that which others have produced for us. We think the feelings experienced by people of our day and our class are very important and varied; but in reality almost all the feelings of people of our class amount to but three very insignificant and simple feelings, — the feeling of pride, the feeling of sexual desire, and the feeling of weariness of life. These three feelings, with their outgrowths, form almost the only subject-matter of the art of the rich classes.

At first, at the very beginning of the separation of the exclusive art of the upper classes from universal art, its chief subject-matter was the feeling of pride. It was so at the time of the Renaissance and after it, when the chief subject of works of art was the laudation of the strong, — popes, kings, and dukes: odes and madrigals were written in their honor, and they were extolled in cantatas and hymns; their portraits were painted, and their statues carved, in various adulatory ways. Next, the element of sexual desire began more and more to enter into art, and (with very few exceptions, and in novels and dramas almost without exception) it has now become an essential feature of every art-product of the rich classes.

The third feeling transmitted by the art of the rich — that of discontent with life — appeared yet later in modern art. This feeling, which, at the commencement of the present century, was expressed only by exceptional men: by Byron, by Leopardi, and afterward by Heine, has latterly become fashionable, and is expressed by most ordinary and empty people. Most justly does the French critic Doumic characterize the works of the new writers: "*C'est la lassitude de vivre, le mépris de l'époque présente, le regret d'un autre temps aperçu à travers l'illusion de l'art, le goût du paradoxe, le besoin de se singulariser, une aspiration de raffinés vers la simplicité, l'adoration enfantine du merveilleux, la séduction maladive de la rêverie, l'ébranlement des nerfs, — surtout l'appel exaspéré de la sensualité*" ("Les Jeunes," René Doumic).[1] And, as a matter of fact, of these three feelings it is sensuality, the lowest (accessible not only to all men, but even to all animals), which forms the chief subject-matter of works of art of recent times.

From Boccaccio to Marcel Prévost, all the novels,

---

[1] It is the weariness of life, contempt for the present epoch, regret for another age seen through the illusion of art, a taste for paradox, a desire to be singular, a sentimental aspiration after simplicity, an infantine adoration of the marvelous, a sickly tendency toward reverie, a shattered condition of nerves, and, above all, the exasperated demand of sensuality.

poems, and verses invariably transmit the feeling of sexual love in its different forms. Adultery is not only the favorite, but almost the only theme of all the novels. A performance is not a performance unless, under some pretense, women appear with naked busts and limbs. Songs and *romances* — all are expressions of lust, idealized in various degrees.

A majority of the pictures by French artists represent female nakedness in various forms. In recent French literature there is hardly a page or a poem in which nakedness is not described, and in which, relevantly or irrelevantly, their favorite thought and word *nu* is not repeated a couple of times. There is a certain writer, René de Gourmond, who gets printed, and is considered talented. To get an idea of the new writers, I read his novel, "Les Chevaux de Diomède." It is a consecutive and detailed account of the sexual connections some gentleman had with various women. Every page contains lust-kindling descriptions. It is the same in Pierre Louÿs' book, "Aphrodite," which met with success; it is the same in a book I lately chanced upon, Huysmans' "Certains," and, with but few exceptions, it is the same in all the French novels. They are all the productions of people suffering from erotic mania. And these people are evidently convinced that as their whole life, in consequence of their diseased condition, is concentrated on amplifying various sexual abominations, therefore the life of all the world is similarly concentrated. And these people, suffering from erotic mania, are imitated throughout the whole artistic world of Europe and America.

Thus in consequence of the lack of belief and the exceptional manner of life of the wealthy classes, the art of those classes became impoverished in its subject-matter, and has sunk to the transmission of the feelings of pride, discontent with life, and, above all, of sexual desire.

CHAPTER X

In consequence of their unbelief, the art of the upper classes became poor in subject-matter. But besides that, becoming continually more and more exclusive, it became at the same time continually more and more involved, affected, and obscure.

When a universal artist (such as were some of the Grecian artists or the Jewish prophets) composed his work, he naturally strove to say what he had to say in such a manner that his production should be intelligible to all men. But when an artist composed for a small circle of people placed in exceptional conditions, or even for a single individual and his courtiers, — for popes, cardinals, kings, dukes, queens, or for a king's mistress, — he naturally only aimed at influencing these people, who were well known to him, and lived in exceptional conditions familiar to him. And this was an easier task, and the artist was involuntarily drawn to express himself by allusions comprehensible only to the initiated, and obscure to every one else. In the first place, more could be said in this way ; and secondly, there is (for the initiated) even a certain charm in the cloudiness of such a manner of expression. This method, which showed itself both in euphemism and in mythological and historical allusions, came more and more into use, until it has, apparently, at last reached its utmost limits in the so-called art of the Decadents. It has come, finally, to this : that not only is haziness, mysteriousness, obscurity, and exclusiveness (shutting out the masses) elevated to the rank of a merit and a condition of poetic art, but even incorrectness, indefiniteness, and lack of eloquence are held in esteem.

Théophile Gautier, in his preface to the celebrated " Fleurs du Mal," says that Baudelaire, as far as possible, banished from poetry eloquence, passion, and truth too strictly copied (" *l'éloquence, la passion, et la vérité calquée trop exactement* ").

And Baudelaire not only expressed this, but maintained his thesis in his verses, and yet more strikingly in the prose of his "Petits Poèmes en Prose," the meanings of which have to be guessed like a rebus, and remain for the most part undiscovered.

The poet Verlaine (who followed next after Baudelaire, and was also esteemed great) even wrote an "Art Poétique," in which he advises this style of composition : —

> *De la musique avant toute chose,*
> *Et pour cela préfère l'Impair*
> *Plus vague et plus soluble dans l'air,*
> *Sans rien en lui qui pèse ou qui pose.*
>
> *Il faut aussi que tu n'ailles point*
> *Choisir tes mots sans quelque méprise :*
> *Rien de plus cher que la chanson grise*
> *Où l'Indécis au Précis se joint.*

 *   *   *   *   *

And again : —

> *De la musique encore et toujours!*
> *Que ton vers soit la chose envolée*
> *Qu'on sent qui fuit d'une âme en allée*
> *Vers d'autres cieux à d'autres amours.*
>
> *Que ton vers soit la bonne aventure*
> *Eparse au vent crispé du matin,*
> *Qui va fleurant la menthe et le thym ...*
> *Et tout le reste est littérature.*[1]

[1] Music, music before all things
The eccentric still prefer,
Vague in air, and nothing weighty,
Soluble. Yet do not err,

Choosing words; still do it lightly,
Do it too with some contempt;
Dearest is the song that's tipsy,
Clearness, dimness not exempt.

 *   *   *   *   *

After these two comes Mallarmé, considered the most important of the young poets, and he plainly says that the charm of poetry lies in our having to guess its meaning — that in poetry there should always be a puzzle : —

Je pense qu'il faut qu'il n'y ait qu'allusion, says he. *La contemplation des objets, l'image s'envolant des rê-veries suscitées par eux, sont le chant : les Parnassiens, eux, prennent la chose entièrement et la montrent ; par là ils manquent de mystère ; ils retirent aux esprits cette joie délicieuse de croire qu'ils créent.* Nommer un ob-jet, c'est supprimer les trois quarts de la jouissance du poème, qui est faite du bonheur de deviner peu à peu : le suggérer, voilà le rêve. *C'est le parfait usage de ce mystère qui constitue le symbole : évoquer petit à petit un objet pour montrer un état d'âme, ou, inversement, choisir un objet et en dégager un état d'âme, par une sèrie de déchiffrements.*

.... Si un être d'une intelligence moyenne, et d'une préparation littéraire insuffisante, ouvre par hasard un livre ainsi fait et prétend en jouir, il y a malentendu, il faut remettre les choses à leur place. Il doit y avoir toujours énigme en poèsie, *et c'est le but de la littérature, il n'y en a pas d'autre, — d'évoquer les objets.* — " En-quête sur l'Évolution Littéraire," Jules Huret, pp. 60, 61.[1]

> Music always, now and ever
> Be thy verse the thing that flies
> From a soul that 's gone, escaping,
> Gone to other loves and skies.
>
> Gone to other loves and regions,
> Following fortunes that allure,
> Mint and thyme and morning crispness ....
> All the rest 's mere literature.

[1] I think there should be nothing but allusions. The contemplation of objects, the flying image of reveries evoked by them, are the song. The Parnassiens state the thing completely, and show it, and thereby lack mystery; they deprive the mind of that delicious joy of imagining that it creates. To *name an object is to take three-quarters from the enjoyment of the poem, which consists in the happiness of guessing little by little : to suggest, that is the dream.* It is the perfect use of this mystery that con-stitutes the symbol: little by little, to evoke an object in order to show a

Thus is obscurity elevated into a dogma among the new poets. As the French critic Doumic (who has not yet accepted the dogma) quite correctly says : —

"*Il serait temps aussi d'en finir avec cette fameuse 'théorie de l'obscurite' que la nouvelle école a élevée, en effet, à la hauteur d'un dogme.*" — " Les Jeunes, par René Doumic."[1]

But it is not French writers only who think thus. The poets of all other countries think and act in the same way : German, and Scandinavian, and Italian, and Russian, and English. So also do the artists of the new period in all branches of art : in painting, in sculpture, and in music. Relying on Nietzsche and Wagner, the artists of the new age conclude that it is unnecessary for them to be intelligible to the vulgar crowd ; it is enough for them to evoke poetic emotion in " the finest nurtured," to borrow a phrase from an English æsthetician.

In order that what I am saying may not seem to be mere assertion, I will quote at least a few examples from the French poets who have led this movement. The name of these poets is legion. I have taken French writers, because they, more decidedly than any others, indicate the new direction of art, and are imitated by most European writers.

Besides those whose names are already considered famous, such as Baudelaire and Verlaine, here are the names of a few of them : Jean Moréas, Charles Morice, Henri de Régnier, Charles Vignier, Adrien Remacle, René Ghil, Maurice Maeterlinck, G. Albert Aurier, Rémy de Gourmont, Saint-Pol-Roux-le-Magnifique, Georges Rodenbach, le comte Robert de Montesquiou-Fezensac.

state of the soul; or, inversely, to choose an object, and from it to disengage a state of the soul by a series of decipherings.

.... If a being of mediocre intelligence and insufficient literary preparation chance to open a book made in this way and pretends to enjoy it, there is a misunderstanding — things must be returned to their places. *There should always be an enigma in poetry*, and the aim of literature — it has no other — is to evoke objects.

[1] It were time also to have done with this famous " theory of obscurity," which the new school have practically raised to the height of a dogma.

These are Symbolists and Decadents.   Next we have
the "Magi": Joséphin Péladan, Paul Adam, Jules Bois,
M. Papus, and others.

Besides these, there are yet one hundred and forty-one
others, whom Doumic mentions in the book referred to
above.

Here are some examples from the work of those of
them who are considered to be the best, beginning with
that most celebrated man, acknowledged to be a great
artist worthy of a monument — Baudelaire.   This is a
poem from his celebrated " Fleurs du Mal ":—

No. XXIV

Je t'adore à l'égal de la voûte nocturne,
O vase de tristesse, ô grande taciturne,
Et t'aime d'autant plus, belle, que tu me fuis,
Et que tu me parais, ornement de mes nuits,
Plus ironiquement accumuler les lieues
Qui séparent mes bras des immensités bleues.

Je m'avance à l'attaque, et je grimpe aux assauts,
Comme après un cadavre un chœur de vermisseaux,
Et je chéris, ô bête implacable et cruelle,
Jusqu'à cette froideur par où tu m'es plus belle ! [1]

And this is another by the same writer:—

No. XXXVI

DUELLUM

Deux guerriers ont couru l'un sur l'autre; leurs armes
Ont éclaboussé l'air de lueurs et de sang.
Ces jeux, ces cliquetis du fer sont les vacarmes
D'une jeunesse en proie à l'amour vagissant.

[1] For translation, see Appendix **IV.**

Les glaives sont brisés ! comme notre jeunesse,
Ma chère ! Mais les dents, les ongles acérés,
Vengent bientôt l'épée et la dague traîtresse.
O fureur des cœurs mûrs par l'amour ulcérés !

Dans le ravin hanté des chats-pards et des onces
Nos héros, s'étreignant méchamment, ont roulé,
Et leur peau fleurira l'aridité des ronces.

Ce gouffre, c'est l'enfer, de nos amis peuplé !
Roulons-y sans remords, amazone inhumaine,
Afin d'éterniser l'ardeur de notre haine ! [1]

To be exact, I should mention that the collection contains verses less comprehensible than these, but not one
poem which is plain and can be understood without a
certain effort — an effort seldom rewarded; for the feelings which the poet transmits are evil and very low ones.
And these feelings are always, and purposely, expressed
by him with eccentricity and lack of clearness. This
premeditated obscurity is especially noticeable in his
prose, where the author could, if he liked, speak plainly.
Take, for instance, the first piece from his "Petits
Poèmes" : —

L'ETRANGER

Qui aimes-tu le mieux, homme énigmatique, dis ? ton
père, ta mère, ta sœur, ou ton frère ?
Je n'ai ni père, ni mère, ni sœur, ni frère.
Tes amis ?
Vous vous servez là d'une parole dont le sens m'est resté
jusqu'à ce jour inconnu.
Ta patrie ?
J'ignore sous quelle latitude elle est située.
La beauté ?
Je l'aimerais volontiers, desse et immortelle.
L'or ?
Je le hais comme vous haïssez Dieu.

[1] For translation, see Appendix IV.

Et qu'aimes-tu donc, extraordinaire étranger?
J'aime les nuages .... les nuages qui passent .... là bas,
les merveilleux nuages ! [1]

The piece called "La Soupe et les Nuages" is probably
intended to express the unintelligibility of the poet even
to her whom he loves.   This is the piece in question : —

Ma petite folle bien-aimée me donnait à dîner, et par la
fenêtre ouverte de la salle à manger je contemplais les
mouvantes architectures que Dieu fait avec les vapeurs,
les merveilleuses constructions de l'impalpable.   Et je me
disais, à travers ma contemplation: "Toutes ces fantas-
magories sont presque aussi belles que les yeux de ma belle
bien-aimée, la petite folle monstrueuse aux yeux verts."
Et tout à coup je reçus un violent coup de poing dans le
dos, et j'entendis une voix rauque et charmante, une voix
hystérique et comme enrouée par l'eau-de-vie, la voix de
ma chère petite bien-aimée, qui me disait, "Allez-vous
bientôt manger votre soupe, s .... b .... de marchand de
nuages ?" [1]

However artificial these two pieces may be, it is still
possible, with some effort, to guess at what the author
meant them to express, but some of the pieces are absolutely incomprehensible — at least to me.   "Le Galant
Tireur" is a piece I was quite unable to understand.

LE GALANT TIREUR

Comme la voiture traversait le bois, il la fit arrêter
dans le voisinage d'un tir, disant qu'il lui serait agréable
de tirer quelques balles pour tuer le Temps.   Tuer ce
monstre-là, n'est-ce pas l'occupation la plus ordinaire et la
plus légitime de chacun? — Et il offrit galamment la
main à sa chère, délicieuse et exécrable femme, à cette
mystérieuse femme à laquelle il doit tant de plaisirs, tant
de douleurs, et peut-être aussi une grande partie de son
génie.

[1] For translation, see Appendix IV.

Plusieurs balles frappèrent loin du but proposé, l'une d'elles s'enfonça même dans le plafond; et comme la charmante créature riait follement, se moquant de la maladresse de son époux, celui-ci se tourna brusquement vers elle, et lui dit: "Observez cette poupée, là-bas, à droite, qui porte le nez en l'air et qui a la mine si hautaine. Eh bien! cher ange, je me figure que c'est vous." *Et il ferma les yeux et il lâcha la détente. La poupée fut nettement décapitée.*

Alors s' inclinant vers sa chère, sa délicieuse, son exécrable femme, son inévitable et impitoyable Muse, et lui baisant respectueusement la main, il ajouta: "Ah! mon cher ange, combien je vous remercie de mon adresse!" [1]

The productions of another celebrity, Verlaine, are not less affected and unintelligible. This, for instance, is the first poem in the section called " Ariettes Oubliés."

> " *Le vent dans la plaine*
> *Suspend son haleine.*" — FAVART.

C'est l'extase langoureuse,
C'est la fatigue amoureuse,
C'est tous les frissons des bois
Parmi l'étreinte des brises,
C'est, vers les ramures grises,
Le chœur des petites voix.

O le frêle et frais murmure!
Cela gazouille et susurre,
Cela ressemble au cri doux
Que l'herbe agitée expire ....
Tu dirais, sous l'eau qui vire,
Le roulis sourd des cailloux.

Cette âme qui se lamente
En cette plainte dormante
C'est la nôtre, n'est-ce pas ?

---

[1] For translation, see Appendix IV.

La mienne, dis, et la tienne,
Dont s'exhale l'humble antienne
Par ce tiède soir, tout bas?[1]

What "*chœur des petites voix*"? and what "*cri doux que l'herbe agitée expire*"? and what it all means, remains altogether unintelligible to me.

And here is another "Ariette":—

VIII

Dans l'interminable
Ennui de la plaine,
La neige incertaine
Luit comme du sable.

Le ciel est de cuivre,
Sans lueur aucune.
On croirait voir vivre
Et mourir la lune.

Comme des nuées
Flottent gris les chênes
Des forêts prochaines
Parmi les buées.

Le ciel est de cuivre,
Sans lueur aucune.
On croirait voir vivre
Et mourir la lune.

Corneille poussive
Et vous, les loups maigres,
Par ces bises aigres
Quoi donc vous arrive?

Dans l'interminable
Ennui de la plaine,

---

[1] For translation, see Appendix **IV.**

La neige incertaine
Luit comme du sable.[1]

How does the moon seem to live and die in a copper heaven? And how can snow shine like sand? The whole thing is not merely unintelligible, but, under pretense of conveying an impression, it passes off a string of incorrect comparisons and words.

Besides these artificial and obscure poems there are others which are intelligible, but which make up for it by being altogether bad, both in form and in subject. Such are all the poems under the heading " La Sagesse." The chief place in these verses is occupied by a very poor expression of the most commonplace Roman Catholic and patriotic sentiments. For instance, one meets with verses such as this : —

Je ne veux plus penser qu'à ma mère Marie,
Siège de la sagesse et source de pardons,
Mère de France aussi de qui nous attendons
Inébranlablement l'honneur de la patrie.[2]

Before citing examples from other poets, I must pause to note the amazing celebrity of these two versifiers, Baudelaire and Verlaine, who are now accepted as being great poets. How the French, who had Chénier, Musset, Lamartine, and, above all, Hugo, — and among whom quite recently flourished the so-called Parnassiens: Leconte de Lisle, Sully-Prudhomme, etc., — could attribute such importance to these two versifiers, who were far from skilful in form and most contemptible and commonplace in subject-matter, is to me incomprehensible. The conception of life of one of them, Baudelaire, consisted in elevating gross egotism into a theory, and replacing morality by a cloudy conception of beauty, and

---

[1] For translation, see Appendix IV.

[2] I do not wish to think any more, except about **my mother Mary,**
Seat of wisdom and source of pardon,
Also Mother of France, *from whom we*
Steadfastly expect the honor of our country.

especially artificial beauty. Baudelaire had a preference, which he expressed, for a woman's face painted rather than showing its natural color, and for metal trees and a theatrical imitation of water rather than real trees and real water.

The life-conception of the other, Verlaine, consisted in weak profligacy, confession of his moral impotence, and, as an antidote to that impotence, in the grossest Roman Catholic idolatry. Both, moreover, were quite lacking in naïveté, sincerity, and simplicity, and both overflowed with artificiality, forced originality and self-assurance. So that in their least bad productions one sees more of M. Baudelaire or M. Verlaine than of what they were describing. But these two indifferent versifiers form a school, and lead hundreds of followers after them.

There is only one explanation of this fact : it is that the art of the society in which these versifiers lived is not a serious, important matter of life, but is a mere amusement. And all amusements grow wearisome by repetition. And, in order to make wearisome amusement again tolerable, it is necessary to find some means to freshen it up. When, at cards, ombre grows stale, whist is introduced ; when whist grows stale, écarté is substituted ; when écarté grows stale, some other novelty is invented, and so on. The substance of the matter remains the same, only its form is changed. And so it is with this kind of art. The subject-matter of the art of the upper classes growing continually more and more limited, it has come at last to this, that to the artists of these exclusive classes it seems as if everything has already been said, and that to find anything new to say is impossible. And therefore, to freshen up this art, they look out for fresh forms.

Baudelaire and Verlaine invent such a new form, furbish it up, moreover, with hitherto unused pornographic details, and — the critics and the public of the upper classes hail them as great writers.

This is the only explanation of the success, not of Baudelaire and Verlaine only, but of all the Decadents.

For instance, there are poems by Mallarmé and Maeterlinck which have no meaning, and yet for all that, or perhaps on that very account, are printed by tens of thousands, not only in various publications, but even in collections of the best works of the younger poets.

This, for example, is a sonnet by Mallarmé:—

A la nue accablante tu
Basse de basalte et de laves
A même les échos esclaves
Par une trompe sans vertu.

Quel sépulcral naufrage (tu
Le soir, écume, mais y baves)
Suprême une entre les épaves
Abolit le mât dévêtu.

Ou cela que furibond faute
De quelque perdition haute
Tout l'abîme vain éployé
Dans le si blanc cheveu qui traîne
Avarement aura noyé
Le flanc enfant d'une sirène.[1]

("Pan," 1895, No. 1.)

This poem is not exceptional in its incomprehensibility. I have read several poems by Mallarmé, and they also had no meaning whatever. I give a sample of his prose in Appendix I. There is a whole volume of this prose called "Divagations." It is impossible to understand any of it. And that is evidently what the author intended.

And here is a song by Maeterlinck, another cele-brated author of to-day:—

Quand il est sorti,
(J'entendis la porte)

---

[1] This sonnet seems too unintelligible for translation.—TR.

Quand il est sorti
Elle avait souri ....

Mais quand il entra
(J'entendis la lampe)
Mais quand il entra
Une autre était là ....

Et j'ai vu la mort,
(J'entendis son âme)
Et j'ai vu la mort
Qui l'attend encore ....

On est venu dire,
(Mon enfant j'ai peur)
On est venu dire
Qu'il allait partir....

Ma lampe allumée,
(Mon enfant j'ai peur)
Ma lampe allumée
Me suis approchée ....

A la première porte,
(Mon enfant j'ai peur)
A la première porte,
La flamme a tremblé ....

A la seconde porte,
(Mon enfant j'ai peur)
A la seconde porte,
La flamme a parlé ....

A la troisième porte,
(Mon enfant j'ai peur)
A la troisième porte,
La lumière est morte ....

Et s'il revenait un jour
Que faut-il lui dire?

Dites-lui, qu'on l'attendit
Jusqu'à s'en mourir ....

Et s'il demande où vous êtes
Que faut-il répondre ?
Donnez-lui mon anneau d'or
Sans rien lui répondre ....

Et s'il m'interroge alors
Sur la dernière heure ?
Dites lui que j'ai souri
De peur qu'il ne pleure ....

Et s'il m'interroge encore
Sans me reconnaître ?
Parlez-lui comme une sœur,
Il souffre peut-être ....

Et s'il veut savoir pourquoi
La salle est déserte ?
Montrez lui la lampe éteinte
Et la porte ouverte ....[1]

("Pan," 1895, No. 2.)

Who went out? Who came in? Who is speaking? Who died?

I beg the reader to be at the pains of reading through the samples I cite in Appendix II. of the celebrated and esteemed young poets — Griffin, Verhaeren, Moréas, and Montesquiou. It is important to do so in order to form a clear conception of the present position of art, and not to suppose, as many do, that Decadentism is an accidental and transitory phenomenon. To avoid the reproach of having selected the worst verses, I have copied out of each volume the poem which happened to stand on page 28.

All the other productions of these poets are equally unintelligible, or can only be understood with great

---

[1] For translation, see Appendix IV.

difficulty, and then not fully. All the productions of
those hundreds of poets, of whom I have named a few,
are the same in kind.   And among the Germans,
Swedes, Norwegians, Italians, and us Russians, similar
verses are printed.   And such productions are printed
and made up into book form, if not by the million, then
by the hundred thousand (some of these works sell in
tens of thousands). For type-setting, paging, printing,
and binding these books, millions and millions of working days are spent — not less, I think, than went to
build the great pyramid. And this is not all. The
same is going on in all the other arts : millions and
millions of working days are being spent on the production of equally incomprehensible works in painting,
in music, and in the drama.

Painting not only does not lag behind poetry in this
matter, but rather outstrips it. Here is an extract from
the diary of an amateur of art, written when visiting
the Paris exhibitions in 1894 : —

".I was to-day at three exhibitions : the Symbolists',
the Impressionists', and the Neo-Impressionists'.   I
looked at the pictures conscientiously and carefully, but
again felt the same stupefaction and ultimate indignation.   The first exhibition, that of Camille Pissarro, was
comparatively the most comprehensible, though the pictures were out of drawing, had no subject, and the col-
orings were most improbable.   The drawing was so
indefinite that you were sometimes unable to make out
which way an arm or a head was turned.   The subject
was generally 'effets' — *Effet de brouillard, Effet du
soir, Soleil couchant.* There were some pictures with
figures, but without subjects.

"In the coloring, bright blue and bright green pre-
dominated. And each picture had its special color, with
which the whole picture was, as it were, splashed. For
instance, in 'A Girl Guarding Geese,' the special color
is *vert de gris*, and dots of it were splashed about everywhere ; on the face, the hair, the hands, and the clothes.
In the same gallery — 'Durand Ruel' — were other pic·
tures by Puvis de Chavannes, Manet, Monet, Renoir,

Sisley — who are all Impressionists. One of them, whose name I could not make out, — it was something like Redon, — had painted a blue face in profile. On the whole face there is only this blue tone, with white-of-lead. Pissarro has a water-color all done in dots. In the foreground is a cow, entirely painted with various-colored dots. The general color cannot be distinguished, however much one stands back from, or draws near to, the picture. From there I went to see the Symbolists. I looked at them long without asking any one for an explanation, trying to guess the meaning; but it is beyond human comprehension. One of the first things to catch my eye was a wooden *haut-relief*, wretchedly executed, representing a woman (naked) who with both hands is squeezing from her two breasts streams of blood. The blood flows down, becoming lilac in color. Her hair first descends, and then rises again, and turns into trees. The figure is all colored yellow, and the hair is brown.

" Next — a picture : a yellow sea, on which swims something which is neither a ship nor a heart; on the horizon is a profile with a halo and yellow hair, which changes into a sea, in which it is lost. Some of the painters lay on their colors so thickly that the effect is something between painting and sculpture. A third exhibit was even less comprehensible : a man's profile ; before him a flame and black stripes — leeches, as I was afterwards told. At last I asked a gentleman who was there what it meant, and he explained to me that the *haut-relief* was a symbol, and that it represented '*La Terre.*' The heart swimming in a yellow sea was '*Illusion perdue,*' and the gentleman with the leeches '*Le Mal.*' There were also some Impressionist pictures : elementary profiles, holding some sort of flowers in their hands : in monotone, out of drawing, and either quite blurred or else marked out with wide black outlines."

This was in 1894; the same tendency is now even more strongly defined, and we have Böcklin, Stuck, Klinger, Sasha Schneider, and others.

The same thing is taking place in the drama. The
play-writers give us an architect who, for some reason,
has not fulfilled his former high intentions, and who
consequently climbs on to the roof of a house he has
erected, and tumbles down head foremost; or an incomprehensible old woman (who exterminates rats), and
who, for an unintelligible reason, takes a poetic child to
the sea, and there drowns him; or some blind men who,
sitting on the seashore, for some reason always repeat
one and the same thing; or a bell of some kind, which
flies into a lake, and there rings.

And the same is happening in music — in that art
which, more than any other, one would have thought,
should be intelligible to everybody.

An acquaintance of yours, a musician of repute, sits
down to the piano and plays you what he says is a new
composition of his own, or of one of the new composers.
You hear the strange, loud sounds, and admire the gymnastic exercises performed by his fingers; and you see
that the performer wishes to impress upon you that the
sounds he is producing express various poetic strivings
of the soul.   You see his intention, but no feeling whatever is transmitted to you except weariness.   The execution lasts long, or at least it seems very long to you,
because you do not receive any clear impression, and
involuntarily you remember the words of Alphonse
Karr, "*Plus ça va vite, plus ça dure longtemps.*" [1]   And
it occurs to you that perhaps it is all a mystification;
perhaps the performer is trying you — just throwing his
hands and fingers wildly about the keyboard in the
hope that you will fall into the trap and praise him,
and then he will laugh and confess that he only wanted
to see if he could hoax you.   But when at last the piece
does finish, and the perspiring and agitated musician
rises from the piano evidently anticipating praise, you
see that it was all done in earnest.

The same thing takes place at all the concerts, with
pieces by Liszt, Wagner, Berlioz, Brahms, and (newest
of all) Richard Strauss, and the numberless other com

[1] The quicker it goes the longer it lasts.

posers of the new school, who unceasingly produce opera after opera, symphony after symphony, piece after piece.

The same is occurring in a domain in which it seemed hard to be unintelligible, — in the sphere of novels and short stories.

Read "Là Bas," by Huysmans, or some of Kipling's short stories, or "L'Annonciateur," by Villiers de l'Isle Adam in his "Contes Cruels," etc., and you will find them not only "abscons" (to use a word adopted by the new writers), but absolutely unintelligible both in form and in substance. Such, again, is the work by E. Morel, "Terre Promise," now appearing in the *Revue Blanche*, and such are most of the new novels. The style is very high-flown, the feelings seem to be most elevated, but you can't make out what is happening, to whom it is happening, and where it is happening. And such is the bulk of the young art of our time.

People who grew up in the first half of this century, admiring Goethe, Schiller, Musset, Hugo, Dickens, Beethoven, Chopin, Raphael, da Vinci, Michael Angelo, Delaroche, being unable to make head or tail of this new art, simply attribute its productions to tasteless insanity, and wish to ignore them. But such an attitude toward this new art is quite unjustifiable, because, in the first place, that art is spreading more and more, and has already conquered for itself a firm position in society, similar to the one occupied by the Romanticists in the third decade of this century ; and, secondly and chiefly, because, if it is permissible to judge in this way of the productions of the latest form of art, called by us Decadent art, merely because we do not understand it, then remember there are an enormous number of people, — all the laborers, and many of the non-laboring folk, — who, in just the same way, do not comprehend those productions of art which we consider admirable . the verses of our favorite artists — Goethe, Schiller, and Hugo ; the novels of Dickens, the music of Beethoven and Chopin, the pictures of Raphael, Michael Angelo, da Vinci, etc.

If I have a right to think that great masses of people do not understand and do not like what I consider un doubtedly good because they are not sufficiently devel- oped, then I have no right to deny that perhaps the reason why I cannot understand and cannot like the new productions of art is merely that I am still insuffi- ciently developed to understand them.   If I have a right to say that I, and the majority of people who are in sympathy with me, do not understand the productions of the new art, simply because there is nothing in it to understand, and because it is bad art, then, with just the same right, the still larger majority, the whole laboring mass, who do not understand what I consider admirable art, can say that what I reckon as good art is bad art, and there is nothing in it to understand.

I once saw the injustice of such condemnation of the new art with especial clearness, when, in my presence, a certain poet, who writes incomprehensible verses, ridiculed incomprehensible music with gay self-assurance; and, shortly afterwards, a certain mu- sician, who composes incomprehensible symphonies, laughed at incomprehensible poetry with equal self- confidence.   I have no right, and no authority, to con- demn the new art on the ground that I (a man educated in the first half of the century) do not under- stand it; I can only say that it is incomprehensible to me.   The only advantage the art I acknowledge has over the Decadent art, lies in the fact that the art I recognize is comprehensible to a somewhat larger number of people than the present-day art.

The fact that I am accustomed to a certain exclusive art, and can understand it, but am unable to under- stand another still more exclusive art, does not give me a right to conclude that my art is the real true art, and that the other one, which I do not understand, is an unreal, a bad art.   I can only conclude that art, becoming ever more and more exclusive, has become more and more incomprehensible to an ever increas- ing number of people, and that, in this its progress toward greater and greater incomprehensibility (on one level of which I am standing, with the art familiar to me), it has reached a point where it is understood by a very small number of the elect, and the number of these chosen people is ever becoming smaller and smaller.

As soon as ever the art of the upper classes separated itself from universal art, a conviction arose that art may be art and yet be incomprehensible to the masses. And as soon as this position was admitted, it had inevitably to be admitted also that art may be intelligible only to the very smallest number of the elect, and, eventually, to two, or to one, of our nearest friends, or to oneself alone. Which is practically what is being said by modern artists: "I create and understand myself, and if any one does not understand me, so much the worse for him."

The assertion that art may be good art, and at the same time incomprehensible to a great number of people, is extremely unjust, and its consequences are ruinous to art itself ; but at the same time it is so common and has so eaten into our conceptions, that it is impossible sufficiently to elucidate all the absurdity of it.

Nothing is more common than to hear it said of reputed works of art, that they are very good but very difficult to understand. We are quite used to such assertions, and yet to say that a work of art is good, but incomprehensible to the majority of men, is the same as saying of some kind of food that it is very good, but that most people can't eat it. The majority of men may not like rotten cheese or putrefying grouse — dishes esteemed by people with perverted tastes; but bread and fruit are only good when they please the majority of men. And it is the same with art. Perverted art may not please the majority of men, but good art always pleases every one.

It is said that the very best works of art are such that they cannot be understood by the mass, but are accessible only to the elect who are prepared to understand these great works. But if the majority of men

do not understand, the knowledge necessary to enable
them to understand should be taught and explained
to them.   But it turns out that there is no such knowledge, that the works cannot be explained, and that
those who say the majority do not understand good
works of art, still do not explain those works, but only
tell us that, in order to understand them, one must
read, and see, and hear these same works over and
over again.   But this is not to explain, it is only to
habituate!   And people may habituate themselves to
anything, even to the very worst things.   As people
may habituate themselves to bad food, to spirits, to-
bacco, and opium, just in the same way they may
habituate themselves to bad art — and that is exactly
what is being done.

Moreover, it cannot be said that the majority of
people lack the taste to esteem the highest works of
art.   The majority always have understood, and still
understand, what we also recognize as being the very
best art: the epic of Genesis, the gospel parables,
folk-legends, fairy-tales, and folk-songs, are understood
by all.   How can it be that the majority has suddenly
lost its capacity to understand what is high in our
art?

Of a speech it may be said that it is admirable, but
incomprehensible to those who do not know the language in which it is delivered.   A speech delivered in
Chinese may be excellent, and may yet remain incomprehensible to me if I do not know Chinese; but what
distinguishes a work of art from all other mental activity is just the fact that its language is understood
by all, and that it infects all without distinction.   The
tears and laughter of a Chinese infect me just as
the laughter and tears of a Russian; and it is the
same with painting and music and poetry, when it is
translated into a language I understand.   The songs
of a Kirghiz or of a Japanese touch me, though in a
lesser degree than they touch a Kirghiz or a Japanese.
I am also touched by Japanese painting, Indian architecture, and Arabian stories.   If I am but little touched

by a Japanese song and a Chinese novel, it is not that I do not understand these productions, but that I know and am accustomed to higher works of art. It is not because their art is above me. Great works of art are only great because they are accessible and comprehensible to every one. The story of Joseph, translated into the Chinese language, touches a Chinese. The story of Sakya Muni touches us. And there are, and must be, buildings, pictures, statues, and music of similar power. So that, if art fails to move men, it cannot be said that this is due to the spectators' or hearers' lack of understanding; but the conclusion to be drawn may and should be, that such art is either bad art, or is not art at all.

Art is differentiated from activity of the understanding, which demands preparation and a certain sequence of knowledge (so that one cannot learn trigonometry before knowing geometry), by the fact that it acts on people independently of their state of development and education, that the charm of a picture, sounds, or of forms, infects any man whatever his plane of development.

The business of art lies just in this, — to make that understood and felt which, in the form of an argument, might be incomprehensible and inaccessible Usually it seems to the recipient of a truly artistic impression that he knew the thing before but had been unable to express it.

And such has always been the nature of good, supreme art; the "Iliad," the "Odyssey," the stories of Isaac, Jacob, and Joseph, the Hebrew prophets, the psalms, the gospel parables, the story of Sakya Muni, and the hymns of the Vedas: all transmit very elevated feelings, and are nevertheless quite comprehensible now to us, educated or uneducated, as they were comprehensible to the men of those times, long ago, who were even less educated than our laborers. People talk about incomprehensibility; but if art is the transmission of feelings flowing from man's religious perception, how can a feeling be incomprehensible

which is founded on religion, *i.e.* on man's relation
to God? Such art should be, and has actually always
been, comprehensible to everybody, because every man's
relation to God is one and the same.   And therefore
the churches and the images in them were always
comprehensible to every one.   The hindrance to understanding the best and highest feelings (as is said in the
gospel) does not at all lie in deficiency of development
or learning, but, on the contrary, in false development
and false learning.   A good and lofty work of art may
be incomprehensible, but not to simple, unperverted
peasant laborers (all that is highest is understood by
them) — it may be, and often is, unintelligible to
erudite, perverted people destitute of religion.   And
this continually occurs in our society, in which the
highest feelings are simply not understood.   For instance, I know people who consider themselves most
refined, and who say that they do not understand the
poetry of love to one's neighbor, of self-sacrifice, or
of chastity.

So that good, great, universal, religious art may be
incomprehensible to a small circle of spoilt people, but
certainly not to any large number of plain men.

Art cannot be incomprehensible to the great masses
only because it is very good — as artists of our day are
fond of telling us.   Rather we are bound to conclude
that this art is unintelligible to the great masses only
because it is very bad art, or even is not art at all.   So
that the favorite argument (naïvely accepted by the
cultured crowd), that in order to feel art one has first
to understand it (which really only means habituate
oneself to it), is the truest indication that what we are
asked to understand by such a method is either very
bad, exclusive art, or is not art at all.

People say that works of art do not please the people because they are incapable of understanding them.
But if the aim of works of art is to infect people with
the emotion the artist has experienced, how can one
talk about not understanding?

A man of the people reads a book, sees a picture,

hears a play or a symphony, and is touched by no feeling. He is told that this is because he cannot understand. People promise to let a man see a certain show;
he enters and sees nothing. He is told that this is because his sight is not prepared for this show. But the
man well knows that he sees quite well, and if he does
not see what people promised to show him, he only concludes (as is quite just) that those who undertook to
show him the spectacle have not fulfilled their engage-
ment. And it is perfectly just for a man who does feel
the influence of some works of art to come to this conclusion concerning artists who do not, by their works,
evoke feeling in him. To say that the reason a man is
not touched by my art is because he is still too stupid,
besides being very self-conceited and also rude, is to
reverse the rôles, and for the sick to send the hale to
bed.

Voltaire said that " *Tous les genres sont bons, hors le
genre ennuyeux;* " [1] but with even more right one may
say of art that *Tous les genres sont bons, hors celui
qu'on ne comprend pas,* or *qui ne produit pas son effet,*[2]
for of what value is an article which fails to do that for
which it was intended?

Mark this above all: if only it be admitted that art
may be art and yet be unintelligible to any one of sound
mind, there is no reason why any circle of perverted
people should not compose works tickling their own
perverted feelings and comprehensible to no one but
themselves, and call it "art," as is actually being done
by the so-called Decadents.

The direction art has taken may be compared to
placing on a large circle other circles, smaller and
smaller, until a cone is formed, the apex of which is no
longer a circle at all. That is what has happened to
the art of our times.

---

[1] All styles are good except the wearisome style.
[2] All styles are good except that which is not understood, *or* which fails
to produce its effect.

CHAPTER XI

BECOMING ever poorer and poorer in subject-matter, and more and more unintelligible in form, the art of the upper classes, in its latest productions, has even lost all the characteristics of art, and has been replaced by imitations of art. Not only has upper-class art, in consequence of its separation from universal art, become poor in subject-matter, and bad in form, *i.e.* ever more and more unintelligible, it has, in course of time, ceased even to be art at all, and has been replaced by counterfeits.

This has resulted from the following causes: Universal art arises only when some one of the people, having experienced a strong emotion, feels the necessity of transmitting it to others. The art of the rich classes, on the other hand, arises not from the artist's inner impulse, but chiefly because people of the upper classes demand amusement and pay well for it. They demand from art the transmission of feelings that please them, and this demand artists try to meet. But it is a very difficult task; for people of the wealthy classes, spending their lives in idleness and luxury, desire to be continually diverted by art; and art, even the lowest, cannot be produced at will, but has to generate spontaneously in the artist's inner self. And therefore, to satisfy the demands of people of the upper classes, artists have had to devise methods of producing imitations of art. And such methods have been devised.

These methods are those of (1) borrowing, (2) imitating, (3) striking (effects), and (4) interesting.

The first method consists in borrowing whole subjects, or merely separate features, from former works recognized by every one as being poetical, and in so re-shaping them, with sundry additions, that they should have an appearance of novelty.

Such works, evoking in people of a certain class memories of artistic feelings formerly experienced, produce an impression similar to art, and, provided only that they conform to other needful conditions, they pass for art among those who seek for pleasure from art. Subjects borrowed from previous works of art are usually called poetical subjects. Objects and people thus borrowed are called poetical objects and people. Thus, in our circle, all sorts of legends, sagas, and ancient traditions are considered poetical subjects. Among poetical people and objects we reckon maidens, warriors, shepherds, hermits, angels, devils of all sorts, moonlight, thunder, mountains, the sea, precipices, flowers, long hair, lions, lambs, doves, and nightingales. In general, all those objects are considered poetical which have been most frequently used by former artists in their productions.

Some forty years ago a stupid but highly cultured — *ayant beaucoup d'acquis* — lady (since deceased) asked me to listen to a novel written by herself. It began with a heroine who, in a poetic white dress, and with poetically flowing hair, was reading poetry near some water in a poetic wood. The scene was in Russia, but suddenly from behind the bushes the hero appears, wearing a hat with a feather *à la Guillaume Tell* (the book specially mentioned this) and accompanied by two poetical white dogs. The authoress deemed all this highly poetical, and it might have passed muster if only it had not been necessary for the hero to speak. But as soon as the gentleman in the hat *à la Guillaume Tell* began to converse with the maiden in the white dress, it became obvious that the authoress had nothing to say, but had merely been moved by poetic memories of other works, and imagined that by ringing the changes on those memories she could produce an artistic impression. But an artistic impression, *i.e.* infection, is only received when an author has, in the manner peculiar to himself, experienced the feeling which he transmits, and not when he passes on another man's feeling previously transmitted to him. Such poetry from poetry cannot infect people, it can only simulate a work of art, and even that only to people of perverted æsthetic taste. The lady in question being very stupid and devoid of talent, it was at once apparent how the case stood; but when such borrowing is resorted to by people who are erudite and talented and have cultivated the technique of their art, we get those borrowings from the Greek, the antique, the Christian or mythological world which have become so numerous, and which, particularly in our day, continue to increase and multiply, and are accepted by the public as works of art, if only the borrowings are well mounted by means of the technique of the particular art to which they belong.

As a characteristic example of such counterfeits of art in the realm of poetry, take Rostand's " Princesse Lointaine," in which there is not a spark of art, but which seems very poetical to many people, and probably also to its author.

The second method of imparting a semblance of art is that which I have called imitating. The essence of this method consists in supplying details accompanying the thing described or depicted. In literary art this method consists in describing, in the minutest details, the external appearance, the faces, the clothes, the gestures, the tones, and the habitations of the characters represented, with all the occurrences met with in life. For instance, in novels and stories, when one of the characters speaks, we are told in what voice he spoke, and what he was doing at the time. And the things said are not given so that they should have as much sense as possible, but, as they are in life, disconnectedly, and with interruptions and omissions. In dramatic art, besides such imitation of real speech, this method consists in having all the accessories and all the people just like those in real life. In painting, this method assimilates painting to photography, and destroys the difference between them. And, strange to say, this method is used also in music: music tries to imitate, not only by its rhythm but also by its very sounds, the sounds which in real life accompany the thing it wishes to represent.

The third method is by action, often purely physical, on the outer senses. Work of this kind is said to be " striking," " effectful." In all arts these effects con-

sist chiefly in contrasts; in bringing together the terrible and the tender, the beautiful and the hideous, the
loud and the soft, darkness and light, the most ordinary
and the most extraordinary. In verbal art, besides effects
of contrast, there are also effects consisting in the description of things that have never before been described.
These are usually pornographic details evoking sexual
desire, or details of suffering and death evoking feelings
of horror, as, for instance, when describing a murder, to
give a detailed medical account of the lacerated tissues,
of the swellings, of the smell, quantity, and appearance
of the blood. It is the same in painting: besides all
kinds of other contrasts, one is coming into vogue which
consists in giving careful finish to one object and being
careless about all the rest. The chief and usual effects
in painting are effects of light and the depiction of the
horrible. In the drama, the most common effects, besides contrasts, are tempests, thunder, moonlight, scenes
at sea or by the seashore, changes of costume, exposure
of the female body, madness, murders, and death generally: the dying person exhibiting in detail all the
phases of agony. In music the most usual effects are a
crescendo, passing from the softest and simplest sounds
to the loudest and most complex crash of the full
orchestra; a repetition of the same sounds *arpeggio* in
all the octaves and on various instruments; or that the
harmony, tone, and rhythm be not at all those naturally
flowing from the course of the musical thought, but such
as strike one by their unexpectedness. Besides these,
the commonest effects in music are produced in a purely
physical manner by strength of sound, especially in an
orchestra.

Such are some of the most usual effects in the various
arts, but there yet remains one common to them all;
namely, to convey by means of one art what it would be
natural to convey by another: for instance, to make
music describe (as is done by the programme music of
Wagner and his followers), or to make painting, the
drama, or poetry, induce a frame of mind (as is aimed
at by all the Decadent art).

The fourth method is that of interesting (that is, absorbing the mind) in connection with works of art. The interest may lie in an intricate plot—a method till quite recently much employed in English novels and French plays, but now going out of fashion and being replaced by authenticity, *i.e.* by detailed description of some historical period or some branch of contemporary life. For example, in a novel, interestingness may consist in a description of Egyptian or Roman life, the life of miners, or that of the clerks in a large shop. The reader becomes interested and mistakes this interest for an artistic impression. The interest may also depend on the very method of expression; a kind of interest that has now come much into use. Both verse and prose, as well as pictures, plays, and music, are constructed so that they must be guessed like riddles, and this process of guessing again affords pleasure and gives a semblance of the feeling received from art.

It is very often said that a work of art is very good because it is poetic, or realistic, or striking, or interesting; whereas not only can neither the first, nor the second, nor the third, nor the fourth of these attributes supply a standard of excellence in art, but they have not even anything in common with art.

Poetic — means borrowed. All borrowing merely recalls to the reader, spectator, or listener some dim recollection of artistic impressions they have received from previous works of art, and does not infect them with feeling which the artist has himself experienced. A work founded on something borrowed, like Goethe's "Faust," for instance, may be very well executed and be full of mind and every beauty, but because it lacks the chief characteristic of a work of art — completeness, oneness, the inseparable unity of form and contents expressing the feeling the artist has experienced — it cannot produce a really artistic impression. In availing himself of this method, the artist only transmits the feeling received by him from a previous work of art; therefore every borrowing, whether it be of whole subjects, or of various scenes, situations, or descriptions, is but a reflection of art, a simulation of it, but not art itself. And therefore, to say that a certain production is good because it is poetic — *i.e.* resembles a work of art — is like saying of a coin that it is good because it resembles real money.

Equally little can imitation, realism, serve, as many people think, as a measure of the quality of art. Imitation cannot be such a measure; for the chief characteristic of art is the infection of others with the feelings the artist has experienced, and infection with a feeling is not only not identical with description of the accessories of what is transmitted, but is usually hindered by superfluous details. The attention of the receiver of the artistic impression is diverted by all these well-observed details, and they hinder the transmission of feeling even when it exists.

To value a work of art by the degree of its realism, by the accuracy of the details reproduced, is as strange as to judge of the nutritive quality of food by its external appearance. When we appraise a work according to its realism, we only show that we are talking, not of a work of art, but of its counterfeit.

Neither does the third method of imitating art — by the use of what is striking or effectual — coincide with real art any better than the two former methods; for in effectfulness — the effects of novelty, of the unexpected, of contrasts, of the horrible — there is no transmission of feeling, but only an action on the nerves. If an artist were to paint a bloody wound admirably, the sight of the wound would strike me, but it would not be art. One prolonged note on a powerful organ will produce a striking impression, will often even cause tears, but there is no music in it, because no feeling is transmitted. Yet such physiological effects are constantly mistaken for art by people of our circle, and this not only in music, but also in poetry, painting, and the drama. It is said that art has become refined. On the contrary, thanks to the pursuit of effectfulness, it has become very coarse. A new piece is brought out and accepted all over Europe, such, for instance, as " Hannele," in

which play the author wishes to transmit to the spec
tators pity for a persecuted girl.   To evoke this feeling
in the audience by means of art, the author should
either make one of the characters express this pity in
such a way as to infect every one, or he should describe
the girl's feelings correctly.   But he cannot, or will not,
do this, and chooses another way, more complicated in
stage management, but easier for the author.   He makes
the girl die on the stage ; and, still further to increase
the physiological effect on the spectators, he extinguishes
the lights in the theater, leaving the audience in the
dark, and to the sound of dismal music he shows how
the girl is pursued and beaten by her drunken father.
The girl shrinks — screams — groans — and falls.
Angels appear and carry her away.   And the audience,
experiencing some excitement while this is going on,
are fully convinced that this is true æsthetic feeling.
But there is nothing æsthetic in such excitement; for
there is no infecting of man by man, but only a mingled
feeling of pity for another, and of self-congratulation
that it is not I who am suffering : it is like what we
feel at the sight of an execution, or what the Romans
felt in their circuses.

The substitution of effectfulness for æsthetic feeling
is particularly noticeable in musical art — that art which
by its nature has an immediate physiological action on
the nerves.   Instead of transmitting by means of a melody the feelings he has experienced, a composer of the
new school accumulates and complicates sounds, and
by now strengthening, now weakening them, he produces on the audience a physiological effect of a kind
that can be measured by an apparatus invented for the
purpose.[1]   And the public mistake this physiological
effect for the effect of art.

As to the fourth method — that of interesting — it also
is frequently confounded with art.   One often hears it
said, not only of a poem, a novel, or a picture, but even

[1] An apparatus exists by means of which a very sensitive arrow, in
dependence on the tension of a muscle of the arm, will indicate the
physiological action of music on the nerves and muscles.

of a musical work, that it is interesting. What does this mean? To speak of an interesting work of art means either that we receive from a work of art information new to us, or that the work is not fully intelligible, and that little by little, and with effort, we arrive at its meaning, and experience a certain pleasure in this process of guessing it. In neither case has the interest anything in common with artistic impression. Art aims at infecting people with feeling experienced by the artist. But the mental effort necessary to enable the spectator, listener, or reader to assimilate the new information contained in the work, or to guess the puzzles propounded, by distracting him, hinders the infection. And therefore the interestingness of a work, not only has nothing to do with its excellence as a work of art, but rather hinders than assists artistic impression.

We may, in a work of art, meet with what is poetic, and realistic, and striking, and interesting, but these things cannot replace the essential of art, — feeling experienced by the artist. Latterly, in upper-class art, most of the objects given out as being works of art are of the kind which only resemble art, and are devoid of its essential quality, — feeling experienced by the artist. And, for the diversion of the rich, such objects are continually being produced in enormous quantities by the artisans of art.

Many conditions must be fulfilled to enable a man to produce a real work of art. It is necessary that he should stand on the level of the highest life-conception of his time, that he should experience feeling and have the desire and capacity to transmit it, and that he should, moreover, have a talent for some one of the forms of art. It is very seldom that all these conditions necessary to the production of true art are combined. But in order — aided by the customary methods of borrowing, imitating, introducing effects, and interesting — unceasingly to produce counterfeits of art which pass for art in our society and are well paid for, it is only necessary to have a talent for some branch of art; and this is very often to be met with. By talent I mean ability: in literary art, the ability to express one's thoughts and impressions easily and to notice and re-member characteristic details; in the depictive arts, to distinguish and remember lines, forms, and colors; in music, to distinguish the intervals, and to remember and transmit the sequence of sounds. And a man, in our times, if only he possesses such a talent and selects some specialty, may, after learning the methods of counterfeiting used in his branch of art, — if he has patience and if his æsthetic feeling (which would ren-der such productions revolting to him) be atrophied, — unceasingly, till the end of his life, turn out works which will pass for art in our society.

To produce such counterfeits, definite rules or recipes exist in each branch of art. So that the talented man, having assimilated them, may produce such works *à froid*, cold drawn, without any feeling.

In order to write poems a man of literary talent needs only these qualifications: to acquire the knack, con-formably with the requirements of rhyme and rhythm, of using, instead of the one really suitable word, ten others meaning approximately the same; to learn how to take any phrase which, to be clear, has but one natural order of words, and despite all possible dis-locations still to retain some sense in it; and lastly, to be able, guided by the words required for the rhymes, to devise some semblance of thoughts, feelings, or descriptions to suit these words. Having acquired these qualifications, he may unceasingly produce poems — short or long, religious, amatory, or patriotic, according to the demand.

If a man of literary talent wishes to write a story or novel, he need only form his style — *i.e.* learn how to describe all that he sees — and accustom himself to remember or note down details. When he has accus-tomed himself to this, he can, according to his inclina-tion or the demand, unceasingly produce novels or stories — historical, naturalistic, social, erotic, psycho-logical, or even religious, for which latter kind a de-mand and fashion begins to show itself. He can take subjects from books or from the events of life, and can copy the characters of the people in his book from his acquaintances.

And such novels and stories, if only they are decked out with well-observed and carefully noted details, preferably erotic ones, will be considered works of art, even though they may not contain a spark of feeling experienced.

To produce art in dramatic form, a talented man, in addition to all that is required for novels and stories, must also learn to furnish his characters with as many smart and witty sentences as possible, must know how to utilize theatrical effects, and how to entwine the action of his characters so that there should not be any long conversations, but as much bustle and movement on the stage as possible. If the writer is able to do this, he may produce dramatic works one after another without stopping, selecting his subjects from the reports of the law courts, or from the latest society topic, such as hypnotism, heredity, etc., or from deep antiquity, or even from the realms of fancy.

In the sphere of painting and sculpture it is still easier for the talented man to produce imitations of art. He need only learn to draw, paint, and model — especially naked bodies. Thus equipped he can continue to paint pictures, or model statues, one after another, choosing subjects according to his bent — mythological, or religious, or fantastic, or symbolical; or he may depict what is written about in the papers — a coronation, a strike, the Turko-Grecian war, famine scenes; or, commonest of all, he may just copy anything he thinks beautiful — from naked women to copper basins.

For the production of musical art the talented man needs still less of what constitutes the essence of art, *i.e.* feeling wherewith to infect others : but on the other hand, he requires more physical, gymnastic labor than for any other art, unless it be dancing. To produce works of musical art, he must first learn to move his fingers on some instrument as rapidly as those who have reached the highest perfection ; next, he must know how in former times polyphonic music was written, must study what are called counterpoint and fugue; and, furthermore, he must learn orchestration, *i.e.* how to utilize the effects of the instruments.   But once he has learned all this, the composer may unceasingly produce one work after another; whether programme-music, opera, or song (devising sounds more or less corresponding to the words), or chamber music, *i.e.* he may take another man's themes and work them up into definite forms by means of counterpoint and fugue; or, what is commonest of all, he may compose fantastic music, *i.e.* he may take a conjunction of sounds which happens to come to hand, and pile every sort of complication and ornamentation on to this chance combination.

Thus, in all realms of art, counterfeits of art are manufactured to a ready-made, prearranged recipe, and these counterfeits the public of our upper classes accept for real art.

And this substitution of counterfeits for real works of art was the third and most important consequence of the separation of the art of the upper classes from universal art.

CHAPTER XII

IN our society three conditions coöperate to cause the production of objects of counterfeit art.   They are — (1) the considerable remuneration of artists for their productions, and the professionalization of artists which this has produced, (2) art criticism, and (3) schools of art.

While art was as yet undivided, and only religious art was valued and rewarded while indiscriminate art was left unrewarded, there were no counterfeits of art, or, if any existed, being exposed to the criticism of the whole people, they quickly disappeared.   But as soon as that division occurred, and the upper classes ac-

claimed every kind of art as good if only it afforded
them pleasure, and began to reward such art more
highly than any other social activity, immediately a
large number of people devoted themselves to this
activity, and art assumed quite a different character,
and became a profession.

And as soon as this occurred, the chief and most
precious quality of art — its sincerity — was at once
greatly weakened and eventually quite destroyed.

The professional artist lives by his art, and has con
tinually to invent subjects for his works, and does in
vent them. And it is obvious how great a difference
must exist between works of art produced on the one
hand by men such as the Jewish prophets, the authors
of the Psalms, Francis of Assisi, the authors of the
" Iliad " and " Odyssey," of folk-stories, legends, and folk·
songs, many of whom not only received no remuneration
for their work, but did not even attach their names to
it; and, on the other hand, works produced by court
poets, dramatists and musicians receiving honors and
remuneration; and later on by professional artists, who
lived by the trade, receiving remuneration from newspaper editors, publishers, impresarios, and in general
from those agents who come between the artists and
the town public — the consumers of art.

Professionalism is the first condition of the diffusion
of false, counterfeit art.

The second condition is the growth, in recent times,
of artistic criticism, *i.e.* the valuation of art, not by everybody, and, above all, not by plain men, but by erudite,
that is, by perverted and at the same time self-confident
individuals.

A friend of mine, speaking of the relation of critics to
artists, half jokingly defined it thus : " Critics are the
stupid who discuss the wise." However partial, inexact,
and rude this definition may be, it is yet partly true, and
is incomparably juster than the definition which con·
siders critics to be men who can explain works of art.

"Critics explain!" What do they explain?

The artist, if a real artist, has by his work transmitted

to others the feeling he experienced. What is there, then, to explain?

If a work be good as art, then the feeling expressed by the artist — be it moral or immoral — transmits itself to other people. If transmitted to others, then they feel it, and all interpretations are superfluous. If the work does not infect people, no explanation can make it contagious. An artist's work cannot be interpreted. Had it been possible to explain in words what he wished to convey, the artist would have expressed himself in words. He expressed it by his art only because the feeling he experienced could not be otherwise transmitted. The interpretation of works of art by words only indicates that the interpreter is himself incapable of feeling the infection of art. And this is actually the case; for, however strange it may seem to say so, critics have always been people less susceptible than other men to the contagion of art. For the most part they are able writers, educated and clever, but with their capacity of being infected by art quite perverted or atrophied. And therefore their writings have always largely contributed, and still contribute, to the perversion of the taste of that public which reads them and trusts them.

Artistic criticism did not exist — could not and cannot exist — in societies where art is undivided, and where, consequently, it is appraised by the religious understanding of life common to the whole people. Art criticism grew, and could grow, only on the art of the upper classes, who did not acknowledge the religious perception of their time.

Universal art has a definite and indubitable internal criterion, — religious perception; upper-class art lacks this, and therefore the appreciators of that art are obliged to cling to some external criterion. And they find it in "the judgments of the finest-nurtured," as an English æsthetician has phrased it, that is, in the authority of the people who are considered educated, nor in this alone, but also in a tradition of such authorities. This tradition is extremely misleading, both because the opinions of "the finest-nurtured" are often mistaken, and also because judgments which were valid once cease to be so with the lapse of time. But the critics, having no basis for their judgments, never cease to repeat their traditions. The classical tragedians were once considered good, and therefore criticism considers them to be so still. Dante was esteemed a great poet, Raphael a great painter, Bach a great musician — and the critics, lacking a standard by which to separate good art from bad, not only consider these artists great, but regard all their productions as admirable and worthy of imitation. Nothing has contributed, and still contributes, so much to the perversion of art as these authorities set up by criticism. A man produces a work of art, like every true artist expressing in his own peculiar manner a feeling he has experienced. Most people are infected by the artist's feeling; and his work becomes known. Then criticism, discussing the artist, says that the work is not bad, but all the same the artist is not a Dante, nor a Shakespear, nor a Goethe, nor a Raphael, nor what Beethoven was in his last period. And the young artist sets to work to copy those who are held up for his imitation, and he produces not only feeble works, but false works, — counterfeits of art.

Thus, for instance, our Pushkin writes his short poems, "Evgeniy Onegin," "The Gipsies," and his stories — works all varying in quality, but all true art. But then, under the influence of false criticism extolling Shakespear, he writes "Boris Godunoff," a cold, brain-spun work, and this production is lauded by the critics, set up as a model, and imitations of it appear: "Minin," by Ostrovsky, and "Tsar Boris," by Alexée Tolstoï, and such imitations of imitations as crowd all literatures with insignificant productions. The chief harm done by the critics is this, — that themselves lacking the capacity to be infected by art (and that is the characteristic of all critics; for did they not lack this they could not attempt the impossible — the interpretation of works of art), they pay most attention to, and eulogize, brain-spun, invented works, and set these up as models worthy of imitation. That is the reason they so confidently extol, in literature, the Greek tragedians, Dante, Tasso, Milton, Shakespear, Goethe (almost all he wrote), and, among recent writers, Zola and Ibsen ; in music, Beethoven's last period, and Wagner. To justify their praise of these brain-spun, invented works, they devise entire theories (of which the famous theory of beauty is one); and not only dull but also talented people compose works in strict deference to these theories ; and often even real artists, doing violence to their genius, submit to them.

Every false work extolled by the critics serves as a door through which the hypocrites of art at once crowd in.

It is solely due to the critics, who in our times still praise rude, savage, and, for us, often meaningless works of the ancient Greeks : Sophocles, Euripides, Æschylus, and especially Aristophanes ; or, of modern writers, Dante, Tasso, Milton, Shakespear ; in painting, all of Raphael, all of Michael Angelo, including his absurd " Last Judgment"; in music, the whole of Bach, and the whole of Beethoven, including his last period, — thanks only to them have the Ibsens, Maeterlincks, Verlaines, Mallarmés, Puvis de Chavannes, Klingers, Böcklins, Stucks, Schneiders ; in music, the Wagners, Liszts, Berliozes, Brahmses, and Richard Strausses, etc., and all that immense mass of good-for-nothing imitators of these imitators, become possible in our day.

As a good illustration of the harmful influence of criticism, take its relation to Beethoven. Among his innumerable hasty productions written to order, there are, notwithstanding their artificiality of form, works of true art. But he grows deaf, cannot hear, and begins to write invented, unfinished works, which are consequently often meaningless and musically unintelligible. I know that musicians can imagine sounds vividly enough, and can almost hear what they read, but imaginary sounds can never replace real ones, and every composer must hear his production in order to perfect it. Beethoven, however, could not hear, could not perfect his work, and consequently published productions which are artistic ravings. But criticism, having once acknowledged him to be a great composer, seizes on just these abnormal works with special gusto, and searches for extraordinary beauties in them. And, to justify its laudations (perverting the very meaning of musical art), it attributed to music the property of describing what it cannot describe. And imitators appear — an innumerable host of imitators of these abnormal attempts at artistic productions which Beethoven wrote when he was deaf.

Then Wagner appears, who at first in critical articles praises just Beethoven's last period, and connects this music with Schopenhauer's mystical theory that music is the expression of Will — not of separate manifestations of will objectivized on various planes, but its very essence — which is in itself as absurd as this music of Beethoven. And afterward he composes music of his own on this theory, in conjunction with another still more erroneous system of the union of all the arts. After Wagner yet new imitators appear, diverging yet further from art: Brahms, Richard Strauss, and others.

Such are the results of criticism. But the third condition of the perversion of art, namely, art schools, is almost more harmful still.

As soon as art became, not art for the whole people, but for a rich class, it became a profession; as soon as it became a profession, methods were devised to teach it; people who chose this profession of art began to learn these methods, and thus professional schools sprang up: classes of rhetoric or literature in the public schools, academies for painting, conservatoires for music, schools for dramatic art.

In these schools art is taught! But art is the transmission to others of a special feeling experienced by the artist. How can this be taught in schools?

No school can evoke feeling in a man, and still less can it teach him how to manifest it in the one particular manner natural to him alone. But the essence of art lies in these things.

The one thing these schools can teach is how to transmit feelings experienced by other artists in the way those other artists transmitted them. And this is just what the professional schools do teach; and such instruction not only does not assist the spread of true art, but, on the contrary, by diffusing counterfeits of art, does more than anything else to deprive people of the capacity to understand true art.

In literary art people are taught how, without having anything they wish to say, to write a many-paged composition on a theme about which they have never thought, and, moreover, to write it so that it should resemble the work of an author admitted to be celebrated. This is taught in schools.

In painting, the chief training consists in learning to draw and paint from copies and models, the naked body chiefly (the very thing that is never seen, and which a man occupied with real art hardly ever has to depict), and to draw and paint as former masters drew and painted. The composition of pictures is taught by giving out themes similar to those which have been treated by former acknowledged celebrities.

So also in dramatic schools, the pupils are taught to recite monologues just as tragedians, considered celebrated, declaimed them.

It is the same in music. The whole theory of music is nothing but a disconnected repetition of those methods which the acknowledged masters of composition made use of.

I have elsewhere quoted the profound remark of the Russian artist Bruloff on art, but I cannot here refrain from repeating it, because nothing better illustrates what can and what cannot be taught in the schools. Once when correcting a pupil's study, Bruloff just touched it in a few places, and the poor dead study immediately became animated. "Why, you only touched it a *wee bit*, and it is quite another thing!" said one of the pupils. "Art begins where the *wee bit* begins," replied Bruloff, indicating by these words just what is most characteristic of art. The remark is true of all the arts, but its justice is particularly noticeable in the performance of music. That musical execution should be artistic, should be art, *i.e.* should infect, three chief

conditions must be observed, — there are many others
needed for musical perfection; the transition from one
sound to another must be interrupted or continu-
ous; the sound must increase or diminish steadily;
it must be blended with one and not with another
sound; the sound must have this or that timbre, and
much besides, — but take the three chief conditions;
the pitch, the time, and the strength of the sound.
Musical execution is only then art, only then infects,
when the sound is neither higher nor lower than it should
be, that is, when exactly the infinitely small center of
the required note is taken; when that note is continued
exactly as long as is needed; and when the strength of
the sound is neither more nor less than is required.
The slightest deviation of pitch in either direction, the
slightest increase or decrease in time, or the slightest
strengthening or weakening of the sound beyond what
is needed, destroys the perfection and, consequently,
the infectiousness of the work. So that the feeling of
infection by the art of music, which seems so simple
and so easily obtained, is a thing we receive only when
the performer finds those infinitely minute degrees
which are necessary to perfection in music. It is the
same in all arts: a wee bit lighter, a wee bit darker,
a wee bit higher, lower, to the right or the left — in
painting; a wee bit weaker or stronger in intonation,
or a wee bit sooner or later — in dramatic art; a
wee bit omitted, over-emphasized, or exaggerated — in
poetry, and there is no contagion. Infection is only
obtained when an artist finds those infinitely minute
degrees of which a work of art consists, and only to the
extent to which he finds them. And it is quite impossible to teach people by external means to find these
minute degrees; they can only be found when a man
yields to his feeling. No instruction can make a dancer
catch just the tact of the music, or a singer or a fiddler
take exactly the infinitely minute center of his note,
or a sketcher draw of all possible lines the only right
one, or a poet find the only meet arrangement of the
only suitable words. All this is found only by feeling.

And therefore schools may teach what is necessary in order to produce something resembling art, but not art itself.

The teaching of the schools stops there where the *wet bit* begins — consequently where art begins.

Accustoming people to something resembling art, disaccustoms them to the comprehension of real art. And that is how it comes about that none are more dull to art than those who have passed through the professional schools and been most successful in them. Professional schools produce an hypocrisy of art precisely akin to that hypocrisy of religion which is produced by theological colleges for training priests, pastors, and religious teachers generally. As it is impossible in a school to train a man so as to make a religious teacher of him, so it is impossible to teach a man how to become an artist.

Art schools are thus doubly destructive of art : first, in that they destroy the capacity to produce real art in those who have the misfortune to enter them and go through a seven or eight years' course ; secondly, in that they generate enormous quantities of that counterfeit art which perverts the taste of the masses and overflows our world. In order that born artists may know the methods of the various arts elaborated by former artists, there should exist in all elementary schools such classes for drawing and music (singing) that, after passing through them, every talented scholar may, by using existing models accessible to all, be able to perfect himself in his art independently.

These three conditions — the professionalization of artists, art criticism, and art schools — have had this effect : that most people in our times are quite unable even to understand what art is, and accept as art the grossest counterfeits of it.

CHAPTER XIII

To what an extent people of our circle and time have lost the capacity to receive real art, and have become accustomed to accept as art things that have nothing in common with it, is best seen from the works of Richard Wagner, which have latterly come to be more and more esteemed, not only by the Germans, but also by the French and the English, as the very highest art, revealing new horizons to us.

The peculiarity of Wagner's music, as is known, consists in this, — that he considered that music should serve poetry, expressing all the shades of a poetical work.

The union of the drama with music, devised in the fifteenth century in Italy for the revival of what they imagined to have been the ancient Greek drama with music, is an artificial form which had, and has, success only among the upper classes, and that only when gifted composers, such as Mozart, Weber, Rossini, and others, drawing inspiration from a dramatic subject, yielded freely to the inspiration and subordinated the text to the music, so that in their operas the important thing to the audience was merely the music on a certain text, and not the text at all, which latter, even when it was utterly absurd, as, for instance, in the "Magic Flute," still did not prevent the music from producing an artistic impression.

Wagner wishes to correct the opera by letting music submit to the demands of poetry and unite with it. But each art has its own definite realm, which is not identical with the realm of other arts, but merely comes in contact with them; and therefore, if the manifestation of, I will not say several, but even of two arts — the dramatic and the musical — be united in one complete production, then the demands of the one art will make it impossible to fulfil the demands of the other, as has always occurred in the ordinary operas, where the dramatic art has submitted to, or rather yielded place to, the musical. Wagner wishes that musical art should submit to dramatic art, and that both should appear in full strength. But this is impossible; for every work of art, if it be a true one, is an expression of intimate feelings of the artist, which are quite exceptional, and not like anything else. Such is a musical production, and such is a dramatic work, if they be true art. And therefore, in order that a production in the one branch of art should coincide with a production in the other branch, it is necessary that the impossible should happen : that two works from different realms of art should be absolutely exceptional, unlike anything that existed before, and yet should coincide, and be exactly alike.

And this cannot be, just as there cannot be two men, or even two leaves on a tree, exactly alike. Still less can two works from different realms of art, the musical and the literary, be absolutely alike. If they coincide, then either one is a work of art and the other a counterfeit, or both are counterfeits. Two live leaves cannot be exactly alike, but two artificial leaves may be. And so it is with works of art. They can only coincide completely when neither the one nor the other is art, but only cunningly devised semblances of it.

If poetry and music may be joined, as occurs in hymns, songs, and *romances* — (though even in these the music does not follow the changes of each verse of the text, as Wagner wants to, but the song and the music merely produce a coincident effect on the mind) — this occurs only because lyrical poetry and music have, to some extent, one and the same aim : to produce a mental condition and the conditions produced by lyrical poetry and by music can, more or less, coincide. But even in these conjunctions the center of gravity always lies in one of the two productions, so that it is one of them that produces the artistic impression while the other remains unregarded. And still less is it possible for such union to exist between epic or dramatic poetry and music.

Moreover, one of the chief conditions of artistic creation is the complete freedom of the artist from every kind of preconceived demand. And the necessity of adjusting his musical work to a work from another realm of

art is a preconceived demand of such a kind as to destroy
all possibility of creative power; and therefore works of
this kind, adjusted to one another, are, and must be, as
has always happened, not works of art, but only imitations of art, like the music of a melodrama, signatures
to pictures, illustrations, and librettos to operas.

And such are Wagner's productions. And a confirmation of this is to be seen in the fact that Wagner's
new music lacks the chief characteristic of every true
work of art; namely, such entirety and completeness
that the smallest alteration in its form would disturb the
meaning of the whole work. In a true work of art —
poem, drama, picture, song, or symphony — it is impossible to extract one line, one scene, one figure, or one
bar from its place and put it in another, without infringing the significance of the whole work; just as it is
impossible, without infringing the life of an organic being, to extract an organ from one place and insert it
in another. But in the music of Wagner's last period,
with the exception of certain parts of little importance
which have an independent musical meaning, it is possible to make all kinds of transpositions, putting what
was in front behind, and *vice versa*, without altering the
musical sense. And the reason why these transpositions
do not alter the sense of Wagner's music is because the
sense lies in the words and not in the music.

The musical score of Wagner's later operas is like what
the result would be should one of those versifiers — of
whom there are now many, with tongues so broken that
they can write verses on any theme to any rhymes in
any rhythm, which sound as if they had a meaning —
conceive the idea of illustrating by his verses some symphony or sonata of Beethoven, or some ballade of
Chopin, in the following manner. To the first bars, of
one character, he writes verses corresponding in his opinion to those first bars. Next come some bars of a different character, and he also writes verses corresponding
in his opinion to them, but with no internal connection
with the first verses, and, moreover, without rhymes and
without rhythm. Such a production, without the music,

would be exactly parallel in poetry to what Wagner's operas are in music, if heard without the words.

But Wagner is not only a musician, he is also a poet, or both together; and therefore, to judge of Wagner, one must know his poetry also — that same poetry which the music has to subserve. The chief poetical production of Wagner is "The Nibelung's Ring." This work has attained such enormous importance in our time, and has such influence on all that now professes to be art, that it is necessary for every one to-day to have some idea of it. I have carefully read through the four booklets which contain this work, and have drawn up a brief summary of it, which I give in Appendix III. I would strongly advise the reader (if he has not perused the poem itself, which would be the best thing to do) at least to read my account of it, so as to have an idea of this extraordinary work. It is a model work of counterfeit art, so gross as to be even ridiculous.

But we are told that it is impossible to judge of Wagner's works without seeing them on the stage. The Second Day of this drama, which, as I was told, is the best part of the whole work, was given in Moscow last winter, and I went to see the performance.

When I arrived the enormous theater was already filled from top to bottom. There were grand dukes, and the flower of the aristocracy, of the merchant class, of the learned, and of the middle-class official public. Most of them held the libretto, fathoming its meaning. Musicians — some of them elderly, gray-haired men — followed the music, score in hand. Evidently the performance of this work was an event of importance.

I was rather late, but I was told that the short prelude, with which the act begins, was of little importance, and that it did not matter having missed it. When I arrived, an actor sat on the stage amid decorations intended to represent a cave, and before something which was meant to represent a smith's forge. He was dressed in trico-tights, with a cloak of skins, wore a wig and an artificial beard, and with white, weak genteel hands (his easy movements, and especially the shape of his stomach

and his lack of muscle revealed the actor) beat an impossible sword with an unnatural hammer in a way in which
no one ever uses a hammer; and at the same time, opening his mouth in a strange way, he sang something
incomprehensible. The music of various instruments
accompanied the strange sounds which he emitted.
From the libretto one was able to gather that the actor
had to represent a powerful gnome, who lived in the cave,
and who was forging a sword for Siegfried, whom he
had reared. One could tell he was a gnome by the fact
that the actor walked all the time bending the knees of
his trico-covered legs. This gnome, still opening his
mouth in the same strange way, long continued to sing
or shout. The music meanwhile runs over something
strange, like beginnings which are not continued and do
not get finished. From the libretto one could learn that
the gnome is telling himself about a ring which a giant
had obtained, and which the gnome wishes to procure
through Siegfried's aid, while Siegfried wants a good
sword, on the forging of which the gnome is occupied.
After this conversation or singing to himself has gone
on rather a long time, other sounds are heard in the orchestra, also like something beginning and not finishing,
and another actor appears, with a horn slung over his
shoulder, and accompanied by a man running on all fours
dressed up as a bear, whom he sets at the smith-gnome.
The latter runs away without unbending the knees of
his trico-covered legs. This actor with the horn represented the hero, Siegfried. The sounds which were
emitted in the orchestra on the entrance of this actor
were intended to represent Siegfried's character, and
are called Siegfried's *leit-motiv*. And these sounds are
repeated each time Siegfried appears. There is one
fixed combination of sounds, or *leit-motiv*, for each character, and this *leit-motiv* is repeated every time the person whom it represents appears; and when any one is
mentioned the *motiv* is heard which relates to that person. Moreover, each article also has its own *leit-motiv*
or chord. There is a *motiv* of the ring, a *motiv* of the
helmet, a *motiv* of the apple, a *motiv* of fire, spear, sword,

water, etc.; and as soon as the ring, helmet, or apple is
mentioned, the *motiv* or chord of the ring, helmet, or
apple is heard. The actor with the horn opens his
mouth as unnaturally as the gnome, and long continues
in a chanting voice to shout some words, and in a similar
chant Mime (that is the gnome's name) answers something or other to him. The meaning of this conversation can only be discovered from the libretto; and it is
that Siegfried was brought up by the gnome, and therefore, for some reason, hates him and always wishes to
kill him. The gnome has forged a sword for Siegfried,
but Siegfried is dissatisfied with it. From a ten-page
conversation (by the libretto), lasting half an hour and
conducted with the same strange openings of the mouth
and chantings, it appears that Siegfried's mother gave
birth to him in the wood, and that concerning his father
all that is known is that he had a sword which was broken,
the pieces of which are in Mime's possession, and that
Siegfried does not know fear and wishes to go out of
the wood. Mime, however, does not want to let him go.
During the conversation the music never omits, at the
mention of father, sword, etc., to sound the *motiv* of
these people and things. After these conversations
fresh sounds are heard — those of the god Wotan —
and a wanderer appears. This wanderer is the god
Wotan. Also dressed up in a wig, and also in tights,
this god Wotan, standing in a stupid pose with a spear,
thinks proper to recount what Mime must have known
before, but what it is necessary to tell the audience.
He does not tell it simply, but in the form of riddles
which he orders himself to guess, staking his head (one
does not know why) that he will guess right. Moreover,
whenever the wanderer strikes his spear on the ground,
fire comes out of the ground, and in the orchestra the
sounds of spear and of fire are heard. The orchestra
accompanies the conversation, and the *motiv* of the
people and things spoken of are always artfully intermingled. Besides this the music expresses feelings in
the most naïve manner: the terrible by sounds in the
bass, the frivolous by rapid touches in the treble, etc.

The riddles have no meaning except to tell the audience what the *nibelungs* are, what the giants are, what
the gods are, and what has happened before. This
conversation also is chanted with strangely opened
mouths and continues for eight libretto pages, and correspondingly long on the stage. After this the wanderer departs, and Siegfried returns and talks with
Mime for thirteen pages more. There is not a single
melody the whole of this time, but merely intertwinings
of the *leit-motiv* of the people and things mentioned.
The conversation tells that Mime wishes to teach Siegfried fear, and that Siegfried does not know what fear
is. Having finished this conversation, Siegfried seizes
one of the pieces of what is meant to represent the
broken sword, saws it up, puts it on what is meant to
represent the forge, melts it, and then forges it and sings :
Heiho! heiho! heiho! Ho! ho! Aha! oho! aha!
Heiaho! heiaho! heiaho! Ho! ho! Hahei! hoho!
hahei! and Act I. finishes.

As far as the question I had come to the theater to
decide was concerned, my mind was fully made up, as
surely as on the question of the merits of my lady
acquaintance's novel when she read me the scene between the loose-haired maiden in the white dress and
the hero with two white dogs and a hat with a feather
à la Guillaume Tell.

From an author who could compose such spurious
scenes, outraging all æsthetic feeling, as those which I
had witnessed, there was nothing to be hoped ; it may
safely be decided that all that such an author can write
will be bad, because he evidently does not know what
a true work of art is. I wished to leave, but the friends
I was with asked me to remain, declaring that one could
not form an opinion by that one act, and that the second
would be better. So I stopped for the second act.

Act II., night. Afterward, dawn. In general, the
whole piece is crammed with lights, clouds, moonlight,
darkness, magic fires, thunder, etc.

The scene represents a wood, and in the wood there
is a cave. At the entrance of the cave sits a third

actor in tights, representing another gnome. It dawns.
Enter the god Wotan, again with a spear, and again in
the guise of a wanderer. Again his sounds, together
with fresh sounds of the deepest bass that can be produced. These latter indicate that the dragon is speaking. Wotan awakens the dragon. The same bass
sounds are repeated, growing yet deeper and deeper.
First the dragon says, "I want to sleep," but afterward
he crawls out of the cave. The dragon is represented
by two men; it is dressed in a green, scaly skin, waves
a tail at one end, while at the other it opens a kind of
crocodile's jaw that is fastened on, and from which
flames appear. The dragon (who is meant to be dread-
ful, and may appear so to five-year-old children) speaks
some words in a terribly bass voice. This is all so
stupid, so like what is done in a booth at a fair, that it
is surprising that people over seven years of age can
witness it seriously; yet thousands of quasi-cultured
people sit and attentively hear and see it, and are
delighted.

Siegfried, with his horn, reappears, as does Mime also.
In the orchestra the sounds denoting them are emitted,
and they talk about whether Siegfried does or does not
know what fear is. Mime goes away, and a scene commences which is intended to be most poetical. Siegfried,
in his tights, lies down in a would-be beautiful pose, and
alternately keeps silent and talks to himself. He pon-
ders, listens to the song of birds, and wishes to imitate
them. For this purpose he cuts a reed with his sword
and makes a pipe. The dawn grows brighter and
brighter; the birds sing. Siegfried tries to imitate the
birds. In the orchestra is heard the imitation of birds,
alternating with sounds corresponding to the words he
speaks. But Siegfried does not succeed with his pipe-
playing, so he plays on his horn instead. This scene
is unendurable. Of music, *i.e.* of art serving as a means
to transmit a state of mind experienced by the author,
there is not even a suggestion. There is something that
is absolutely unintelligible musically. In a musical sense
a hope is continually experienced, followed by disap-

pointment, as if a musical thought were commenced only to be broken off. If there are something like musical commencements, these commencements are so short, so encumbered with complications of harmony and orchestration and with effects of contrast, are so obscure and unfinished, and what is happening on the stage meanwhile is so abominably false, that it is difficult even to perceive these musical snatches, let alone to be infected by them. Above all, from the very beginning to the very end, and in each note, the author's purpose is so audible and visible that one sees and hears neither Siegfried nor the birds, but only a limited, self-opinionated German, of bad taste and bad style, who has a most false conception of poetry, and who, in the rudest and most primitive manner, wishes to transmit to me these false and mistaken conceptions of his.

Every one knows the feeling of distrust and resistance which is always evoked by an author's evident predetermination. A narrator need only say in advance, Prepare to cry or to laugh, and you are sure neither to cry nor to laugh. But when you see that an author prescribes emotion at what is not touching, but only laughable or disgusting, and when you see, moreover, that the author is fully assured that he has captivated you, a painfully tormenting feeling results, similar to what one would feel if an old, deformed woman put on a ball-dress, and smilingly coquetted before you, confident of your approbation. This impression was strengthened by the fact that around me I saw a crowd of three thousand people, who not only patiently witnessed all this absurd nonsense, but even considered it their duty to be delighted with it.

I somehow managed to sit out the next scene also, in which the monster appears, to the accompaniment of his bass notes intermingled with the *motiv* of Siegfried; but after the fight with the monster, and all the roars, fires, and sword-wavings, I could stand no more of it, and escaped from the theater with a feeling of repulsion which, even now, I cannot forget.

Listening to this opera, I involuntarily thought of a

respected, wise, educated country laborer, — one, for instance, of those wise and truly religious men whom I know among the peasants, — and I pictured to myself the terrible perplexity such a man would be in were he to witness what I was seeing that evening.

What would he think if he knew of all the labor spent on such a performance, and saw that audience, those great ones of the earth, — old, bald-headed, gray-bearded men, whom he had been accustomed to respect, — sit silent and attentive, listening to and looking at all these stupidities for five hours on end? Not to speak of an adult laborer, one can hardly imagine even a child of over seven occupying himself with such a stupid, incoherent fairy tale.

And yet an enormous audience, the cream of the cultured upper classes, sits out five hours of this insane performance, and goes away imagining that by paying tribute to this nonsense it has acquired a fresh right to esteem itself advanced and enlightened.

I speak of the Moscow public. But what is the Moscow public? It is but a hundredth part of that public which, while considering itself most highly enlightened, esteems it a merit to have so lost the capacity of being infected by art, that not only can it witness this stupid sham without being revolted, but can even take delight in it.

In Bayreuth, where these performances were first given, people who consider themselves finely cultured assembled from the ends of the earth, spent, say one hundred pounds each, to see this performance, and for four days running they went to see and hear this nonsensical rubbish, sitting it out for six hours each day.

But why did people go, and why do they still go to these performances, and why do they admire them? The question naturally presents itself: How is the success of Wagner's works to be explained?

That success I explain to myself in this way; thanks to his exceptional position in having at his disposal the resources of a king, Wagner was able to command all the methods for counterfeiting art which have been developed by long usage, and, employing these methods with great ability, he produced a model work of coun-terfeit art. The reason why I have selected his work for my illustration is, that in no other counterfeit of art known to me are all the methods by which art is coun-terfeited — namely, borrowings, imitation, effects, and interestingness — so ably and powerfully united.

From the subject, borrowed from antiquity, to the clouds and the risings of the sun and moon, Wagner, in this work, has made use of all that is considered poeti-cal. We have here the sleeping beauty, and nymphs, and subterranean fires, and gnomes, and battles, and swords, and love, and incest, and a monster, and singing-birds — the whole arsenal of the poetical is brought into action.

Moreover, everything is imitative; the decorations are imitated, and the costumes are imitated. All are just as, according to the data supplied by archæology, they would have been in antiquity. The very sounds are imi-tative; for Wagner, who was not destitute of musical talent, invented just such sounds as imitate the strokes of a hammer, the hissing of molten iron, the singing of birds, etc.

Furthermore, in this work everything is in the high-est degree striking in its effects and in its peculiarities: its monsters, its magic fires, and its scenes under water; the darkness in which the audience sit, the invisibility of the orchestra, and the hitherto unemployed combina-tions of harmony.

And besides, it is all interesting. The interest lies not only in the question who will kill whom, and who will marry whom, and who is whose son, and what will happen next? — the interest lies also in the relation of the music to the text. The rolling waves of the Rhine —now how is that to be expressed in music? An evil gnome appears — how is the music to express an evil gnome? — and how is it to express the sensuality of this gnome? How will bravery, fire, or apples be ex-pressed in music? How are the *leit-motiv* of the people speaking to be interwoven with the *leit-motiv* of the people and objects about whom they speak? Besides, the music has a further interest. It diverges from all formerly accepted laws, and most unexpected and totally new modulations crop up (as is not only possible, but even easy in music having no inner law of its being); the dissonances are new, and are allowed in a new way —and this, too, is interesting.

And it is this poeticality, imitativeness, effectfulness,, and interestingness which, thanks to the peculiarities of Wagner's talent, and to the advantageous position in which he was placed, are in these productions carried to the highest pitch of perfection, that so act on the spectator, hypnotizing him as one would be hypnotized who should listen for several consecutive hours to the ravings of a maniac pronounced with great oratorical power.

People say: "You cannot judge without having seen Wagner performed at Bayreuth: in the dark, where the orchestra is out of sight concealed under the stage, and where the performance is brought to the highest perfection." And this just proves that we have here no question of art, but one of hypnotism. It is just what the spiritualists say. To convince you of the reality of their apparitions they usually say, "You cannot judge; you must try it, be present at several séances," *i.e.* come and sit silent in the dark for hours together in the same room with semi-sane people, and repeat this some ten times over, and you shall see all that we see.

Yes, naturally! Only place yourself in such conditions, and you may see what you will. But this can be still more quickly attained by getting drunk or smoking opium. It is the same when listening to an opera of Wagner's. Sit in the dark for four days in company with people who are not quite normal, and, through the auditory nerves, subject your brain to the strongest action of the sounds best adapted to excite it, and you will no doubt be reduced to an abnormal condition, and be enchanted by absurdities. But to attain this end you do not even need four days; the five hours during which one "day" is enacted, as in Moscow, are quite enough.

Nor are five hours needed; even one hour is enough
for people who have no clear conception of what art
should be, and who have come to the conclusion in advance that what they are going to see is excellent, and
that indifference or dissatisfaction with this work will
serve as a proof of their inferiority and lack of culture.

I observed the audience present at this representation. The people who led the whole audience and gave
the tone to it were those who had previously been hypnotized, and who again succumbed to the hypnotic influence to which they were accustomed. These hypnotized
people, being in an abnormal condition, were perfectly
enraptured. Moreover, all the art critics, who lack the
capacity to be infected by art and therefore always
especially prize works like Wagner's opera where it is
all an affair of the intellect, also, with much profundity,
expressed their approval of a work affording such ample
material for ratiocination. And following these two
groups went that large city crowd (indifferent to art, with
their capacity to be infected by it perverted and partly
atrophied), headed by the princes, millionaires, and
art patrons, who, like sorry harriers, keep close to those
who most loudly and decidedly express their opinion.

"Oh, yes, certainly! What poetry! Marvelous! Especially the birds!" "Yes, yes! I am quite vanquished!"
exclaim these people, repeating in various tones what they
have just heard from men whose opinion appears to
them authoritative.

If some people do feel insulted by the absurdity and
spuriousness of the whole thing, they are timidly silent,
as sober men are timid and silent when surrounded by
tipsy ones.

And thus, thanks to the masterly skill with which it
counterfeits art while having nothing in common with it, a
meaningless, coarse, spurious production finds acceptance
all over the world, costs millions of roubles to produce,
and assists more and more to pervert the taste of people
of the upper classes and their conception of what is art

CHAPTER XIV

I KNOW that most men — not only those considered clever, but even those who are very clever, and capable of understanding most difficult scientific, mathematical, or philosophic problems — can very seldom discern even the simplest and most obvious truth if it be such as to oblige them to admit the falsity of conclusions they have formed, perhaps with much difficulty — conclusions of which they are proud, which they have taught to others, and on which they have built their lives. And therefore I have little hope that what I adduce as to the perversion of art and taste in our society will be accepted or even seriously considered. Nevertheless, I must state fully the inevitable conclusion to which my investigation into the question of art has brought me. This investigation has brought me to the conviction that almost all that our society considers to be art, good art, and the whole of art, far from being real and good art, and the whole of art, is not even art at all, but only a counterfeit of it. This position, I know, will seem very strange and paradoxical; but if we once acknowledge art to be a human activity by means of which some people transmit their feelings to others (and not a service of Beauty, nor a manifestation of the Idea, and so forth), we shall inevitably have to admit this further conclusion also. If it is true that art is an activity by means of which one man, having experienced a feeling, intentionally transmits it to others, then we have inevitably to admit further, that of all that among us is termed the art of the upper classes — of all those novels, stories, dramas, comedies, pictures, sculptures, symphonies, operas, operettas, ballets, etc., which profess to be works of art — scarcely one in a hundred thousand proceeds from an emotion felt by its author, all the rest being but manufactured counterfeits of art, in which borrowing, imitating, effects, and interestingness replace the contagion of feeling. That the proportion of real productions of art is to the counterfeits as one to some hundreds of thousands or even more, may be seen by the following calculation. I have read somewhere that the artist painters in Paris alone number 30,000; there will probably be as many in England, as many in Germany, and as many in Russia, Italy, and the smaller states combined. So that in all there will be in Europe, say, 120,000 painters; and there are probably as many musicians and as many literary artists. If these 360,000 individuals produce three works a year each (and many of them produce ten or more), then each year yields over a million so-called works of art. How many, then, must have been produced in the last ten years, and how many in the whole time since upper-class art broke off from the art of the whole people? Evidently millions. Yet who of all the connoisseurs of art has received impressions from all these pseudo works of art? Not to mention all the laboring classes who have no conception of these productions, even people of the upper classes cannot know one in a thousand of them all, and cannot remember those they have known. These works all appear under the guise of art, produce no impression on any one (except when they serve as pastimes for the idle crowd of rich people), and vanish utterly.

In reply to this it is usually said that without this enormous number of unsuccessful attempts we should not have the real works of art. But such reasoning is as though a baker, in reply to a reproach that his bread was bad, were to say that if it were not for the hundreds of spoiled loaves there would not be any well-baked ones. It is true that where there is gold there is also much sand; but that cannot serve as a reason for talking a lot of nonsense in order to say something wise.

We are surrounded by productions considered artistic. Thousands of verses, thousands of poems, thousands of novels, thousands of dramas, thousands of pictures, thousands of musical pieces, follow one after another. All the verses describe love, or nature, or the author's state of mind, and in all of them rhyme and rhythm are observed. All the dramas and comedies are splendidly mounted and are performed by admirably trained actors. All the novels are divided into chapters; all of them describe love, contain effective situations, and correctly describe the details of life. All the symphonies contain *allegro, andante, scherzo,* and *finale;* all consist of modulations and chords, and are played by highly trained musicians. All the pictures, in gold frames, saliently depict faces and sundry accessories. But among these productions in the various branches of art, there is in each branch one among hundreds of thousands, not only somewhat better than the rest, but differing from them as a diamond differs from paste. The one is priceless, the others not only have no value, but are worse than valueless, for they deceive and pervert taste. And yet, externally, they are, to a man of perverted or atrophied artistic perception, precisely alike.

In our society the difficulty of recognizing real works of art is further increased by the fact that the external quality of the work in false productions is not only no worse, but often better, than in real ones; the counterfeit is often more effective than the real, and its subject more interesting. How is one to discriminate? How is one to find a production in no way distinguished in externals from hundreds of thousands of others intentionally made to imitate it precisely?

For a country peasant of unperverted taste this is as easy as it is for an animal of unspoilt scent to follow the trace he needs among a thousand others in wood or forest. The animal unerringly finds what he needs. So also the man, if only his natural qualities have not been perverted, will, without fail, select from among thousands of objects the real work of art he requires, — that infecting him with the feeling experienced by the artist. But it is not so with those whose taste has been perverted by their education and life. The receptive feeling for art of these people is atrophied, and in valuing artistic productions they must be guided by discussion and study, which discussion and study completely confuse them. So that most people in our society are quite unable to distinguish a work of art from the grossest counterfeit. People sit for whole hours in concert-rooms and theaters listening to the new composers, consider it a duty to read the novels of the famous modern novelists, and to look at pictures representing either something incomprehensible, or just the very things they see much better in real life ; and, above all, they consider it incumbent on them to be enraptured by all this, imagining it all to be art, while at the same time they will pass real works of art by, not only without attention, but even with contempt, merely because, in their circle, these works are not included in the list of works of art.

A few days ago I was returning home from a walk feeling depressed, as occurs sometimes. On nearing the house I heard the loud singing of a large choir of peasant women. They were welcoming my daughter, celebrating her return home after her marriage. In this singing, with its cries and clanging of scythes, such a definite feeling of joy, cheerfulness, and energy was expressed, that, without noticing how it infected me, I continued my way toward the house in a better mood, and reached home smiling, and quite in good spirits. That same evening, a visitor, an admirable musician, famed for his execution of classical music, and particularly of Beethoven, played us Beethoven's sonata, Opus 101. For the benefit of those who might otherwise attribute my judgment of that sonata of Beethoven to non-comprehension of it, I should mention that, whatever other people understand of that sonata and of other productions of Beethoven's later period, I, being very susceptible to music, equally understood. For a long time I used to attune myself so as to delight in those shapeless improvisations which form the subject-matter of the works of Beethoven's later period, but I had only to consider the question of art seriously, and to compare the impression I received from Beethoven's later works with those pleasant, clear, and strong musical impressions which are transmitted, for instance, by the melodies of Bach (his arias), Haydn, Mozart, Chopin, (when his melodies are not overloaded with complications and ornamentation), and of Beethoven himself in his earlier period, and, above all, with the impressions produced by folk-songs, — Italian, Norwegian, or Russian, — by the Hungarian *tzardas*, and other such simple, clear, and powerful music, and the obscure, almost unhealthy excitement from Beethoven's later pieces that I had artificially evoked in myself was immediately destroyed.

On the completion of the performance (though it was noticeable that every one had become dull) those present, in the accepted manner, warmly praised Beethoven's profound production, and did not forget to add that formerly they had not been able to understand that last period of his, but that they now saw that he was really then at his very best. And when I ventured to compare the impression made on me by the singing of the peasant women — an impression which had been shared by all who heard it — with the effect of this sonata, the admirers of Beethoven only smiled contemptuously, not considering it necessary to reply to such strange remarks.

But, for all that, the song of the peasant women was real art, transmitting a definite and strong feeling ; while the 101st sonata of Beethoven was only an unsuccessful attempt at art, containing no definite feeling, and therefore not infectious.

For my work on art I have this winter read diligently, though with great effort, the celebrated novels and stories, praised by all Europe, written by Zola, Bourget, Huysmans, and Kipling. At the same time I chanced on a story in a child's magazine, and by a quite unknown writer, which told of the Easter preparations in a poor widow's family. The story tells how the mother managed with difficulty to obtain some wheat-flour, which she poured on the table ready to knead. She then went out to procure some yeast, telling the children not to leave the hut, and to take care of the flour. When the mother had gone, some other children ran shouting near the window, calling those in the hut to come to play. The children forgot their mother's warning, ran into the street, and were soon engrossed in the game. The mother, on her return with the yeast, finds a hen on the table throwing the last of the flour to her chickens, who were busily picking it out of the dust of the earthen floor. The mother, in despair, scolds the children, who cry bitterly. And the mother begins to feel pity for them — but the white flour has all gone. So to mend matters she decides to make the Easter cake with sifted rye-flour, brushing it over with white of egg, and surrounding it with eggs. "Rye-bread which we bake is akin to any cake," says the mother, using a rhyming proverb to console the children for not having an Easter cake made with white flour. And the children, quickly passing from despair to rapture, repeat the proverb and await the Easter cake more merrily even than before.

Well! the reading of the novels and stories by Zola, Bourget, Huysmans, Kipling, and others, handling the most harrowing subjects, did not touch me for one moment, and I was provoked with the authors all the while, as one is provoked with a man who considers you so naïve that he does not even conceal the trick by which he intends to take you in. From the first lines you see the intention with which the book is written, and the details all become superfluous, and one feels dull. Above all, one knows that the author had no other feeling all the time than a desire to write a story or a novel, and so one receives no artistic impression. On the other hand, I could not tear myself away from the unknown author's tale of the children and the chickens, because I was at once infected by the feeling which the author had evidently experienced, reëvoked in himself, and transmitted.

Vasnetsoff is one of our Russian painters. He has painted ecclesiastical pictures in Kieff Cathedral, and every one praises him as the founder of some new, elevated kind of Christian art. He worked at those pictures for ten years, was paid tens of thousands of roubles for them, and they are all simply bad imitations of imitations of imitations, destitute of any spark of feeling. And this same Vasnetsoff drew a picture for Tourgenieff's story, "The Quail" (in which it is told how, in his son's presence, a father killed a quail and felt pity for it), showing the boy asleep with pouting upper lip, and above him, as a dream the quail. And this picture is a true work of art.

In the English Academy of 1897 two pictures were exhibited together; one of which, by J. C. Dolman, was the temptation of St. Anthony. The saint is on his knees praying. Behind him stands a naked woman and animals of some kind. It is apparent that the naked woman pleased the artist very much, but that Anthony did not concern him at all; and that, so far from the temptation being terrible to him (the artist) it is highly agreeable. And therefore if there be any art in this picture, it is very nasty and false. Next in the same book of academy pictures comes a picture by Langley, showing a stray beggar-boy, who has evidently been called in by a woman who has taken pity on him. The boy, pitifully drawing his bare feet under the bench, is eating; the woman is looking on, probably considering whether he will not want some more; and a girl of about seven, leaning on her arm, is carefully and seriously looking on, not taking her eyes from the hungry boy, and evidently understanding for the first time what poverty is, and what inequality among people is, and asking herself why she has everything provided for her while this boy goes barefoot and hungry? She feels sorry, and yet pleased. And she loves both the boy and goodness. .... And one feels that the artist loved this girl, and that she too loves. And this picture, by an artist who, I think, is not very widely known, is an admirable and true work of art.

I remember seeing a performance of "Hamlet" by Rossi. Both the tragedy itself and the performer who took the chief part are considered by our critics to represent the climax of supreme dramatic art. And yet, both from the subject-matter of the drama and from the performance, I experienced all the time that peculiar suffering which is caused by false imitations of works of art. And I lately read of a theatrical performance among the savage tribe, the Voguls. A spectator describes the play. A big Vogul and a little one, both dressed in reindeer skins, represent a reindeer-doe and its young. A third Vogul, with a bow, represents a huntsman on snow-shoes, and a fourth imitates with his voice a bird that warns the reindeer of their danger. The play is that the huntsman follows the track that the doe with its young one has traveled. The deer run off the scene, and again reappear. (Such performances take place in a small tent-house.) The huntsman gains more and more on the pursued. The little deer is tired, and presses against its mother. The doe stops to draw breath. The hunter comes up with them and draws his bow. But just then the bird sounds its note, warning the deer of their danger. They escape. Again there is a chase, and again the hunter gains on them, catches them, and lets fly his arrow. The arrow strikes the young deer. Unable to run, the little one presses against its mother. The mother licks its wound. The hunter draws another arrow. The audience, as the eye-witness describes them, are paralyzed with suspense; deep groans and even weeping is heard among them. And, from the mere description, I felt that this was a true work of art.

What I am saying will be considered irrational paradox, at which one can only be amazed; but for all that I must say what I think; namely, that people of our circle, of whom some compose verses, stories, novels, operas, symphonies, and sonatas, paint all kinds of pictures and make statues, while others hear and look at these things, and again others appraise and criticize it all, discuss, condemn, triumph, and raise monuments to one another, generation after generation, — that all these people, with very few exceptions, artists, and public, and critics, have never (except in childhood and earliest youth, before hearing any discussions on art) experienced that simple feeling familiar to the plainest man and even to a child, that sense of infection with another's feeling, — compel

ling us to joy in another's gladness, to sorrow at another's grief, and to mingle souls with another, — which
is the very essence of art. And therefore these people
not only cannot distinguish true works of art from counterfeits, but continually mistake for real art the worst
and most artificial, while they do not even perceive works
of real art, because the counterfeits are always more
ornate, while true art is modest.

CHAPTER XV

ART, in our society, has been so perverted that not
only has bad art come to be considered good, but even
the very perception of what art really is has been lost. In
order to be able to speak about the art of our society, it
is, therefore, first of all necessary to distinguish art from
counterfeit art.

There is one indubitable indication distinguishing real
art from its counterfeit, namely, the infectiousness of
art. If a man, without exercising effort and without
altering his standpoint, on reading, hearing, or seeing
another man's work, experiences a mental condition
which unites him with that man and with other people
who also partake of that work of art, then the object
evoking that condition is a work of art. And however
poetical, realistic, effectful, or interesting a work may be,
it is not a work of art if it does not evoke that feeling
(quite distinct from all other feelings) of joy, and of
spiritual union with another (the author) and with others
(those who are also infected by it).

It is true that this indication is an *internal* one, and
that there are people who have forgotten what the action
of real art is, who expect something else from art (in our
society the great majority are in this state), and that
therefore such people may mistake for this æsthetic feeling the feeling of divertisement and a certain excitement
which they receive from counterfeits of art. But though
it is impossible to undeceive these people, just as it is
impossible to convince a man suffering from " Dalton-

ism " that green is not red, yet, for all that, this indica
tion remains perfectly definite to those whose feeling for
art is neither perverted nor atrophied, and it clearly distinguishes the feeling produced by art from all other
feelings.

The chief peculiarity of this feeling is that the receiver
of a true artistic impression is so united to the artist that
he feels as if the work were his own and not some one
else's, — as if what it expresses were just what he had
long been wishing to express. A real work of art destroys, in the consciousness of the receiver, the separation between himself and the artist; nor that alone, but
also between himself and all whose minds receive this
work of art. In this freeing of our personality from its
separation and isolation, in this uniting of it with others,
lies the chief characteristic and the great attractive force
of art.

If a man is infected by the author's condition of soul,
if he feels this emotion and this union with others, then
the object which has effected this is art; but if there be
no such infection, if there be not this union with the author and with others who are moved by the same work
— then it is not art. And not only is infection a sure
sign of art, but the degree of infectiousness is also the
sole measure of excellence in art.

The stronger the infection the better is the art; as art,
speaking now apart from its subject-matter, *i.e.* not
considering the quality of the feelings it transmits.

And the degree of the infectiousness of art depends
on three conditions : —

(1) On the greater or lesser individuality of the feeling transmitted; (2) on the greater or lesser clearness
with which the feeling is transmitted; (3) on the sincerity of the artist, *i.e.* on the greater or lesser force with
which the artist himself feels the emotion he transmits.

The more individual the feeling transmitted the more
strongly does it act on the receiver; the more individual
the state of soul into which he is transferred the more
pleasure does the receiver obtain, and therefore the more
readily and strongly does he join in it.

The clearness of expression assists infection, because the receiver, who mingles in consciousness with the author, is the better satisfied the more clearly the feeling is transmitted, which, as it seems to him, he has long known and felt, and for which he has only now found expression.

But most of all is the degree of infectiousness of art increased by the degree of sincerity in the artist. As soon as the spectator, hearer, or reader feels that the artist is infected by his own production, and writes, sings, or plays for himself, and not merely to act on others, this mental condition of the artist infects the receiver; and, contrariwise, as soon as the spectator, reader, or hearer feels that the author is not writing, singing, or playing for his own satisfaction, — does not himself feel what he wishes to express, — but is doing it for him, the receiver, a resistance immediately springs up, and the most individual and the newest feelings and the cleverest technique not only fail to produce any infection, but actually repel.

I have mentioned three conditions of contagiousness in art, but they may be all summed up into one, the last, sincerity, *i.e.* that the artist should be impelled by an inner need to express his feeling. That condition includes the first; for if the artist is sincere he will express the feeling as he experienced it. And as each man is different from every one else, his feeling will be individual for every one else; and the more individual it is, — the more the artist has drawn it from the depths of his nature, — the more sympathetic and sincere will it be. And this same sincerity will impel the artist to find a clear expression of the feeling which he wishes to transmit.

Therefore this third condition — sincerity — is the most important of the three. It is always complied with in peasant art, and this explains why such art always acts so powerfully; but it is a condition almost entirely absent from our upper-class art, which is continually produced by artists actuated by personal aims of covetousness or vanity.

Such are the three conditions which divide art from its counterfeits, and which also decide the quality of every work of art apart from its subject-matter.

The absence of any one of these conditions excludes a work from the category of art and relegates it to that of art's counterfeits. If the work does not transmit the artist's peculiarity of feeling, and is therefore not individual, if it is unintelligibly expressed, or if it has not proceeded from the author's inner need for expression — it is not a work of art. If all these conditions are present, even in the smallest degree, then the work, even if a weak one, is yet a work of art.

The presence in various degrees of these three conditions — individuality, clearness, and sincerity — decides the merit of a work of art, as art, apart from subject-matter. All works of art take rank of merit according to the degree in which they fulfil the first, the second, and the third of these conditions. In one the individuality of the feeling transmitted may predominate; in another, clearness of expression; in a third, sincerity; while a fourth may have sincerity and individuality, but be deficient in clearness; a fifth, individuality and clearness, but less sincerity; and so forth, in all possible degrees and combinations.

Thus is art divided from not art, and thus is the quality of art, as art, decided, independently of its subject-matter, *i.e.* apart from whether the feelings it transmits are good or bad.

But how are we to define good and bad art with reference to its subject-matter?

CHAPTER XVI

How in art are we to decide what is good and what is bad in subject-matter?

Art, like speech, is a means of communication, and therefore of progress, *i.e.* of the movement of humanity forward toward perfection. Speech renders accessible to men of the latest generations all the knowledge dis covered by the experience and reflection, both of preceding generations and of the best and foremost men of their own times; art renders accessible to men of the latest generations all the feelings experienced by their predecessors, and those also which are being felt by their best and foremost contemporaries. And as the evolution of knowledge proceeds by truer and more necessary knowledge dislodging and replacing what is mistaken and unnecessary, so the evolution of feeling proceeds through art, — feelings less kind and less needful for the well-being of mankind are replaced by others kinder and more needful for that end. That is the purpose of art. And, speaking now of its subject-matter, the more art fulfils that purpose the better the art, and the less it fulfils it the worse the art.

And the appraisement of feelings (*i.e.* the acknowledgment of these or those feelings as being more or less good, more or less necessary for the well-being of mankind) is made by the religious perception of the age.

In every period of history, and in every human society, there exists an understanding of the meaning of life which represents the highest level to which men of that society have attained, — an understanding defining the highest good at which that society aims. And this understanding is the religious perception of the given time and society. And this religious perception is always clearly expressed by some advanced men, and more or less vividly perceived by all the members of the society. Such a religious perception and its corresponding expression exists always in every society. If it appears to us that in our society there is no religious perception, this is not because there really is none, but only because we do not want to see it. And we often wish not to see it because it exposes the fact that our life is inconsistent with that religious perception.

Religious perception in a society is like the direction of a flowing river. If the river flows at all, it must have a direction. If a society lives, there must be a religious perception indicating the direction in which, more or less consciously, all its members tend.

And so there always has been, and there is, a religious perception in every society. And it is by the standard of this religious perception that the feelings transmitted by art have always been estimated. Only on the basis of this religious perception of their age have men always chosen from the endlessly varied spheres of art that art which transmitted feelings making religious perception operative in actual life. And such art has always been highly valued and encouraged; while art transmitting feelings already outlived, flowing from the antiquated religious perceptions of a former age, has always been condemned and despised. All the rest of art, transmitting those most diverse feelings by means of which people commune together, was not condemned, and was tolerated, if only it did not transmit feelings contrary to religious perception. Thus, for instance, among the Greeks, art transmitting the feeling of beauty, strength, and courage (Hesiod, Homer, Phidias) was chosen, approved, and encouraged; while art transmitting feelings of rude sensuality, despondency, and effeminacy was condemned and despised. Among the Jews, art transmitting feelings of devotion and submission to the God of the Hebrews and to His will (the epic of Genesis, the prophets, the Psalms) was chosen and encouraged, while art transmitting feelings of idolatry (the golden calf) was condemned and despised. All the rest of art — stories, songs, dances, ornamentation of houses, of utensils, and of clothes — which was not contrary to religious perception, was neither distinguished nor discussed. Thus, in regard to its subject-matter, has art been appraised always and everywhere, and thus it should be appraised; for this attitude toward art proceeds from the fundamental characteristics of human nature, and those characteristics do not change.

I know that according to an opinion current in our times religion is a superstition which humanity has outgrown, and that it is therefore assumed that no such thing exists as a religious perception, common to us all, by which art, in our time, can be estimated. I know that this is the opinion current in the pseudo-cultured

circles of to-day.   People who do not acknowledge
Christianity in its true meaning because it undermines
all their social privileges, and who, therefore, invent all
kinds of philosophic and æsthetic theories to hide from
themselves the meaninglessness and wrongness of their
lives, cannot think otherwise.   These people intentionally, or sometimes unintentionally, confusing the conception of a religious cult with the conception of religious
perception, think that by denying the cult they get rid
of religious perception.   But even the very attacks on
religion, and the attempts to establish a life-conception
contrary to the religious perception of our times, most
clearly demonstrate the existence of a religious perception condemning the lives that are not in harmony
with it.

If humanity progresses, *i.e.* moves forward, there
must inevitably be a guide to the direction of that movement.   And religions have always furnished that guide.
All history shows that the progress of humanity is accomplished not otherwise than under the guidance of
religion.   But if the race cannot progress without the
guidance of religion,— and progress is always going on,
and consequently also in our own times, — then there
must be a religion of our times.   So that, whether it
pleases or displeases the so-called cultured people of to-
day, they must admit the existence of religion, — not of
a religious cult, Catholic, Protestant, or another, but of
religious perception, — which, even in our times, is the
guide always present where there is any progress.   And
if a religious perception exists amongst us, then our art
should be appraised on the basis of that religious perception ; and, as has always and everywhere been the
case, art transmitting feelings flowing from the religious
perception of our time should be chosen from all the
indifferent art, should be acknowledged, highly esteemed,
and encouraged ; while art running counter to that perception should be condemned and despised, and all the
remaining indifferent art should neither be distinguished
nor encouraged.

The religious perception of our time, in its widest

and most practical application, is the consciousness that our well-being, both material and spiritual, individual and collective, temporal and eternal, lies in the growth of brotherhood among all men — in their loving harmony with one another. This perception is not only expressed by Christ and all the best men of past ages, it is not only repeated in the most varied forms and from most diverse sides by the best men of our own times, but it already serves as a clue to all the complex labor of humanity, consisting as this labor does, on the one hand, in the destruction of physical and moral obstacles to the union of men, and, on the other hand, in establishing the principles common to all men which can and should unite them into one universal brotherhood. And it is on the basis of this perception that we should appraise all the phenomena of our life, and, among the rest, our art also ; choosing from all its realms whatever transmits feelings flowing from this religious perception, highly prizing and encouraging such art, rejecting whatever is contrary to this perception, and not attributing to the rest of art an importance not properly pertaining to it.

The chief mistake made by people of the upper classes of the time of the so-called Renaissance — a mistake which we still perpetuate — was not that they ceased to value and to attach importance to religious art (people of that period could not attach importance to it, because, like our own upper classes, they could not believe in what the majority considered to be religion), but their mistake was that they set up in place of religious art, which was lacking, an insignificant art which aimed only at giving pleasure, *i.e.* they began to choose, to value, and to encourage, in place of religious art, something which, in any case, did not deserve such esteem and encouragement.

One of the Fathers of the Church said that the great evil is, not that men do not know God, but that they have set up, instead of God, that which is not God. So also with art. The great misfortune of the people of the upper classes of our time is not so much that they are without a religious art, as that, instead of a supreme religious art, chosen from all the rest as being specially important and valuable, they have chosen a most in-significant and, usually, harmful art, which aims at pleasing certain people, and which, therefore, if only by its exclusive nature, stands in contradiction to that Christian principle of universal union which forms the religious perception of our time. Instead of religious art, an empty and often vicious art is set up, and this hides from men's notice the need of that true religious art which should be present in life in order to improve it.

It is true that art which satisfies the demands of the religious perception of our time is quite unlike former art, but, notwithstanding this dissimilarity, to a man who does not intentionally hide the truth from himself, it is very clear and definite what does form the religious art of our age. In former times, when the highest religious perception united only some people (who, even if they formed a large society, were yet but one society sur-rounded by others — Jews, or Athenian or Roman citi-zens), the feelings transmitted by the art of that time flowed from a desire for the might, greatness, glory, and prosperity of that society, and the heroes of art might be people who contributed to that prosperity by strength, by craft, by fraud, or by cruelty (Ulysses, Jacob, David, Samson, Hercules, and all the heroes). But the religious perception of our times does not select any one society of men ; on the contrary, it demands the union of all, — absolutely of all people without exception, — and above every other virtue it sets brotherly love to all men. And, therefore, the feelings transmitted by the art of our time not only cannot coincide with the feelings transmitted by former art, but must run counter to them.

Christian, truly Christian, art has been so long in estab-lishing itself, and has not yet established itself, just be-cause the Christian religious perception was not one of those small steps by which humanity advances regularly, but was an enormous revolution, which, if it has not already altered, must inevitably alter the entire life-conception of mankind, and, consequently, the whole internal organization of their life. It is true that the life of humanity, like that of an individual, moves regularly; but in that regular movement come, as it were, turning-points, which sharply divide the preceding from the subsequent life. Christianity was such a turning-point; such, at least, it must appear to us who live by the Christian perception of life. Christian perception gave another, a new, direction to all human feelings, and therefore completely altered both the contents and the significance of art. The Greeks could make use of Persian art and the Romans could use Greek art, or, similarly, the Jews could use Egyptian art, — the fundamental ideals were one and the same. Now the ideal was the greatness and prosperity of the Persians, now the greatness and prosperity of the Greeks, now that of the Romans. The same art was transferred into other conditions, and served new nations. But the Christian ideal changed and reversed everything, so that, as the gospel puts it, "That which was exalted among men has become an abomination in the sight of God." The ideal is no longer the greatness of Pharaoh or of a Roman emperor, not the beauty of a Greek, nor the wealth of Phœnicia, but humility, purity, compassion, love. The hero is no longer Dives, but Lazarus the beggar; not Mary Magdalene in the day of her beauty, but in the day of her repentance; not those who acquire wealth, but those who have abandoned it; not those who dwell in palaces, but those who dwell in catacombs and huts; not those who rule over others, but those who acknowledge no authority but God's. And the greatest work of art is no longer a cathedral of victory [1] with statues of conquerors, but the representation of a human soul so transformed by love that a man who is tormented and murdered yet pities and loves his persecutors.

And the change is so great that men of the Christian world find it difficult to resist the inertia of the heathen art to which they have been accustomed all their lives.

[1] There is in Moscow a magnificent "Cathedral of our Saviour," erected to commemorate the defeat of the French in the war of 1812. — Tr.

The subject-matter of Christian religious art is so new
to them, so unlike the subject-matter of former art, that
it seems to them as though Christian art were a denial
of art, and they cling desperately to the old art.   But
this old art, having no longer, in our day, any source in
religious perception, has lost its meaning, and we shall
have to abandon it whether we wish to or not.

The essence of the Christian perception consists in
the recognition by every man of his sonship to God, and
of the consequent union of men with God and with one
another, as is said in the gospel (John xvii. 21[1]).   Therefore the subject-matter of Christian art is such feeling
as can unite men with God and with one another.

The expression *unite men with God and with one
another* may seem obscure to people accustomed to the
misuse of these words which is so customary, but the
words have a perfectly clear meaning nevertheless.
They indicate that the Christian union of man (in contradiction to the partial, exclusive union of only some
men) is that which unites all without exception.

Art, all art, has this characteristic, that it unites people.   Every art causes those to whom the artist's feeling
is transmitted to unite in soul with the artist, and also
with all who receive the same impression.   But non-
Christian art, while uniting some people together, makes
that very union a cause of separation between these
united people and others; so that union of this kind is
often a source, not only of division, but even of enmity
toward others.   Such is all patriotic art, with its
anthems, poems, and monuments; such is all Church
art, *i.e.* the art of certain cults, with their images, statues,
processions, and other local ceremonies.   Such art is
belated and non-Christian art, uniting the people of one
cult only to separate them yet more sharply from the
members of other cults, and even to place them in relations of hostility to each other.   Christian art is only
such as tends to unite all without exception, either by
evoking in them the perception that each man and all

[1] "That they may be one; even as thou, Father, art in me and I in
thee, that they also may be in us."

men stand in like relation toward God and toward their neighbor, or by evoking in them identical feelings, which may even be the very simplest, provided only that they are not repugnant to Christianity and are natural to every one without exception.

Good Christian art of our time may be unintelligible to people because of imperfections in its form, or because men are inattentive to it, but it must be such that all men can experience the feelings it transmits. It must be the art, not of some one group of people, nor of one class, nor of one nationality, nor of one religious cult; that is, it must not transmit feelings which are accessible only to a man educated in a certain way, or only to an aristocrat, or a merchant, or only to a Russian, or a native of Japan, or a Roman Catholic, or a Buddhist, etc., but it must transmit feelings accessible to every one. Only art of this kind can be acknowledged in our time to be good art, worthy of being chosen out from all the rest of art and encouraged.

Christian art, *i.e.* the art of our time, should be catholic in the original meaning of the word, *i.e.* universal, and therefore it should unite all men. And only two kinds of feeling do unite all men : first, feelings flowing from the perception of our sonship to God and of the brother-hood of man ; and next, the simple feelings of common life, accessible to every one without exception — such as the feeling of merriment, of pity, of cheerfulness, of tranquillity, etc. Only these two kinds of feelings can now supply material for art good in its subject-matter.

And the action of these two kinds of art, apparently so dissimilar, is one and the same. The feelings flow-ing from perception of our sonship to God and of the brotherhood of man — such as a feeling of sureness in truth, devotion to the will of God, self-sacrifice, respect for and love of man — evoked by Christian religious per-ception ; and the simplest feelings — such as a softened or a merry mood caused by a song or an amusing jest intelligible to every one, or by a touching story, or a drawing, or a little doll : both alike produce one and the same effect, — the loving union of man with man. Sometimes people who are together are, if not hostile to one another, at least estranged in mood and feeling, till perchance a story, a performance, a picture, or even a building, but oftenest of all, music, unites them all as by an electric flash, and, in place of their former isolation or even enmity, they are all conscious of union and mutual love. Each is glad that another feels what he feels; glad of the communion established, not only between him and all present, but also with all now living who will yet share the same impression; and more than that, he feels the mysterious gladness of a communion which, reaching beyond the grave, unites us with all men of the past who have been moved by the same feelings, and with all men of the future who will yet be touched by them. And this effect is produced both by the religious art which transmits feelings of love to God and one's neighbor, and by universal art, transmitting the very simplest feelings common to all men.

The art of our time should be appraised differently from former art chiefly in this, that the art of our time, *i.e.* Christian art (basing itself on a religious perception which demands the union of man), excludes from the domain of art good in subject-matter everything transmitting exclusive feelings, which do not unite but divide men. It relegates such work to the category of art bad in its subject-matter, while, on the other hand, it includes in the category of art good in subject-matter a section not formerly admitted to deserve to be chosen out and respected, namely, universal art, transmitting even the most trifling and simple feelings if only they are accessible to all men without exception, and therefore unite them. Such art cannot, in our time, but be esteemed good, for it attains the end which the religious perception of our time, *i.e.* Christianity, sets before humanity.

Christian art either evokes in men those feelings which, through love of God and of one's neighbor, draw them to greater and ever greater union, and make them ready for and capable of such union; or evokes in them those feelings which show them that they are already united in the joys and sorrows of life. And therefore the Christian

art of our time can be and is of two kinds : (1) art transmitting feelings flowing from a religious perception of
man's position in the world in relation to God and to his
neighbor — religious art in the limited meaning of the
term ; and (2) art transmitting the simplest feelings of
common life, but such, always, as are accessible to all men
in the whole world — the art of common life — the art of
a people — universal art. Only these two kinds of art
can be considered good art in our time.

The first, religious art, — transmitting both positive
feelings of love to God and one's neighbor, and negative
feelings of indignation and horror at the violation of
love, — manifests itself chiefly in the form of words, and
to some extent also in painting and sculpture : the second
kind (universal art), transmitting feelings accessible to
all, manifests itself in words, in painting, in sculpture,
in dances, in architecture, and, most of all, in music.

If I were asked to give modern examples of each of
these kinds of art, then, as examples of the highest art,
flowing from love of God and man (both of the higher,
positive, and of the lower, negative kind), in literature
I should name, "The Robbers," by Schiller ; Victor
Hugo's "Les Pauvres Gens " and " Les Misérables " ; the
novels and stories of Dickens, — "The Tale of Two
Cities," "The Christmas Carol," "The Chimes," and
others ; " Uncle Tom's Cabin ; " Dostoievsky's works —
especially his "Memoirs from the House of Death" ;
and "Adam Bede," by George Eliot.

In modern painting, strange to say, works of this kind,
directly transmitting the Christian feeling of love of God
and of one's neighbor, are hardly to be found, especially
among the works of the celebrated painters. There are
plenty of pictures treating of the gospel stories ; they,
however, depict historical events with great wealth of
detail, but do not, and cannot, transmit religious feeling
not possessed by their painters. There are many pictures treating of the personal feelings of various people,
but of pictures representing great deeds of self-sacrifice
and of Christian love there are very few, and what there
are, are principally by artists who are not celebrated,

and are, for the most part, not pictures, but merely sketches. Such, for instance, is the drawing by Kram-skoy (worth many of his finished pictures), showing a drawing-room with a balcony, past which troops are marching in triumph on their return from the war. On the balcony stands a wet-nurse holding a baby and a boy. They are admiring the procession of the troops, but the mother, covering her face with a handkerchief, has fallen back on the sofa, sobbing. Such also is the picture by Walter Langley, to which I have already referred, and such again is a picture by the French artist Morlon, de-picting a lifeboat hastening, in a heavy storm, to the relief of a steamer that is being wrecked. Approaching these in kind are pictures which represent the hard-working peasant with respect and love. Such are the pictures by Millet, and, particularly, his drawing, "The Man with the Hoe"; also pictures in this style by Jules Breton, L'Hermitte, Defregger, and others. As examples of pictures evoking indignation and horror at the violation of love to God and man, Gay's picture, "Judgment," may serve, and also Leizen-Mayer's, "Signing the Death Warrant." But there are also very few of this kind. Anxiety about the technique and the beauty of the picture for the most part obscures the feeling. For instance, Gérôme's "Pollice Verso" expresses, not so much horror at what is being perpetrated as attraction by the beauty of the spectacle.[1]

To give examples, from the modern art of our upper classes, of art of the second kind, good universal art or even of the art of a whole people, is yet more difficult, especially in literary art and music. If there are some works which by their inner contents might be assigned to this class (such as "Don Quixote," Molière's comedies, "David Copperfield" and "The Pickwick Papers" by Dickens, Gogol's and Pushkin's tales, and some things of Maupassant's), these works are for the most part — from the exceptional nature of the feelings they

---

[1] In this picture the spectators in the Roman Amphitheater are turning down their thumbs to show that they wish the vanquished gladiator to be killed. — TR.

transmit, and the superfluity of special details of time
and locality, and, above all, on account of the poverty
of their subject-matter in comparison with examples of
universal ancient art (such, for instance, as the story of
Joseph) — comprehensible only to people of their own
circle. That Joseph's brethren, being jealous of his
father's affection, sell him to the merchants; that Potiphar's wife wishes to tempt the youth; that having attained the highest station, he takes pity on his brothers,
including Benjamin, the favorite, — these and all the rest
are feelings accessible alike to a Russian peasant, a Chinese, an African, a child, or an old man, educated or uneducated; and it is all written with such restraint, is so
free from any superfluous detail, that the story may be
told to any circle and will be equally comprehensible and
touching to every one. But not such are the feelings of
Don Quixote or of Molière's heroes (though Molière is
perhaps the most universal, and therefore the most excellent, artist of modern times), nor of Pickwick and his
friends. These feelings are not common to all men, but
very exceptional; and therefore, to make them infectious,
the authors have surrounded them with abundant details
of time and place. And this abundance of detail makes
the stories difficult of comprehension to all people not living within reach of the conditions described by the author.

The author of the novel of Joseph did not need to
describe in detail, as would be done nowadays, the
blood-stained coat of Joseph, the dwelling and dress
of Jacob, the pose and attire of Potiphar's wife, and
how, adjusting the bracelet on her left arm, she said,
"Come to me," and so on, because the subject-matter
of feelings in this novel is so strong that all details,
except the most essential, — such as that Joseph went
out into another room to weep, — are superfluous, and
would only hinder the transmission of feelings. And
therefore this novel is accessible to all men, touches
people of all nations and classes, young and old, and
has lasted to our times, and will yet last for thousands of years to come. But strip the best novels of
our times of their details, and what will remain?

It is therefore impossible in modern literature to in‑ dicate works fully satisfying the demands of univer‑ sality. Such works as exist are, to a great extent, spoilt by what is usually called "realism," but would be better termed "provincialism," in art.

In music the same occurs as in verbal art, and for similar reasons. In consequence of the poorness of the feeling they contain, the melodies of the modern composers are amazingly empty and insignificant. And to strengthen the impression produced by these empty melodies, the new musicians pile complex mod‑ ulations on to each trivial melody, not only in their own national manner, but also in the way charac‑ teristic of their own exclusive circle and particular musical school. Melody — every melody — is free, and may be understood of all men; but as soon as it is bound up with a particular harmony, it ceases to be accessible except to people trained to such harmony, and it becomes strange, not only to common men of another nationality, but to all who do not belong to the circle whose members have accustomed themselves to certain forms of harmonization. So that music, like poetry, travels in a vicious circle. Trivial and exclu‑ sive melodies, in order to make them attractive, are laden with harmonic, rhythmic, and orchestral com‑ plications, and thus become yet more exclusive; and, far from being universal, are not even national, *i.e.* they are not comprehensible to the whole people but only to some people.

In music, besides marches and dances by various composers, which satisfy the demands of universal art, one can indicate very few works of this class: Bach's famous violin *aria*, Chopin's nocturne in E-flat major, and perhaps a dozen bits (not whole pieces, but parts) selected from the works of Haydn, Mozart, Schubert, Beethoven, and Chopin.[1]

---

[1] While offering as examples of art those that seem to me the best, I attach no special importance to my selection; for, besides being in‑ sufficiently informed in all branches of art, I belong to the class of people whose taste has, by false training, been perverted. And there‑

Although in painting the same thing is repeated as in poetry and music, — namely, that in order to make them more interesting, works weak in conception are surrounded by minutely studied accessories of time and place, which give them a temporary and local interest but make them less universal, — still, in painting, more than in the other spheres of art, may be found works satisfying the demands of universal Christian art; that is to say, there are more works expressing feelings in which all men may participate.

In the arts of painting and sculpture, all pictures and statues in so-called genre style, depictions of animals, landscapes and caricatures with subjects comprehensible to every one, and also all kinds of ornaments, are universal in subject-matter. Such productions in painting and sculpture are very numerous (*e.g.* china dolls), but for the most part such objects (for instance, ornaments of all kinds) are either not considered to be art or are considered to be art of a low quality. In reality all such objects, if only they transmit a true feeling experienced by the artist and comprehensible to every one (however insignificant it may seem to us to be) are works of real good Christian art.

I fear it will here be urged against me that having denied that the conception of beauty can supply a standard for works of art, I contradict myself by acknowledging ornaments to be works of good art. The reproach is unjust, for the subject-matter of all kinds of ornamentation consists not in the beauty, but in the feeling (of admiration of, and delight in, the combination of lines and colors) which the artist has experienced and with which he infects the spectator. Art remains what

---

fore my old, inured habits may cause me to err, and I may mistake for absolute merit the impression a work produced on me in my youth. My only purpose in mentioning examples of works of this or that class is to make my meaning clearer, and to show how, with my present views, I understand excellence in art in relation to its subject-matter. I must, moreover, mention that I consign my own artistic productions to the category of bad art, excepting the story "God sees the Truth," which seeks a place in the first class, and "The Prisoner of the Caucasus," which belongs to the second.

it was and what it must be : nothing but the infection by one man of another, or of others, with the feelings ex-perienced by the infector. Among those feelings is the feeling of delight at what pleases the sight. Objects pleasing the sight may be such as please a small or a large number of people, or such as please all men. And ornaments for the most part are of the latter kind. A landscape representing a very unusual view, or a genre picture of a special subject, may not please every one, but ornaments, from Yakutsk ornaments to Greek ones, are intelligible to every one and evoke a similar feeling of admiration in all, and therefore this despised kind of art should, in Christian society, be esteemed far above exceptional, pretentious pictures and sculptures.

So that there are only two kinds of good Christian art : all the rest of art not comprised in these two divi-sions should be acknowledged to be bad art, deserving not to be encouraged, but to be driven out, denied, and despised, as being art not uniting but dividing people. Such, in literary art, are all novels and poems which transmit Church or patriotic feelings, and also exclusive feelings pertaining only to the class of the idle rich ; such as aristocratic honor, satiety, spleen, pessimism, and refined and vicious feelings flowing from sex-love — quite incomprehensible to the great majority of man-kind.

In painting we must similarly place in the class of bad art all the Church, patriotic, and exclusive pictures ; all the pictures representing the amusements and allure-ments of a rich and idle life ; all the so-called symbolic pictures, in which the very meaning of the symbol is comprehensible only to the people of a certain circle ; and, above all, pictures with voluptuous subjects — all that odious female nudity which fills all the exhibitions and galleries. And to this class belongs almost all the chamber and opera music of our times, — beginning especially from Beethoven (Schumann, Berlioz, Liszt, Wagner), by its subject-matter devoted to the expres-sion of feelings accessible only to people who have developed in themselves an unhealthy, nervous irritation evoked by this exclusive, artificial, and complex music.

"What! the '*Ninth Symphony*' not a good work of art!" I hear exclaimed by indignant voices.

And I reply, Most certainly it is not. All that I have written I have written with the sole purpose of finding a clear and reasonable criterion by which to judge the merits of works of art. And this criterion, coinciding with the indications of plain and sane sense, indubitably shows me that that symphony by Beethoven is not a good work of art. Of course, to people edu- cated in the adoration of certain productions and of their authors, to people whose taste has been perverted just by being educated in such adoration, the acknowl- edgment that such a celebrated work is bad is amazing and strange. But how are we to escape the indications of reason and of common sense?

Beethoven's " Ninth Symphony " is considered a great work of art. To verify its claim to be such, I must first ask myself whether this work transmits the highest religious feeling? I reply in the negative, for music in itself cannot transmit those feelings; and therefore I ask myself next, Since this work does not belong to the highest kind of religious art, has it the other character- istic of the good art of our time, — the quality of uniting all men in one common feeling: does it rank as Christian universal art? And again I have no option but to reply in the negative; for not only do I not see how the feel- ings transmitted by this work could unite people not specially trained to submit themselves to its complex hypnotism, but I am unable to imagine to myself a crowd of normal people who could understand anything of this long, confused, and artificial production, except short snatches which are lost in a sea of what is incom- prehensible. And therefore, whether I like it or not, I am compelled to conclude that this work belongs to the rank of bad art. It is curious to note in this connection, that attached to the end of this very symphony is a poem of Schiller's which (though somewhat obscurely) expresses this very thought, namely, that feeling (Schil

ler speaks only of the feeling of gladness) unites people
and evokes love in them.   But though this poem is sung
at the end of the symphony, the music does not accord
with the thought expressed in the verses; for the music
is exclusive and does not unite all men, but unites only
a few, dividing them off from the rest of mankind.

And just in this same way, in all branches of art,
many and many works considered great by the upper
classes of our society will have to be judged.   By
this one sure criterion we shall have to judge the celebrated " Divine Comedy " and " Jerusalem Delivered,"
and a great part of Shakespear's and Goethe's works,
and in painting every representation of miracles, including Raphael's " Transfiguration," etc.

Whatever the work may be and however it may have
been extolled, we have first to ask whether this work is
one of real art or a counterfeit.   Having acknowledged,
on the basis of the indication of its infectiousness even
to a small class of people, that a certain production belongs to the realm of art, it is necessary, on the basis of
the indication of its accessibility, to decide the next question, Does this work belong to the category of bad,
exclusive art, opposed to religious perception, or to
Christian art, uniting people?   And having acknowledged an article to belong to real Christian art, we must
then, according to whether it transmits the feelings flowing from love to God and man, or merely the simple
feelings uniting all men, assign it a place in the ranks of
religious art or in those of universal art.

Only on the basis of such verification shall we find it
possible to select from the whole mass of what, in our
society, claims to be art, those works which form real,
important, necessary spiritual food, and to separate them
from all the harmful and useless art, and from the counterfeits of art which surround us.   Only on the basis of
such verification shall we be able to rid ourselves of the
pernicious results of harmful art. and to avail ourselves
of that beneficent action which is the purpose of true
and good art, and which is indispensable for the spiritual
life of man and of humanity,

CHAPTER XVII

ART is one of two organs of human progress. By words man interchanges thoughts, by the forms of art he interchanges feelings, and this with all men, not only of the present time, but also of the past and the future. It is natural to human beings to employ both these organs of intercommunication, and therefore the perversion of either of them must cause evil results to the society in which it occurs. And these results will be of two kinds: first, the absence, in that society, of the work which should be performed by the organ; and secondly, the harmful activity of the perverted organ. And just these results have shown themselves in our society. The organ of art has been perverted, and therefore the upper classes of society have, to a great extent, been deprived of the work that it should have performed. The diffusion in our society of enormous quantities of, on the one hand, those counterfeits of art which only serve to amuse and corrupt people, and, on the other hand, of works of insignificant, exclusive art, mistaken for the highest art, have perverted most men's capacity to be infected by true works of art, and have thus deprived them of the possibility of experiencing the highest feelings to which mankind has attained, and which can only be transmitted from man to man by art.

All the best that has been done in art by man remains strange to people who lack the capacity to be infected by art, and is replaced either by spurious counterfeits of art or by insignificant art, which they mistake for real art. People of our time and of our society are delighted with Baudelaires, Verlaines, Moréases, Ibsens, and Maeterlincks in poetry; with Monets, Manets, Puvis de Chavannes, Burne-Joneses, Stucks, and Böcklins in painting; with Wagners, Liszts, Richard Strausses, in music; and they are no longer capable of comprehending either the highest or the simplest art.

In the upper classes, in consequence of this loss of

capacity to be infected by works of art, people grow up, are educated, and live, lacking the fertilizing, improving influence of art, and therefore not only do not advance toward perfection, do not become kinder, but, on the contrary, possessing highly developed external means of civilization, they yet tend to become continually more savage, more coarse, and more cruel.

Such is the result of the absence from our society of the activity of that essential organ — art. But the consequences of the perverted activity of that organ are yet more harmful. And they are numerous.

The first consequence, plain for all to see, is the enormous expenditure of the labor of working people on things which are not only useless, but which, for the most part, are harmful; and more than that, the waste of priceless human lives on this unnecessary and harmful business. It is terrible to consider with what intensity, and amid what privations, millions of people — who lack time and opportunity to attend to what they and their families urgently require — labor for 10, 12, or 14 hours on end, and even at night, setting the type for pseudo-artistic books which spread vice among mankind, or working for theaters, concerts, exhibitions, and picture-galleries, which, for the most part, also serve vice; but it is yet more terrible to reflect that lively, kindly children, capable of all that is good, are devoted from their early years to such tasks as these: that for 6, 8, or 10 hours a day, and for 10 or 15 years, some of them should play scales and exercises; others should twist their limbs, walk on their toes, and lift their legs above their heads; a third set should sing solfeggios; a fourth set, showing themselves off in all manner of ways, should pronounce verses; a fifth set should draw from busts or from nude models and paint studies; a sixth set should write compositions according to the rules of certain periods; and that in these occupations, unworthy of a human being, which are often continued long after full maturity, they should waste their physical and mental strength and lose all perception of the meaning of life. It is often said that

it is horrible and pitiful to see little acrobats putting
their legs over their necks, but it is not less pitiful to
see children of 10 giving concerts, and it is still worse
to see school-boys of 10 who, as a preparation for
literary work, have learnt by heart the exceptions to
the Latin grammar.   These people not only grow
physically and mentally deformed, but also morally
deformed, and become incapable of doing anything
really needed by man. Occupying in society the rôle
of amusers of the rich, they lose their sense of human
dignity, and develop in themselves such a passion for
public applause that they are always a prey to an in-
flated and unsatisfied vanity which grows in them to
diseased dimensions, and they expend their mental
strength in efforts to obtain satisfaction for this passion.
And what is most tragic of all is that these people, who
for the sake of art are spoilt for life, not only do not
render service to this art, but, on the contrary, inflict
the greatest harm on it.   They are taught in academies,
schools, and conservatoires how to counterfeit art, and
by learning this they so pervert themselves that they
quite lose the capacity to produce works of real art, and
become purveyors of that counterfeit, or trivial, or depraved art which floods our society.   This is the first
obvious consequence of the perversion of the organ of
art.

The second consequence is that the productions of
amusement-art, which are prepared in such terrific
quantities by the armies of professional artists, enable
the rich people of our times to live the lives they do,
lives not only unnatural, but in contradiction to the hu-
mane principles these people themselves profess.   To
live as do the rich, idle people, especially the women,
far from nature and from animals, in artificial conditions,
with muscles atrophied or misdeveloped by gymnastics,
and with enfeebled vital energy, would be impossible
were it not for what is called art — for this occupation
and amusement which hides from them the meaninglessness of their lives, and saves them from the dullness
that oppresses them. Take from all these people the

theaters, concerts, exhibitions, piano-playing, songs, and novels with which they now fill their time, in full confidence that occupation with these things is a very refined, æsthetical, and therefore good occupation; take from the patrons of art who buy pictures, assist musicians, and are acquainted with writers, their rôle of protectors of that important matter art, and they will not be able to continue such a life, but will all be eaten up by ennui and spleen, and will become conscious of the meaninglessness and wrongness of their present mode of life. Only occupation with what, among them, is considered art renders it possible for them to continue to live on, infringing all natural conditions, without perceiving the emptiness and cruelty of their lives. And this support afforded to the false manner of life pursued by the rich is the second consequence, and a serious one, of the perversion of art.

The third consequence of the perversion of art is the perplexity produced in the minds of children and of plain folk. Among people not perverted by the false theories of our society, among workers and children, there exists a very definite conception of what people may be respected and praised for. In the minds of peasants and children the ground for praise or eulogy can only be either physical strength: Hercules, the heroes and conquerors; or moral, spiritual, strength: Sakya Muni giving up a beautiful wife and a kingdom to save mankind, Christ going to the cross for the truth he professed, and all the martyrs and the saints. Both are understood by peasants and children. They understand that physical strength must be respected, for it compels respect; and the moral strength of goodness an unperverted man cannot fail to respect, because all his spiritual being draws him toward it. But these people, children, and peasants, suddenly perceive that besides those praised, respected, and rewarded for physical or moral strength, there are others who are praised, extolled, and rewarded much more than the heroes of strength and virtue, merely because they sing well, compose verses, or dance. They see that singers,

composers, painters, ballet-dancers, earn millions of roubles and receive more honor than the saints do: and
peasants and children are perplexed.

When fifty years had elapsed after Pushkin's death,
and, simultaneously, the cheap edition of his works began to circulate among the people and a monument was
erected to him in Moscow, I received more than a dozen
letters from different peasants asking why Pushkin was
raised to such dignity. And only the other day a literate[1] man from Saratoff called on me who had evidently
gone out of his mind over this very question. He was
on his way to Moscow to expose the clergy for having
taken part in raising a "monament" to Mr. Pushkin.

Indeed, one need only imagine to oneself what the
state of mind of such a man of the people must be
when he learns, from such rumors and newspapers as
reach him, that the clergy, the Government officials,
and all the best people in Russia are triumphantly un-
veiling a statue to a great man, the benefactor, the
pride of Russia — Pushkin, of whom till then he had
never heard. From all sides he reads or hears about
this, and he naturally supposes that if such honors are
rendered to any one, then without doubt he must have
done something extraordinary — either some feat of
strength or of goodness. He tries to learn who Pushkin was, and having discovered that Pushkin was neither
a hero nor a general, but was a private person and a
writer, he comes to the conclusion that Pushkin must
have been a holy man and a teacher of goodness, and
he hastens to read or to hear his life and works. But
what must be his perplexity when he learns that Pushkin was a man of more than easy morals, who was killed
in a duel, *i.e.* when attempting to murder another man,
and that all his service consisted in writing verses about
love, which were often very indecent.

That a hero, or Alexander the Great, or Genghis

[1] In Russian it is customary to make a distinction between literate and
illiterate people, *i.e.* between those who can and those who cannot read.
Literate in this sense does not imply that the man would speak or write
correctly. — TR.

Khan, or Napoleon were great, he understands, because any one of them could have crushed him and a
thousand like him; that Buddha, Socrates, and Christ
were great he also understands, for he knows and feels
that he and all men should be such as they were; but
why a man should be great because he wrote verses
about the love of women he cannot make out.

A similar perplexity must trouble the brain of a Breton
or Norman peasant who hears that a monument, "*une
statue*" (as to the Madonna), is being erected to Baudelaire, and reads, or is told, what the contents of his
"Fleurs du Mal" are; or, more amazing still, to Verlaine, when he learns the story of that man's wretched,
vicious life, and reads his verses. And what confusion
it must cause in the brains of peasants when they learn
that some Patti or Taglioni is paid £10,000 for a sea-
son, or that a painter gets as much for a picture, or
that authors of novels describing love-scenes have
received even more than that.

And it is the same with children. I remember how I
passed through this stage of amazement and stupefaction, and only reconciled myself to this exaltation of
artists to the level of heroes and saints by lowering in
my own estimation the importance of moral excellence,
and by attributing a false, unnatural meaning to works of
art. And a similar confusion must occur in the soul of
each child and each man of the people when he learns
of the strange honors and rewards that are lavished on
artists. This is the third consequence of the false relation in which our society stands toward art.

The fourth consequence is that people of the upper
classes, more and more frequently encountering the contradictions between beauty and goodness, put the ideal
of beauty first, thus freeing themselves from the demands of morality. These people, reversing the rôles,
instead of admitting, as is really the case, that the art
they serve is an antiquated affair, allege that morality is
an antiquated affair, which can have no importance for
people situated on that high plane of development on
which they opine that they are situated.

This result of the false relation to art showed itself in our society long ago; but recently, with its prophet Nietzsche and his adherents, and with the decadents and certain English æsthetes who coincide with him, it is being expressed with especial impudence. The decadents, and æsthetes of the type at one time represented by Oscar Wilde, select as a theme for their productions the denial of morality and the laudation of vice.

This art has partly generated, and partly coincides with, a similar philosophic theory. I recently received from America a book entitled, "The Survival of the Fittest: Philosophy of Power," 1896, by Ragnar Redbeard, Chicago. The substance of this book, as it is expressed in the editor's preface, is that to measure "right" by the false philosophy of the Hebrew prophets and "weepful" Messiahs is madness. Right is not the offspring of doctrine, but of power. All laws, commandments, or doctrines as to not doing to another what you do not wish done to you, have no inherent authority whatever, but receive it only from the club, the gallows, and the sword. A man truly free is under no obligation to obey any injunction, human or divine. Obedience is the sign of the degenerate. Disobedience is the stamp of the hero. Men should not be bound by moral rules invented by their foes. The whole world is a slippery battlefield. Ideal justice demands that the vanquished should be exploited, emasculated, and scorned. The free and brave may seize the world. And, therefore, there should be eternal war for life, for land, for love, for women, for power, and for gold. (Something similar was said a few years ago by the celebrated and refined academician, Vogüé.) The earth and its treasures is "booty for the bold."

The author has evidently by himself, independently of Nietzsche, come to the same conclusions which are professed by the new artists.

Expressed in the form of a doctrine these positions startle us. In reality they are implied in the ideal of art serving beauty. The art of our upper classes has educated people in this ideal of the over-man,[1] — which is, in reality, the old ideal of Nero, Stenka Razin,[2] Genghis Khan, Robert Macaire,[3] or Napoleon, and all their accomplices, assistants, and adulators — and it supports this ideal with all its might.

It is this supplanting of the ideal of what is right by the ideal of what is beautiful, *i.e.* of what is pleasant, that is the fourth consequence, and a terrible one, of the perversion of art in our society. It is fearful to think of what would befall humanity were such art to spread among the masses of the people. And it already begins to spread.

Finally, the fifth and chief result is, that the art which flourishes in the upper classes of European society has a directly vitiating influence, infecting people with the worst feelings and with those most harmful to humanity, — superstition, patriotism, and, above all, sensuality.

Look carefully into the causes of the ignorance of the masses, and you may see that the chief cause does not at all lie in the lack of schools and libraries, as we are accustomed to suppose, but in those superstitions, both ecclesiastical and patriotic, with which the people are saturated, and which are unceasingly generated by all the methods of art. Church superstitions are supported

[1] The over-man (Uebermensch), in the Nietzschean philosophy, is that superior type of man whom the struggle for existence is to evolve, and who will seek only his own power and pleasure, will know nothing of pity, and will have the right, because he will possess the power, to make ordinary people serve him. — TR.

[2] Stenka Razin was by origin a common Cossack. His brother was hung for a breach of military discipline, and to this event Stenka Razin's hatred of the governing classes has been attributed. He formed a robber band, and subsequently headed a formidable rebellion, declaring himself in favor of freedom for the serfs, religious toleration, and the abolition of taxes. Like the government he opposed, he relied on force, and, though he used it largely in defense of the poor against the rich, he still held to

> "The good old rule, the simple plan,
> That they should take who have the power,
> And they should keep who can."

Like Robin Hood, he is favorably treated in popular legends. — TR.

[3] Robert Macaire is a modern type of adroit and audacious rascality He was the hero of a popular play produced in Paris in 1834. — TR.

and produced by the poetry of prayers, hymns, painting, by the sculpture of images and of statues, by singing, by organs, by music, by architecture, and even by dramatic art in religious ceremonies. Patriotic superstitions are supported and produced by verses and stories, which are supplied even in schools, by music, by songs, by triumphal processions, by royal meetings, by martial pictures, and by monuments.

Were it not for this continual activity in all departments of art, perpetuating the ecclesiastical and patriotic intoxication and embitterment of the people, the masses would long ere this have attained to true enlightenment.

But it is not only in Church matters and patriotic matters that art depraves; it is art in our time that serves as the chief cause of the perversion of people in the most important question of social life, — in their sexual relations. We nearly all know by our own experience, and those who are fathers and mothers know in the case of their grown-up children also, what fearful mental and physical suffering, what useless waste of strength, people suffer merely as a consequence of dissoluteness in sexual desire.

Since the world began, since the Trojan war, which sprang from that same sexual dissoluteness, down to and including the suicides and murders of lovers described in almost every newspaper, a great proportion of the sufferings of the human race have come from this source.

And what is art doing? All art, real and counterfeit, with very few exceptions, is devoted to describing, depicting, and inflaming sexual love in every shape and form. When one remembers all those novels and their lust-kindling descriptions of love, from the most refined to the grossest, with which the literature of our society overflows; if one only remembers all those pictures and statues representing women's naked bodies, and all sorts of abominations which are reproduced in illustrations and advertisements ; if one only remembers all the filthy operas and operettas, songs, and *romances* with which our world teems, involuntarily it seems as if existing art had but one definite aim, — to disseminate vice as widely as possible.

Such, though not all, are the most direct consequences of that perversion of art which has occurred in our society. So that what in our society is called art not only does not conduce to the progress of mankind, but, more than almost anything else, hinders the attainment of goodness in our lives.

And therefore the question which involuntarily presents itself to every man free from artistic activity and therefore not bound to existing art by self-interest, the question asked by me at the beginning of this work: Is it just that to what we call art, to a something belonging to but a small section of society, should be offered up such sacrifices of human labor, of human lives, and of goodness as are now being offered up? receives the natural reply: No; it is unjust, and these things should not be! So also replies sound sense and unperverted moral feeling. Not only should these things not be, not only should no sacrifices be offered up to what among us is called art, but, on the contrary, the efforts of those who wish to live rightly should be directed toward the destruction of this art, for it is one of the most cruel of the evils that harass our section of humanity. So that, were the question put: Would it be preferable for our Christian world to be deprived of *all* that is now esteemed to be art, and, together with the false, to lose *all* that is good in it? I think that every reasonable and moral man would again decide the question as Plato decided it for his "Republic," and as all the Church Christian and Mohammedan teachers of mankind decided it, *i.e.* would say, "Rather let there be no art at all than continue the depraving art, or simulation of art, which now exists." Happily, no one has to face this question, and no one need adopt either solution. All that man can do, and that we — the so-called educated people, who are so placed that we have the possibility of understanding the meaning of the phenomena of our life — can and should do, is to understand the error we are involved in, and not harden our hearts in it, but seek for a way of escape.

CHAPTER XVIII

THE cause of the lie into which the art of our society has fallen was that people of the upper classes, having ceased to believe in the Church teaching (called Christian), did not resolve to accept true Christian teaching in its real and fundamental principles of sonship to God and brotherhood to man, but continued to live on without any belief, endeavoring to make up for the absence of belief — some by hypocrisy, pretending still to believe in the nonsense of the Church creeds; others by boldly asserting their disbelief; others by refined agnosticism; and others, again, by returning to the Greek worship of beauty, proclaiming egotism to be right, and elevating it to the rank of a religious doctrine.

The cause of the malady was the non-acceptance of Christ's teaching in its real, *i.e.* its full, meaning. And the only cure for the illness lies in acknowledging that teaching in its full meaning. And such acknowledgment in our time is not only possible, but inevitable. Already to-day a man, standing on the height of the knowledge of our age, whether he be nominally a Catholic or a Protestant, cannot say that he really believes in the dogmas of the Church: in God being a Trinity, in Christ being God, in the scheme of redemption, and so forth; nor can he satisfy himself by proclaiming his unbelief or skepticism, nor by relapsing into the worship of beauty and egotism. Above all, he can no longer say that we do not know the real meaning of Christ's teaching. That meaning has not only become accessible to all men of our times, but the whole life of man to-day is permeated by the spirit of that teaching, and, consciously or unconsciously, is guided by it.

However differently in form people belonging to our Christian world may define the destiny of man; whether they see it in human progress in whatever sense of the words, in the union of all men in a socialistic realm, or in the establishment of a commune; whether they look forward to the union of mankind under the guidance of one universal Church, or to the federation of the world, — however various in form their definitions of the destination of human life may be, all men in our times already admit that the highest well-being attainable by men is to be reached by their union with one another.

However people of our upper classes (feeling that their ascendancy can only be maintained as long as they separate themselves — the rich and learned — from the laborers, the poor, and the unlearned) may seek to devise new conceptions of life by which their privileges may be perpetuated, — now the ideal of returning to antiquity, now mysticism, now Hellenism, now the cult of the superior person (over-man-ism), — they have, willingly or unwillingly, to admit the truth which is elucidating itself from all sides, voluntarily and involuntarily, namely, that our welfare lies only in the unification and the brotherhood of man.

Unconsciously this truth is confirmed by the construction of means of communication, — telegraphs, telephones, the press, and the ever increasing attainability of material well-being for every one, — and consciously it is affirmed by the destruction of superstitions which divide men, by the diffusion of the truths of knowledge, and by the expression of the ideal of the brotherhood of man in the best works of art of our time.

Art is a spiritual organ of human life which cannot be destroyed, and therefore, notwithstanding all the efforts made by people of the upper classes to conceal the religious ideal by which humanity lives, that ideal is more and more clearly recognized by man, and even in our perverted society is more and more often partially expressed by science and by art. During the present century works of the higher kind of religious art have appeared more and more frequently, both in literature and in painting, permeated by a truly Christian spirit, as also works of the universal art of common life, accessible to all. So that even art knows the true ideal of our times, and tends toward it. On the one hand, the best works of art of our times transmit religious feelings urging toward the union and the brotherhood of man (such are the works of Dickens, Hugo, Dostoievsky; and in painting, of Millet, Bastien Lepage, Jules Breton, L'Hermitte, and others); on the other hand, they strive toward the transmission, not of feelings which are natural to people of the upper classes only, but of such feelings as may unite every one without exception. There are as yet few such works, but the need of them is already acknowledged. In recent times we also meet more and more frequently with attempts at publications, pictures, concerts, and theaters for the people. All this is still very far from accomplishing what should be done, but already the direction in which good art instinctively presses forward to regain the path natural to it can be discerned.

The religious perception of our time — which consists in acknowledging that the aim of life (both collective and individual) is the union of mankind — is already so sufficiently distinct that people have now only to reject the false theory of beauty, according to which enjoyment is considered to be the purpose of art, and religious perception will naturally take its place as the guide of the art of our time.

And as soon as the religious perception, which already unconsciously directs the life of man, is consciously acknowledged, then immediately and naturally the division of art, into art for the lower and art for the upper classes, will disappear. There will be one common, brotherly, universal art; and first, that art will naturally be rejected which transmits feelings incompatible with the religious perception of our time, — feelings which do not unite, but divide men, — and then that insignificant, exclusive art will be rejected to which an importance is now attached to which it has no right.

And as soon as this occurs, art will immediately cease to be what it has been in recent times, — a means of making people coarser and more vicious; and it will become, what it always used to be and should be, a means by which humanity progresses toward unity and blessedness.

Strange as the comparison may sound, what has hap

pened to the art of our circle and time is what happens to a woman who sells her womanly attractiveness, intended for maternity, for the pleasure of those who desire such pleasures.

The art of our time and of our circle has become a prostitute. And this comparison holds good even in minute details. Like her it is not limited to certain times, like her it is always adorned, like her it is always salable, and like her it is enticing and ruinous.

A real work of art can only arise in the soul of an artist occasionally as the fruit of the life he has lived, just as a child is conceived by its mother. But counterfeit art is produced by artisans and handicraftsmen continually, if only consumers can be found.

Real art, like the wife of an affectionate husband, needs no ornaments. But counterfeit art, like a prostitute, must always be decked out.

The cause of the production of real art is the artist's inner need to express a feeling that has accumulated, just as for a mother the cause of sexual conception is love. The cause of counterfeit art, as of prostitution, is gain.

The consequence of true art is the introduction of a new feeling into the intercourse of life, as the consequence of a wife's love is the birth of a new man into life.

The consequences of counterfeit art are the perversion of man, pleasure which never satisfies, and the weakening of man's spiritual strength.

And this is what people of our day and of our circle should understand, in order to avoid the filthy torrent of depraved and prostituted art with which we are deluged.

CHAPTER XIX

PEOPLE talk of the art of the future, meaning by "art of the future" some especially refined, new art, which, as they imagine, will be developed out of that exclusive art of one class which is now considered the highest art. But no such new art of the future can or will be found. Our exclusive art, that of the upper classes of Christen dom, has found its way into a blind alley. The direction in which it has been going leads nowhere. Having once let go of that which is most essential for art (namely, the guidance given by religious perception), that art has become ever more and more exclusive, and therefore ever more and more perverted, until, finally, it has come to nothing. The art of the future, that which is really coming, will not be a development of present-day art, but will arise on completely other and new foundations, having nothing in common with those by which our present art of the upper classes is guided.

Art of the future, that is to say, such part of art as will be chosen from among all the art diffused among mankind, will consist, not in transmitting feelings accessible only to members of the rich classes, as is the case to-day, but in transmitting such feelings as embody the highest religious perception of our times. Only those productions will be considered art which transmit feelings drawing men together in brotherly union, or such universal feelings as can unite all men. Only such art will be chosen, tolerated, approved, and diffused. But art transmitting feelings flowing from antiquated, worn-out religious teaching, — Church art, patriotic art, voluptuous art, transmitting feelings of superstitious fear, of pride, of vanity, of ecstatic admiration of national heroes, — art exciting exclusive love of one's own people, or sensuality, will be considered bad, harmful art, and will be censured and despised by public opinion. All the rest of art, transmitting feelings accessible only to a section of people, will be considered unimportant, and will be neither blamed nor praised. And the appraisement of art in general will devolve, not, as is now the case, on a separate class of rich people, but on the whole people; so that for a work to be esteemed good, and to be approved of and diffused, it will have to satisfy the demands, not of a few people living in identical and often unnatural conditions, but it will have to satisfy the demands of all those great masses of people who are situated in the natural conditions of laborious life.

And the artists producing art will also not be, as now,

merely a few people selected from a small section of the nation, members of the upper classes or their hangers-on, but will consist of all those gifted members of the whole people who prove capable of, and are inclined toward, artistic activity.

Artistic activity will then be accessible to all men. It will become accessible to the whole people, because, in the first place, in the art of the future, not only will that complex technique, which deforms the productions of the art of to-day and requires so great an effort and expenditure of time, not be demanded, but, on the contrary, the demand will be for clearness, simplicity, and brevity — conditions mastered, not by mechanical exercises, but by the education of taste. And secondly, artistic activity will become accessible to all men of the people because, instead of the present professional schools which only some can enter, all will learn music and depictive art (singing and drawing) equally with letters in the elementary schools, and in such a way that every man, having received the first principles of drawing and music, and feeling a capacity for, and a call to, one or other of the arts, will be able to perfect himself in it.

People think that if there are no special art schools the technique of art will deteriorate. Undoubtedly, if by technique we understand those complications of art which are now considered an excellence, it will deteriorate; but if by technique is understood clearness, beauty, simplicity, and compression in works of art, then, even if the elements of drawing and music were not to be taught in the national schools, the technique will not only not deteriorate, but, as is shown by all peasant art, will be a hundred times better. It will be improved, because all the artists of genius now hidden among the masses will become producers of art and will give models of excellence, which (as has always been the case) will be the best schools of technique for their successors. For every true artist, even now, learns his technique, chiefly, not in the schools, but in life, from the examples of the great masters; then — when the producers of art will be the best artists of the whole nation, and there will be more such examples, and they will be more accessible — such part of the school training as the future artist will lose will be a hundredfold compensated for by the training he will receive from the numerous examples of good art diffused in society.

Such will be one difference between present and future art. Another difference will be that art will not be produced by professional artists receiving payment for their work and engaged on nothing else besides their art. The art of the future will be produced by all the members of the community who feel the need of such activity, but they will occupy themselves with art only when they feel such need.

In our society people think that an artist will work better, and produce more, if he has a secured maintenance. And this opinion would serve once more to show clearly, were such demonstration still needed, that what among us is considered art is not art, but only its counterfeit. It is quite true that for the production of boots or loaves division of labor is very advantageous, and that the bootmaker or baker who need not prepare his own dinner or fetch his own fuel will make more boots or loaves than if he had to busy himself about these matters. But art is not a handicraft; it is the transmission of feeling the artist has experienced. And sound feeling can only be engendered in a man when he is living on all its sides the life natural and proper to mankind. And therefore security of maintenance is a condition most harmful to an artist's true productiveness, since it removes him from the condition natural to all men, — that of struggle with nature for the maintenance of both his own life and that of others, — and thus deprives him of opportunity and possibility to experience the most important and natural feelings of man. There is no position more injurious to an artist's productiveness than that position of complete security and luxury in which artists usually live in our society.

The artist of the future will live the common life of man, earning his subsistence by some kind of labor. The fruits of that highest spiritual strength which passes

through him he will try to share with the greatest possible number of people, for in such transmission to others
of the feelings that have arisen in him he will find his
happiness and his reward.   The artist of the future will
be unable to understand how an artist, whose chief delight is in the wide diffusion of his works, could give
them only in exchange for a certain payment.

Until the dealers are driven out, the temple of art will
not be a temple.   But the art of the future will drive
them out.

And therefore the subject-matter of the art of the
future, as I imagine it to myself, will be totally unlike
that of to-day.   It will consist, not in the expression of
exclusive feelings : pride, spleen, satiety, and all possible
forms of voluptuousness, available and interesting only
to people who, by force, have freed themselves from the
labor natural to human beings; but it will consist in the
expression of feelings experienced by a man living
the life natural to all men and flowing from the religious
perception of our times, or of such feelings as are open
to all men without exception.

To people of our circle who do not know and cannot
or will not understand the feelings which will form the
subject-matter of the art of the future, such subject-
matter appears very poor in comparison with those sub-
tleties of exclusive art with which they are now occupied.
"What is there fresh to be said in the sphere of the
Christian feeling of love of one's fellow-man? The feelings common to every one are so insignificant and monotonous," think they.   And yet, in our time, the really
fresh feelings can only be religious, Christian feelings,
and such as are open, accessible, to all.   The feelings
flowing from the religious perception of our times, Christian feelings, are infinitely new and varied, only not in
the sense some people imagine, — not that they can be
evoked by the depiction of Christ and of gospel episodes,
or by repeating in new forms the Christian truths of
unity, brotherhood, equality, and love, — but in that all
the oldest, commonest, and most hackneyed phenomena
of life evoke the newest, most unexpected, and touching

emotions as soon as a man regards them from the Christian point of view.

What can be older than the relations between married couples, of parents to children, of children to parents; the relations of men to their fellow-countrymen and to foreigners, to an invasion, to defense, to property, to the land, or to animals? But as soon as a man regards these matters from the Christian point of view, endlessly varied, fresh, complex, and strong emotions immediately arise.

And, in the same way, that realm of subject-matter for the art of the future which relates to the simplest feelings of common life open to all will not be narrowed, but widened. In our former art only the expression of feelings natural to people of a certain exceptional position was considered worthy of being transmitted by art, and even then only on condition that these feelings were transmitted in a most refined manner, incomprehensible to the majority of men; all the immense realm of folk-art, and children's art — jests, proverbs, riddles, songs, dances, children's games, and mimicry — was not esteemed a domain worthy of art.

The artist of the future will understand that to compose a fairy-tale, a little song which will touch, a lullaby or a riddle which will entertain, a jest which will amuse, or to draw a sketch which will delight dozens of generations or millions of children and adults, is incomparably more important and more fruitful than to compose a novel or a symphony, or paint a picture which will divert some members of the wealthy classes for a short time, and then be forever forgotten. The region of this art of the simple feelings accessible to all is enormous, and it is as yet almost untouched.

The art of the future, therefore, will not be poorer, but infinitely richer in subject-matter. And the form of the art of the future will also not be inferior to the present forms of art, but infinitely superior to them. Superior, not in the sense of having a refined and complex technique, but in the sense of the capacity briefly, simply, and clearly to transmit, without any superfluities, the feeling which the artist has experienced and wishes to transmit.

I remember once speaking to a famous astronomer who had given public lectures on the spectrum analysis of the stars of the Milky Way, and saying it would be a good thing if, with his knowledge and masterly delivery, he would give a lecture merely on the formation and movements of the earth, for certainly there were many people at his lecture on the spectrum analysis of the stars of the Milky Way, especially among the women, who did not well know why night follows day and summer follows winter. The wise astronomer smiled as he answered, " Yes, it would be a good thing, but it would be very difficult. To lecture on the spectrum analysis of the Milky Way is far easier."

And so it is in art. To write a rhymed poem dealing with the times of Cleopatra, or paint a picture of Nero burning Rome, or compose a symphony in the manner of Brahms or Richard Strauss, or an opera like Wagner's, is far easier than to tell a simple story without any unnecessary details, yet so that it should transmit the feelings of the narrator, or to draw a pencil-sketch which should touch or amuse the beholder, or to compose four bars of clear and simple melody, without any accompaniment, which should convey an impression and be remembered by those who hear it.

" It is impossible for us, with our culture, to return to a primitive state," say the artists of our time. " It is impossible for us now to write such stories as that of Joseph or the ' Odyssey,' to produce such statues as the Venus of Milo, or to compose such music as the folk-songs."

And indeed, for the artists of our society and day, it is impossible, but not for the future artist, who will be free from all the perversion of technical improvements hiding the absence of subject-matter, and who, not being a professional artist and receiving no payment for his activity, will only produce art when he feels impelled to do so by an irresistible inner impulse.

The art of the future will thus be completely distinct, both in subject-matter and in form, from what is now called art. The only subject-matter of the art of the future will be either feelings drawing men toward union, or such as already unite them; and the forms of art will be such as will be open to every one. And therefore, the ideal of excellence in the future will not be the exclusiveness of feeling, accessible only to some, but, on the contrary, its universality. And not bulkiness, obscurity, and complexity of form, as is now esteemed, but, on the contrary, brevity, clearness, and simplicity of expression. Only when art has attained to that, will art neither divert nor deprave men as it does now, calling on them to expend their best strength on it, but be what it should be, — a vehicle wherewith to transmit religious, Christian perception from the realm of reason and intellect into that of feeling, and really drawing people in actual life nearer to that perfection and unity indicated to them by their religious perception.

CHAPTER XX

THE CONCLUSION

I HAVE accomplished, to the best of my ability, this work which has occupied me for fifteen years, on a subject near to me — that of art. By saying that this subject has occupied me for fifteen years, I do not mean that I have been writing this book fifteen years, but only that I began to write on art fifteen years ago, thinking that when once I undertook the task I should be able to accomplish it without a break. It proved, however, that my views on the matter then were so far from clear that I could not arrange them in a way that satisfied me. From that time I have never ceased to think on the subject, and I have recommenced to write on it six or seven times; but each time, after writing a considerable part of it, I have found myself unable to bring the work to a satisfactory conclusion, and have had to put it aside. Now I have finished it; and however badly I may have performed the task, my hope is that my fundamental thought as to the false direction the art of our society has taken and is following, as to the reasons of this, and as to the real destination of art, is correct, and that therefore my work will not be without avail. But that this should come to pass, and that art should really abandon its false path and take the new direction, it is necessary that another equally important human spiritual activity, — science, — in intimate dependence on which art always rests, should abandon the false path which it too, like art, is following.

Science and art are as closely bound together as the lungs and the heart, so that if one organ is vitiated the other cannot act rightly.

True science investigates and brings to human perception such truths and such knowledge as the people of a given time and society consider most important. Art transmits these truths from the region of perception to the region of emotion. Therefore, if the path chosen by science be false, so also will be the path taken by art. Science and art are like a certain kind of barge with kedge-anchors which used to ply on our rivers. Science, like the boats which took the anchors up-stream and made them secure, gives direction to the forward movement; while art, like the windlass worked on the barge to draw it toward the anchor, causes the actual progression. And thus a false activity of science inevitably causes a correspondingly false activity of art.

As art in general is the transmission of every kind of feeling, but in the limited sense of the word we only call that art which transmits feelings acknowledged by us to be important, so also science in general is the transmission of all possible knowledge; but in the limited sense of the word we call science that which transmits knowledge acknowledged by us to be important.

And the degree of importance, both of the feelings transmitted by art and of the information transmitted by science, is decided by the religious perception of the given time and society, *i.e.* by the common understanding of the purpose of their lives possessed by the people of that time or society.

That which most of all contributes to the fulfilment of that purpose will be studied most; that which contributes less will be studied less; that which does not contribute at all to the fulfilment of the purpose of human life will be entirely neglected, or, if studied, such study will not be accounted science. So it always has been, and so it should be now; for such is the nature of human knowledge and of human life. But the science of the upper classes of our time, which not only does not acknowledge any religion, but considers every religion to be mere superstition, could not and cannot make such distinctions.

Scientists of our day affirm that they study *everything* impartially; but as everything is too much (is in fact an infinite number of objects), and as it is impossible to study all alike, this is only said in the theory, while in practice not everything is studied, and study is applied far from impartially, only that being studied which, on the one hand, is most wanted by, and on the other hand, is pleasantest to, those people who occupy themselves with science. And what the people, belonging to the upper classes, who are occupying themselves with science most want is the maintenance of the system under which those classes retain their privileges; and what is pleasantest are such things as satisfy idle curiosity, do not demand great mental efforts, and can be practically applied.

And therefore one side of science, including theology and philosophy adapted to the existing order, as also history and political economy of the same sort, are chiefly occupied in proving that the existing order is the very one which ought to exist; that it has come into existence and continues to exist by the operation of immutable laws not amenable to human will, and that all efforts to change it are therefore harmful and wrong. The other part, experimental science, — including mathematics, astronomy, chemistry, physics, botany, and all the natural sciences, — is exclusively occupied with things that have no direct relation to human life : with what is curious, and with things of which practical application advantageous to people of the upper classes can be made. And to justify that selection of objects of study which (in conformity to their own position) the men of science of our times have made, they have devised a theory of science for science's sake, quite similar to the theory of art for art's sake.

As by the theory of art for art's sake it appears that occupation with all those things that please us — is art, so, by the theory of science for science's sake, the study of that which interests us — is science.

So that one side of science, instead of studying how people should live in order to fulfil their mission in life, demonstrates the righteousness and immutability of the bad and false arrangements of life which exist around us ; while the other part, experimental science, occupies itself with questions of simple curiosity or with technical improvements.

The first of these divisions of science is harmful, not only because it confuses people's perceptions and gives false decisions, but also because it exists, and occupies the ground which should belong to true science. It does this harm, that each man, in order to approach the study of the most important questions of life, must first refute these erections of lies which have during ages been piled around each of the most essential questions of human life, and which are propped up by all the strength of human ingenuity.

The second division — the one of which modern science is so particularly proud, and which is considered by many people to be the only real science — is harmful in that it diverts attention from the really important subjects to insignificant subjects, and is also directly harmful in that, under the evil system of society which the first division of science justifies and supports, a great part of the technical gains of science are turned, not to the advantage, but to the injury of mankind.

Indeed, it is only to those who are devoting their lives to such study that it seems as if all the inventions which are made in the sphere of natural science were very important and useful things. And to these people it seems so only when they do not look around them and do not see what is really important. They only need tear themselves away from the psychological micro-scope under which they examine the objects of their study, and look about them, in order to see how insig-nificant is all that has afforded them such naïve pride, all that knowledge not only of geometry of n-dimensions, spectrum analysis of the Milky Way, the form of atoms, dimensions of human skulls of the Stone Age, and simi-lar trifles, but even our knowledge of micro-organisms, X-rays, etc., in comparison with such knowledge as we have thrown aside and handed over to the perversions of the professors of theology, jurisprudence, political economy, financial science, etc. We need only look around us to perceive that the activity proper to real science is not the study of whatever happens to interest us, but the study of how man's life should be established, — the study of those questions of religion, morality, and social life, without the solution of which all our knowl-edge of nature will be harmful or insignificant.

We are highly delighted and very proud that our science renders it possible to utilize the energy of a waterfall and make it work in factories, or that we have pierced tunnels through mountains, and so forth. But the pity of it is that we make the force of the waterfall labor, not for the benefit of the workmen, but to enrich capitalists who produce articles of luxury or weapons of man-destroying war. The same dynamite with which we blast the mountains to pierce tunnels we use for wars, from which latter we not only do not intend to abstain, but which we consider inevitable, and for which we unceasingly prepare.

If we are now able to inoculate preventatively with diphtheritic microbes, to find a needle in a body by means of X-rays, to straighten a hunched-back, cure syphilis, and perform wonderful operations, we should not be proud of these acquisitions either (even were they all established beyond dispute) if we fully understood the true purpose of real science. If but one-tenth of the efforts now spent on objects of pure curiosity or of merely practical application were expended on real science organizing the life of man, more than half the people now sick would not have the illnesses from which a small minority of them now get cured in hospitals. There would be no poor-blooded and deformed children growing up in factories, no death-rates, as now, of fifty per cent among children, no deterioration of whole generations, no prostitution, no syphilis, and no murdering of hundreds of thousands in wars, nor those horrors of folly and of misery which our present science considers a necessary condition of human life.

We have so perverted the conception of science that it seems strange to men of our day to allude to sciences which should prevent the mortality of children, prostitution, syphilis, the deterioration of whole generations, and the wholesale murder of men. It seems to us that science is only then real science when a man in a laboratory pours liquids from one jar into another, or analyzes the spectrum, or cuts up frogs and porpoises, or weaves in a specialized, scientific jargon an obscure network of conventional phrases — theological, philosophical, historical, juridical, or politico-economical — semi-intelligible to the man himself, and intended to demonstrate that what now is, is what should be.

But science, true science, — such science as would really deserve the respect which is now claimed by the followers of one (the least important) part of science, — is not at all such as this: real science lies in knowing what we should and what we should not believe, in knowing how the associated life of man should and should not be constituted; how to treat sexual relations, how to educate children, how to use the land, how to cultivate it oneself without oppressing other people, how to treat foreigners, how to treat animals, and much more that is important for the life of man.

Such has true science ever been and such it should be. And such science is springing up in our times; but, on the one hand, such true science is denied and refuted by all those scientific people who defend the existing order of society, and, on the other hand, it is considered empty, unnecessary, unscientific science by those who are engrossed in experimental science.

For instance, books and sermons appear, demonstrating the antiquatedness and absurdity of Church dogmas, as well as the necessity of establishing a reasonable religious perception suitable to our times, and all the theology that is considered to be real science is only engaged in refuting these works and in exercising human intelligence again and again to find support and justification for superstitions long since outlived, and which have now become quite meaningless. Or a sermon appears showing that land should not be an object of private possession, and that the institution of private property in land is a chief cause of the poverty of the masses. Apparently science, real science, should welcome such a sermon and draw further deductions from this position. But the science of our times does nothing of the kind: on the contrary, political economy demonstrates the opposite position; namely, that landed property, like every other form of property, must be more and more concentrated in the hands of a small number of owners. Again, in the same way, one would suppose it to be the business of real science to demonstrate the irrationality, unprofitableness, and immorality of war and of executions; or the inhumanity and harmfulness of prostitution; or the absurdity, harmfulness, and immorality of using narcotics or of eating animals; or the irrationality, harmfulness, and antiquatedness of patriotism. And such works exist, but are all considered unscientific; while works to prove that all these things ought to continue, and works intended to satisfy an idle thirst for knowledge lacking any relation to human life, are considered to be scientific.

The deviation of the science of our time from its true purpose is strikingly illustrated by those ideals which are put forward by some scientists, and are not denied, but admitted, by the majority of scientific men. These ideals are expressed not only in stupid, fashion-

able books, describing the world as it will be in 1000
or 3000 years' time, but also by sociologists who
consider themselves serious men of science. These
ideals are that food, instead of being obtained from the
land by agriculture, will be prepared in laboratories
by chemical means, and that human labor will be almost
entirely superseded by the utilization of natural forces.

Man will not, as now, eat an egg laid by a hen he has
kept, or bread grown on his field, or an apple from
a tree he has reared and which has blossomed and
matured in his sight; but he will eat tasty, nutritious,
food which will be prepared in laboratories by the con-
joint labor of many people in which he will take a small
part. Man will hardly need to labor, so that all men
will be able to yield to idleness as the upper, ruling
classes now yield to it.

Nothing shows more plainly than these ideals to what
a degree the science of our times has deviated from the
true path.

The great majority of men in our times lack good and
sufficient food (as well as dwellings and clothes and all
the first necessaries of life). And this great majority
of men is compelled, to the injury of its well-being, to
labor continually beyond its strength. Both these evils
can easily be removed by abolishing mutual strife,
luxury, and the unrighteous distribution of wealth, in a
word, by the abolition of a false and harmful order and
the establishment of a reasonable, human manner of
life. But science considers the existing order of things
to be as immutable as the movements of the planets,
and therefore assumes that the purpose of science is —
not to elucidate the falseness of this order and to arrange
a new, reasonable way of life — but, under the existing
order of things, to feed everybody and enable all to
be as idle as the ruling classes, who live a depraved
life, now are.

And, meanwhile, it is forgotten that nourishment with
corn, vegetables, and fruit raised from the soil by one's
own labor is the pleasantest, healthiest, easiest, and most
natural nourishment, and that the work of using one's

muscles is as necessary a condition of life as is the oxidation of the blood by breathing.

To invent means whereby people might, while continuing our false division of property and labor, be well nourished by means of chemically prepared food, and might make the forces of nature work for them, is like inventing means to pump oxygen into the lungs of a man kept in a closed chamber, the air of which is bad, when all that is needed is to cease to confine the man in the closed chamber.

In the vegetable and animal kingdoms a laboratory for the production of food has been arranged, such as can be surpassed by no professors, and to enjoy the fruits of this laboratory, and to participate in it, man has only to yield to that ever joyful impulse to labor, without which man's life is a torment. And lo and behold! the scientists of our times, instead of employing all their strength to abolish whatever hinders man from utilizing the good things prepared for him, acknowledge the conditions under which man is deprived of these blessings to be unalterable, and instead of arranging the life of man so that he might work joyfully and be fed from the soil, they devise methods which will cause him to become an artificial abortion. It is like not helping a man out of confinement into the fresh air, but devising means, instead, to pump into him the necessary quantity of oxygen and arranging so that he may live in a stifling cellar instead of living at home.

Such false ideals could not exist if science were not on a false path.

And yet the feelings transmitted by art grow up on the bases supplied by science.

But what feelings can such misdirected science evoke? One side of this science evokes antiquated feelings, which humanity has used up, and which, in our times, are bad and exclusive. The other side, occupied with the study of subjects unrelated to the conduct of human life, by its very nature cannot serve as a basis for art.

So that art in our times, to be art, must either open up its own road independently of science, or must take

direction from the unrecognized science which is denounced by the orthodox section of science. And this
is what art, when it even partially fulfils its mission, is
doing.

It is to be hoped that the work I have tried to perform
concerning art will be performed also for science—that
the falseness of the theory of science for science's sake
will be demonstrated; that the necessity of acknowledging Christian teaching in its true meaning will be
clearly shown, that on the basis of that teaching a re-
appraisement will be made of the knowledge we possess,
and of which we are so proud; that the secondariness
and insignificance of experimental science, and the
primacy and importance of religious, moral, and social
knowledge will be established; and that such knowledge
will not, as now, be left to the guidance of the upper
classes only, but will form a chief interest of all free,
truth-loving men, such as those who, not in agreement
with the upper classes, but in their despite, have always
forwarded the real science of life.

Astronomical, physical, chemical, and biological science, as also technical and medical science, will be
studied only in so far as they can help to free mankind
from religious, juridical, or social deceptions, or can
serve to promote the well-being of all men, and not of
any single class.

Only then will science cease to be what it is now,—on
the one hand a system of sophistries, needed for the
maintenance of the existing worn-out order of society,
and, on the other hand, a shapeless mass of miscella-
neous knowledge, for the most part good for little or
nothing, — and become a shapely and organic whole,
having a definite and reasonable purpose comprehensible
to all men; namely, the purpose of bringing to the
consciousness of men the truths that flow from the religious perception of our times.

And only then will art, which is always dependent on
science, be what it might and should be, an organ co-
equally important with science for the life and progress
of mankind.

Art is not a pleasure, a solace, or an amusement; art is a great matter. Art is an organ of human life, transmitting man's reasonable perception into feeling. In our age the common religious perception of men is the consciousness of the brotherhood of man — we know that the well-being of man lies in union with his fellow-men. True science should indicate the various methods of applying this consciousness to life. Art should transform this perception into feeling.

The task of art is enormous. Through the influence of real art, aided by science guided by religion, that peaceful coöperation of man which is now obtained by external means — by our law-courts, police, charitable institutions, factory inspection, etc. — should be obtained by man's free and joyous activity. Art should cause violence to be set aside.

And it is only art that can accomplish this.

All that now, independently of the fear of violence and punishment, makes the social life of man possible (and already now this is an enormous part of the order of our lives)— all this has been brought about by art. If by art it has been inculcated how people should treat religious objects, their parents, their children, their wives, their relations, strangers, foreigners; how to conduct themselves to their elders, their superiors, to those who suffer, to their enemies, and to animals; and if this has been obeyed through generations by millions of people, not only unenforced by any violence, but so that the force of such customs can be shaken in no way but by means of art — then, by the same art, other customs, more in accord with the religious perception of our time, may be evoked. If art has been able to convey the sentiment of reverence for images, for the eucharist, and for the king's person; of shame at betraying a comrade, devotion to a flag, the necessity of revenge for an insult, the need to sacrifice one's labor for the erection and adornment of churches, the duty of defending one's honor or the glory of one's native land--then that same art can also evoke reverence for the dignity of every man and for the life of every animal; can make men ashamed of luxury, of violence, of revenge, or of using for their pleasure that of which others are in need; can compel people freely, gladly, and without noticing it, to sacrifice themselves in the service of man.

The task for art to accomplish is to make that feeling of brotherhood and love of one's neighbor, now attained only by the best members of society, the customary feeling and the instinct of all men. By evoking, under imaginary conditions, the feeling of brotherhood and love, religious art will train men to experience those same feelings under similar circumstances in actual life; it will lay in the souls of men the rails along which the actions of those whom art thus educates will naturally pass. And universal art, by uniting the most different people in one common feeling, by destroying separation, will educate people to union, will show them, not by reason, but by life itself, the joy of universal union reaching beyond the bounds set by life.

The destiny of art in our time is to transmit from the realm of reason to the realm of feeling the truth that well-being for men consists in being united together, and to set up, in place of the existing reign of force, that kingdom of God, *i.e.* of love, which we all recognize to be the highest aim of human life.

Possibly, in the future, science may reveal to art yet newer and higher ideals, which art may realize; but, in our time, the destiny of art is clear and definite. The task for Christian art is to establish brotherly union among men.

APPENDIX I

This is the first page of Mallarmé's book, "Divagations" : —

LE PHÉNOMÈNE FUTUR

Un ciel pâle, sur le monde qui finit de décrépitude, va peut-être partir avec les nuages : les lambeaux de la pourpre usée des couchants déteignent dans une rivière dormant à l'horizon submergé de rayons et d'eau. Les arbres s'ennuient, et, sous leur feuillage blanchi (de la poussière du temps plutôt que celle des chemins) monte la maison en toile de Montreur de choses Passées : maint réverbère attend le crépuscule et ravive les visages d'une malheureuse foule, vaincue par la maladie immortelle et le péché des siècles, d'hommes près de leurs chétives complices enceintes des fruits misérables avec lesquels périra la terre. Dans le silence inquiet de tous les yeux suppliant là-bas le soleil qui, sous l'eau, s'enfonce avec le désespoir d'un cri, voici le simple boniment : "Nulle enseigne ne vous régale du spectacle intérieur, car il n'est pas maintenant un peintre capable d'en donner une ombre triste. J'apporte, vivante (et préservée à travers les ans par la science souveraine) une Femme d'autrefois. Quelque folie, originelle et naïve, une extase d'or, je ne sais quoi ! par elle nommé sa chevelure, se ploie avec la grâce des étoffes autour d'un visage qu' éclaire la nudité sanglante de ses lèvres. A la place du vêtement vain, elle a un corps ; et les yeux, semblables aux pierres rares ! ne valent pas ce regard qui sort de sa chair heureuse : des seins levés comme s'ils étaient pleins d'un lait éternel, la pointe vers le ciel, les jambes lisses qui gardent le sel de la mer première." Se rappelant leurs pauvres épouses, chauves, morbides et pleines d'horreur, les maris se pressent : elles aussi par curiosité, mélancoliques, veulent voir.

Quand tous auront contemplé la noble créature, vestige de quelque époque déjà maudite, les uns indifférents, car ils n'auront pas eu la force de comprendre, mais d'autres navrés et la paupière humide de larmes résignées, se regarderont ; tandis que les poètes de ces temps, sentant se rallumer leur yeux éteints, s'achemineront vers leur lampe, le cerveau ivre un instant d'une gloire confuse, hantés du Rythme et dans l'oubli d'exister à une époque qui survit à la beauté.

THE FUTURE PHENOMENON — BY MALLARMÉ.

A pale sky, above the world that is ending through decrepitude, going, perhaps, to pass away with the clouds : shreds of worn-out purple of the sunsets wash off their color in a river sleeping on the horizon, submerged with rays and water. The trees are weary and, beneath their foliage, whitened (by the dust of time rather than that of the roads), rises the canvas house of "Showman of things Past." Many a lamp awaits the gloaming, and brightens the faces of a miserable crowd vanquished by the immortal illness and the sin of ages, of men by the sides of their puny accomplices pregnant with the miserable fruit with which the world will perish. In the anxious silence of all the eyes supplicating the sun there, which sinks under the water with the desperation of a cry, this is the plain announcement: "No sign-board now regales you with the spectacle that is inside, for there is no painter now capable of giving even a shadow of it. I bring living (and preserved by sovereign science through the years) a Woman of other days. Some kind of folly, naïve and original, an ecstasy of gold, I know not what, by her called her hair, clings with the grace of some material round a face brightened by the blood-red nudity of her lips. In place of vain clothing, she has a body; and her eyes, resembling precious stones! are not worth that look, which comes from her happy flesh: breasts raised as if full of eternal milk, the points toward the sky; the smooth legs, that keep the salt of the first sea." Remembering their poor spouses, bald, morbid, and full of horrors, the husbands press forward: the women, too, from curiosity, gloomily wish to see.

When all shall have contemplated the noble creature, vestige of some epoch already damned, some indifferently, for they will not have had strength to understand, but others, broken-hearted, and with eyelids wet with tears of resignation, will look at each other; while the poets of those times, feeling their dim eyes rekindled, will make their way toward their lamp, their brain for an instant drunk with confused glory, haunted by Rhythm, and forgetful that they exist at an epoch which has survived beauty.

APPENDIX II [1]

No. 1

The following verses are by Vielé-Griffin, from page 28 of a volume of his Poems:—

OISEAU BLEU COULEUR DU TEMPS

1	2
Sait-tu l'oubli	O chante-moi
D'un vain doux rêve,	Ta folle gamme,
Oiseau moqueur	Car j'ai dormi
De la forêt ?	Ce jour durant ;
Le jour pâlit,	Le lâche emoi
La nuit se lève,	Où fut mon âme
Et dans mon cœur	Sanglote ennui
L'ombre a pleuré ;	Le jour mourant....

[1] The translations in Appendices I., II., and IV., are by Louise Maude. The aim of these renderings has been to keep as close to the originals as

3

Sais-tu le chant
De sa parole
Et de sa voix,
Toi qui redis
Dans le couchant
Ton air frivole
Comme autrefois
Sous les midis ?

4

O chante alors
La mélodie
De son amour,
Mon fol espoir,
Parmi les ors
Et l'incendie
Du vain doux jour
Qui meurt ce soir.

FRANCIS VIELÉ-GRIFFIN

BLUE BIRD

1

Canst thou forget,
In dreams so vain,
Oh, mocking bird
Of forest deep?
The day doth set,
Night comes again,
My heart has heard
The shadows weep;

3

That music sweet,
Ah, do you know
Her voice and speech?
Your airs so light
You who repeat
In sunset's glow,
As you sang, each,
At noonday's height.

2

Thy tones let flow
In maddening scale,
For I have slept
The livelong day;
Emotions low
In me now wail,
My soul they've kept:
Light dies away ....

4

Of my desire,
My hope so bold,
Her love — up, sing,
Sing, 'neath this light,
This flaming fire,
And all the gold
The eve doth bring
Ere comes the night

No. 2

And here are some verses by the esteemed young poet Verhaeren, which I also take from page 28 of his Works : —

the obscurity of meaning allowed. The sense (or absence of sense) has therefore been more considered than the form of the verses.

ATTIRANCES

Lointainement, et si étrangement pareils,
De grands masques d'argent que la brume recule,
Vaguent, au jour tombant, autour des vieux soleils.

Les doux lointaines ! — et comme, au fond du crépuscule,
Ils nous fixent le cœur, immensément le cœur,
Avec les yeux *défunts de leur* visage d'âme.

C'est toujours du silence, à moins, dans la pâleur
Du soir, un jet de feu sondain, un cri de flamme,
Un départ de lumière inattendu vers Dieu.

On se laisse charmer et troubler de mystère,
Et l'on dirait des morts qui taisent un adieu
Trop mystique, pour être écouté par la terre !

Sont-ils le souvenir matériel et clair
Des éphèbes chrétiens couchés aux catacombes
Parmi les lys?   Sont-ils leur regard et leur chair?

Ou seul, ce qui survit de merveilleux aux tombes
De ceux qui sont partis, vers leurs rêves, un soir,
Conquérir la folie à l'assaut des nuées?

Lointainement, combien nous les sentons vouloir
Un peu d'amour pour leurs œuvres destituées,
Pour leur errance et leur tristesse aux horizons.

Toujours ! aux horizons du cœur et des pensées,
Alors que les vieux soirs éclatent en blasons
Soudains, pour les gloires noires et angoissées.

ÉMILE VERHAEREN,
Poèmes.

ATTRACTIONS

Large masks of silver, by mists drawn away,
So strangely alike, yet so far apart,
Float round the old suns when faileth the day.

They transfix our heart, so immensely our heart,
Those distances mild, in the twilight deep,
Looking out of dead faces with their spirit eyes.

All around is now silence, except when there leap
In the pallor of evening, with fiery cries,
Some fountains of flame that God-ward do fly.

Mysterious trouble and charms us infold,ˋ
You might think that the dead spoke a silent good-by,
Oh! too mystical far on earth to be told !

Are they the memories, material and bright,
Of the Christian youths that in catacombs sleep
'Mid the lilies? Are they their flesh or their sight ί

Or the marvel alone that survives, in the deep,
Of those that, one night, returned to their dream
Of conquering folly by assaulting the skies?

For their destitute works — we feel it seems,
For a little love their longing cries
From horizons far — for their errings and pain.

In horizons ever of heart and thought,
While the evenings old in bright blaze wane
Suddenly, for black glories anguish fraught.

No. 3

And the following is a poem by Moréas, evidently
an admirer of Greek beauty. It is from page 28 of a
volume of his Poems : —

ENONE AU CLAIR VISAGE

Enone, j'avais cru qu'en aimant ta beauté
Où l'âme avec le corps trouvent leur unité,
J'allais, m'affermissant et le cœur et l'esprit,
Monter jusqu'à cela qui jamais ne périt,
N'ayant été crée, qui n'est froideur ou feu,
Qui n'est beau quelque part et laid en autre lieu ;
Et me flattais encor' d'une belle harmonie
Que j'eusse composé du meilleur et du pire,

Ainsi que le chanteur qui chérit Polimnie,
En accordant le grave avec l'aigu, retire
Un son bien élevé sur les nerfs de sa lyre.
Mais mon courage, hélas ! se pâmant comme **mort,**
M'enseigna que le trait qui m'avait fait amant
Ne fut pas de cet arc que courbe sans effort
La Vénus qui naquit du mâle seulement,
Mais que j'avais souffert cette Vénus dernière,
Qui a le cœur couard, né d'une faible mère.
Et pourtant, ce mauvais garçon, chasseur habile,
Qui charge son carquois de sagette subtile,
Qui secoue en riant sa torche, pour un jour,
Qui ne pose jamais que sur de tendres fleurs,
C'est sur un teint charmant qu'il essuie les pleurs,
Et c'est encore un Dieu, Enone, cet Amour.
Mais, laisse, les oiseaux du printemps sont partis,
Et je vois les rayons du soleil amortis.
Enone, ma douleur, harmonieux visage,
Superbe humilité, doux honnête langage,
Hier me remirant dans cet étang glacé
Qui au bout du jardin se couvre de feuillage,
Sur ma face je vis que les jours ont passé.

JEAN MORÉAS

ENONE

Enone, in loving thy beauty, I thought,
Where the soul and the body to union are brought,
That mounting by steadying my heart and my mind,
In that which can't perish, myself I should find.
For it ne'er was created, is not ugly and fair;
Is not coldness in one part, while on fire it is there.
Yes, I flattered myself that a harmony fine
I'd succeed to compose of the worst and the best,
Like the bard who adores Polyhymnia divine,
And mingling sounds different from the nerves of his **lyre,**
From the grave and the smart draws melodies higher.
But, alas! my courage, so faint and nigh spent,
The dart that has struck me proves without fail
Not to be from that bow which is easily bent
By the Venus that's born alone of the male.
No, 't was that other Venus that caused me to **smart,**
Born of frail mother with cowardly heart.
And yet that naughty lad, that little hunter bold,

Who laughs and shakes his flowery torch just for a day,
Who never rests but upon tender flowers and gay,
On sweetest skin who dries the tears his eyes that fill,
Yet oh, Enone mine, a God's that Cupid still.
Let it pass ; for the birds of the Spring are away,
And dying I see the sun's lingering ray.
Enone, my sorrow, oh, harmonious face,
Humility grand, words of virtue and grace,
I looked yestere'en in the pond frozen fast,
Strewn with leaves at the end of the garden's fair space,
And I read in my face that those days are now past.

No. 4

And this is also from page 28 of a thick book, full
of similar poems, by M. Montesquiou.

BERCEUSE D'OMBRE

Des formes, des formes, des formes
Blanche, bleue, et rose, et d'or
Descendront du haut des ormes
Sur l'enfant qui se rendort.
    Des formes !

Des plumes, des plumes, des plumes
Pour composer un doux nid.
Midi sonne : les enclumes
Cessent ; la rumeur finit ....
    Des plumes !

Des roses, des roses, des roses
Pour embaumer son sommeil,
Vos pétales sont moroses
Près du sourire vermeil.
    O roses !

Des ailes, des ailes, des ailes
Pour bourdonner à son front,
Abeilles et demoiselles,
Des rythmes qui berceront.
    Des ailes !

Des branches, des branches, des branches
Pour tresser un pavillon,
Par où des clartés moins franches
Descendront sur l'oisillon.
Des branches !

Des songes, des songes, des songes
Dans ses pensers entr' ouverts
Glissez un peu de mensonges
A voir le vie au travers
Des songes !

Des fées, des fées, des fées
Pour filer leurs écheveaux
Des mirages, de bouffées
Dans tous ces petits cerveaux.
Des fées !

Des anges, des anges, des anges
Pour emporter dans l'éther
Les petits enfants étranges
Qui ne veulent pas rester ....
Nos anges !

Comte Robert de Montesquiou-Fezensac,
Les Hortensias Bleus.

THE SHADOW LULLABY

Oh forms, oh forms, oh forms
White, blue, and gold, and red
Descending from the elm trees,
On sleeping baby's head.
Oh forms!

Oh feathers, feathers, feathers
To make a cozy nest.
Twelve striking: stops the clamor;
The anvils are at rest ....
Oh feathers !

Oh roses, roses, roses
To scent his sleep awhile,

Pale are your fragrant petals
Beside his ruby smile.
     Oh roses !

Oh wings, oh wings, oh wings
Of bees and dragon-flies,
To hum around his forehead,
And lull him with your sighs.
     Oh wings !

Branches, branches, branches
A shady bower to twine,
Through which, oh daylight, faintly
Descend on birdie mine.
     Branches !

Oh dreams, oh dreams, oh dreams
Into his opening mind,
Let in a little falsehood
With sights of life behind.
     Dreams !

Oh fairies, fairies, fairies
To twine and twist their threads
With puffs of phantom visions
Into these little heads.
     Fairies !

Angels, angels, angels
To the ether far away,
Those children strange to carry
That here don't wish to stay ....
     Our angels !

APPENDIX III

These are the contents of " The Nibelung's Ring " : —
The first part tells that the nymphs, the daughters of
the Rhine, for some reason guard gold in the Rhine,
and sing : Weia, Waga, Woge du Welle, Walle zur
Wiege, Wagala-weia, Wallala, Weiala, Weia, and so
forth.

These singing nymphs are pursued by a gnome (a
nibelung) who desires to seize them. The gnome cannot catch any of them. Then the nymphs guarding

the gold tell the gnome just what they ought to keep secret, namely, that whoever renounces love will be able to steal the gold they are guarding. And the gnome renounces love, and steals the gold. This ends the first scene.

In the second scene a god and a goddess lie in a field in sight of a castle which giants have built for them. Presently they wake up and are pleased with the castle, and they relate that in payment for this work they must give the goddess Freia to the giants. The giants come for their pay. But the god Wotan objects to parting with Freia. The giants get angry. The gods hear that the gnome has stolen the gold, promise to confiscate it, and to pay the giants with it. But the giants won't trust them, and seize the goddess Freia in pledge.

The third scene takes place underground. The gnome Alberich, who stole the gold, for some reason beats a gnome, Mime, and takes from him a helmet which has the power both of making people invisible and of turning them into other animals. The gods, Wotan and others, appear and quarrel with one another and with the gnomes, and wish to take the gold, but Alberich won't give it up, and (like everybody all through the piece) behaves in a way to insure his own ruin. He puts on the helmet, and becomes first a dragon and then a toad. The gods catch the toad, take the helmet off it, and carry Alberich away with them.

Scene IV. The gods bring Alberich to their home, and order him to command his gnomes to bring them all the gold. The gnomes bring it. Alberich gives up the gold, but keeps a magic ring. The gods take the ring. So Alberich curses the ring, and says it is to bring misfortune on any one who has it. The giants appear; they bring the goddess Freia, and demand her ransom. They stick up staves of Freia's height, and gold is poured in between these staves : this is to be the ransom. There is not enough gold, so the helmet is thrown in, and they also demand the ring. Wotan refuses to give it up, but the goddess Erda appears and commands him to do so, because it brings misfortune. Wotan gives it up. Freia is released. The giants, having received the ring, fight, and one of them kills the other. This ends the Prelude, and we come to the First Day.

The scene shows a house in a tree. Siegmund runs in tired, and lies down. Sieglinda, the mistress of the house (and wife of Hunding), gives him a drugged draught, and they fall in love with each other. Sieglinda's husband comes home, learns that Siegmund belongs to a hostile race, and wishes to fight him next day; but Sieglinda drugs her husband, and comes to Siegmund. Siegmund discovers that Sieglinda is his sister, and that his father drove a sword into the tree so that no one can get it out. Siegmund pulls the sword out, and commits incest with his sister.

Act II. Siegmund is to fight with Hunding. The gods discuss the question to whom they shall award the victory. Wotan, approving of Siegmund's incest with his sister, wishes to spare him, but, under pressure from his wife, Fricka, he orders the Valkyrie Brünnhilda to kill Siegmund. Siegmund goes to fight; Sieglinda faints. Brünnhilda appears and wishes to slay Siegmund. Siegmund wishes to kill Sieglinda also, but Brünnhilda does not allow it; so he fights with Hunding. Brünnhilda defends Siegmund, but Wotan defends Hunding. Siegmund's sword breaks, and he is killed. Sieglinda runs away.

Act III. The Valkyries (divine Amazons) are on the stage. The Valkyrie Brünnhilda arrives on horseback, bringing Siegmund's body. She is flying from Wotan, who is chasing her for her disobedience. Wotan catches her, and as a punishment dismisses her from her post as a Valkyrie. He casts a spell on her, so that she has to go to sleep and to continue asleep until a man wakes her. When some one wakes her she will fall in love with him. Wotan kisses her; she falls asleep. He lets off fire, which surrounds her.

We now come to the Second Day. The gnome Mime forges a sword in a wood. Siegfried appears. He is a

son born from the incest of brother with sister (Siegmund with Sieglinda), and has been brought up in this
wood by the gnome. In general the motives of the
actions of everybody in this production are quite unintelligible. Siegfried learns his own origin, and that the
broken sword was his father's. He orders Mime to
reforge it, and then goes off. Wotan comes in the
guise of a wanderer, and relates what will happen : that
he who has not learnt to fear will forge the sword, and
will defeat everybody. The gnome conjectures that
this is Siegfried, and wants to poison him. Siegfried
returns, forges his father's sword, and runs off, shouting, Heiho! heiho! heiho! Ho! ho! Aha! oho! aha!
Heiaho! heiaho! heiaho! Ho! ho! Hahei! hoho!
hahei!

And we get to Act II. Alberich sits guarding a
giant, who, in form of a dragon, guards the gold he has
received. Wotan appears, and for some unknown reason foretells that Siegfried will come and kill the dragon.
Alberich wakes the dragon, and asks him for the ring,
promising to defend him from Siegfried. The dragon
won't give up the ring. Exit Alberich. Mime and
Siegfried appear. Mime hopes the dragon will teach
Siegfried to fear. But Siegfried does not fear. He
drives Mime away and kills the dragon, after which he
puts his finger, smeared with the dragon's blood, to his
lips. This enables him to know men's secret thoughts,
as well as the language of birds. The birds tell him
where the treasure and the ring are, and also that Mime
wishes to poison him. Mime returns, and says out loud
that he wishes to poison Siegfried. This is meant to
signify that Siegfried, having tasted dragon's blood,
understands people's secret thoughts. Siegfried, having learnt Mime's intentions, kills him. The birds tell
Siegfried where Brünnhilda is, and he goes to find her.

Act III. Wotan calls up Erda. Erda prophesies to
Wotan, and gives him advice. Siegfried appears,
quarrels with Wotan, and they fight. Suddenly Siegfried's sword breaks Wotan's spear, which had been
more powerful than anything else. Siegfried goes into

the fire to Brünnhilda: kisses her; she wakes up, abandons her divinity, and throws herself into Siegfried's arms.

Third Day. Prelude. Three Norns plait a golden rope, and talk about the future. They go away. Siegfried and Brünnhilda appear. Siegfried takes leave of her, gives her the ring, and goes away.

Act I. By the Rhine. A king wants to get married, and also to give his sister in marriage. Hagen, the king's wicked brother, advises him to marry Brünnhilda and to give his sister to Siegfried. Siegfried appears; they give him a drugged draught, which makes him forget all the past and fall in love with the king's sister, Gutrune. So he rides off with Gunther, the king, to get Brünnhilda to be the king's bride. The scene changes. Brünnhilda sits with the ring. A Valkyrie comes to her and tells her that Wotan's spear is broken, and advises her to give the ring to the Rhine nymphs. Siegfried comes, and by means of the magic helmet turns himself into Gunther, demands the ring from Brünnhilda, seizes it, and drags her off to sleep with him.

Act II. By the Rhine. Alberich and Hagen discuss how to get the ring. Siegfried comes, tells how he has obtained a bride for Gunther and spent the night with her, but put a sword between himself and her. Brünnhilda rides up, recognizes the ring on Siegfried's hand, and declares that it was he, and not Gunther, who was with her. Hagen stirs everybody up against Siegfried, and decides to kill him next day when hunting.

Act III. Again the nymphs in the Rhine relate what has happened. Siegfried, who has lost his way, appears. The nymphs ask him for the ring, but he won't give it up. Hunters appear. Siegfried tells the story of his life. Hagen then gives him a draught, which causes his memory to return to him. Siegfried relates how he aroused and obtained Brünnhilda, and every one is astonished. Hagen stabs him in the back, and the scene is changed. Gutrune meets the corpse of Siegfried. Gunther and Hagen quarrel about the ring, and

Hagen kills Gunther. Brünnhilda cries. Hagen wishes to take the ring from Siegfried's hand, but the hand of the corpse raises itself threateningly. Brünnhilda takes the ring from Siegfried's hand, and when Siegfried's corpse is carried to the pyre, she gets on to a horse and leaps into the fire. The Rhine rises, and the waves reach the pyre. In the river are three nymphs. Hagen throws himself into the fire to get the ring, but the nymphs seize him and carry him off. One of them holds the ring ; and that is the end of the matter.

The impression obtainable from my recapitulation is, of course, incomplete. But however incomplete it may be, it is certainly infinitely more favorable than the impression which results from reading the four booklets in which the work is printed.

APPENDIX IV

Translations of French poems and prose quoted in Chapter X.

BAUDELAIRE'S "FLOWERS OF EVIL"

No. XXIV

I adore thee as much as the vaults of night,
O vase full of grief, taciturnity great,
And I love thee the more because of thy flight.
It seemeth, my night's beautifier, that you
Still heap up those leagues — yes ! ironically heap !
That divide from my arms the immensity blue.

I advance to attack, I climb to assault,
Like a choir of young worms at a corpse in the vault;
Thy coldness, oh cruel, implacable beast !
Yet heightens thy beauty, on which my eyes feast !

BAUDELAIRE'S "FLOWERS OF EVIL"

No. XXXVI

DUELLUM

Two warriors come running, to fight they begin,
  With gleaming and blood they bespatter the air;
These games, and this clatter of arms, is the din
  Of youth that's a prey to the surgings of love.

The rapiers are broken! and so is our youth,
  But the dagger's avenged, dear! and so is the sword,
  By the nail that is steeled and the hardened tooth.
Oh, the fury of hearts aged and ulcered by love!

In the ditch, where the ounce and the pard have their lair,
  Our heroes have rolled in an angry embrace;
  Their skin blooms on brambles that erewhile were bare.

That ravine is a friend-inhabited hell!
  Then let us roll in, oh woman inhuman,
  To immortalize hatred that nothing can quell!

FROM BAUDELAIRE'S PROSE WORK ENTITLED "LITTLE POEMS"

THE STRANGER

Whom dost thou love best? say, enigmatical man — thy father,
thy mother, thy brother, or thy sister?
  " I have neither father, nor mother, nor sister, nor brother."
  Thy friends?
  "You there use an expression the meaning of which till now
remains unknown to me."
  Thy country?
  " I ignore in what latitude it is situated."
  Beauty?
  " I would gladly love her, goddess and immortal."
  Gold?
  " I hate it as you hate God."
  Then what do you love, extraordinary stranger?
  " I love the clouds.... the clouds that pass.... there.... the mar-
velous clouds!"

BAUDELAIRE'S PROSE POEM

THE SOUP AND THE CLOUDS

My beloved little silly was giving me my dinner, and I was contemplating, through the open window of the dining-room, those moving architectures which God makes out of vapors, the marvelous constructions of the impalpable.   And I said to myself, amid my contemplations, "All these phantasmagoria are almost as beautiful as the eyes of my beautiful beloved, the monstrous little silly with the green eyes."

Suddenly I felt the violent blow of a fist on my back, and I heard a harsh, charming voice, an hysterical voice, as it were hoarse with brandy, the voice of my dear little well-beloved, saying, "Are you going to eat your soup soon, you d—— b—— of a dealer in clouds?"

BAUDELAIRE'S PROSE POEM

THE GALLANT MARKSMAN

As the carriage was passing through the forest, he ordered it to be stopped near a shooting-gallery, saying that he wished to shoot off a few bullets to *kill* Time.   To kill this monster, is it not the most ordinary and the most legitimate occupation of every one?   And he gallantly offered his arm to his dear, delicious, and execrable wife — that mysterious woman to whom he owed so much pleasure, so much pain, and perhaps also a large part of his genius.

Several bullets struck far from the intended mark — one even penetrated the ceiling; and as the charming creature laughed madly, mocking her husband's awkwardness, he turned abruptly toward her and said, "Look at that doll there on the right with the haughty mien and her nose in the air; well, dear angel, *I imagine to myself that it is you!*"   And he closed his eyes and pulled the trigger. The doll was neatly decapitated.

Then, bowing toward his dear one, his delightful, execrable wife, his inevitable pitiless muse, and kissing her hand respectfully, he added, "Ah! my dear angel, how I thank you for my skill!"

VERLAINE'S "FORGOTTEN AIRS"

No. I

> "The wind in the plain
> Suspends its breath." — **FAVART.**

'T is ecstasy languishing,
Amorous fatigue,
Of woods all the shudderings

Embraced by the breeze,
'T is the choir of small voices
Toward the gray trees.

Oh, the frail and fresh murmuring!
The twitter and buzz,
The soft cry resembling
That's expired by the grass ....
Oh, the roll of the pebbles
'Neath waters that pass!

Oh, this soul that is groaning
In sleepy complaint!
In us is it moaning?
In me and in you?
Low anthem exhaling
While soft falls the dew.

VERLAINE'S "FORGOTTEN AIRS"

No. VIII

In the unending
Dullness of this land,
Uncertain the snow
Is gleaming like sand.

No kind of brightness
In copper-hued sky,
The moon you might see
Now live and now die.

Gray float the oak trees —
Cloudlike they seem —
Of neighboring forests,
The mists in between.

Wolves hungry and lean,
And famishing crow,
What happens to you
When acid winds blow?

In the unending
Dullness of this land,
Uncertain the snow
Is gleaming like sand.

SONG BY MAETERLINCK

When he went away,
(Then I heard the door)
When he went away,
On her lips a smile there lay ...

Back he came to her,
(Then I heard the lamp)
Back he came to her,
Someone else was there ....

It was death I met,
(And I heard her soul)
It was death I met,
For her he 's waiting yet ....

Someone came to say,
(Child, I am afraid)
Someone came to say
That he would go away ....

With my lamp alight,
(Child, I am afraid)
With my lamp alight,
Approached I in affright ....

To one door I came,
(Child, I am afraid)
To one door I came,
A shudder shook the flame ....

At the second door,
(Child, I am afraid)
At the second door
Forth words of flame did pour ...

To the third I came,
(Child, I am afraid)
To the third I came,
Then died the little flame ...

Should he one day return
Then what shall we say?
Waiting, tell him, one
And dying for him lay ...,

If he asks for you,
  Say what answer then?
Give him my gold ring
  And answer not a thing ....

Should he question me
  Concerning the last hour?
Say I smiled for fear
  That he should shed a tear ...

Should he question more
  Without knowing me?
Like a sister speak;
  Suffering he may be ....

Should he question why
  Empty is the hall?
Show the gaping door,
  The lamp alight no more ...

WHAT IS RELIGION?

WHAT IS RELIGION?

AND WHAT IS ITS ESSENCE?

(*February*, 1902)

CHAPTER I

ALWAYS in all human societies, at a certain period of their existence a time comes when their religion begins to diverge from its fundamental meaning, then diverges more and more, loses this fundamental meaning, and finally crystallizes into permanently established forms; — when its influence upon the life of men grows weaker and weaker.

At such periods, the educated minority, though no longer believing in the existing religious teaching, still pretend to believe, finding this religion necessary for holding the masses in the established order of life; whilst the masses, although adhering by the force of inertia to the established religion, are no longer guided in their lives by religious demands, but only by popular customs and state laws.

So it has been, many times, in many human communities. But what is now taking place in our Christian Society has never before occurred. It has never occurred before that the ruling and more educated minority, which has the chief influence on the masses, not only disbelieved in the existing religion, but was certain that in its time religion was no longer necessary at all, and that it taught those who doubted the truth of the accepted faith not some other, more rational and comprehensible religion than that existing, but even persuaded them that religion in general had outlived its time, and had become not only a useless but even a harmful organ of social life, something like the appendix of the cæcum in the human organism.

Religion is studied by this class of men not as something which we know through our inner experience, but as an external phenomenon, a disease as it were to which some people are subject, and which we can understand only in its external symptoms.

Religion, according to some of these men, has sprung from the spiritualization of all the phenomena of nature (animism). According to others, from the idea of the possibility of communicating with departed ancestors. According to others again, from the fear of the powers of nature. And as science has proved — the scientists of our day further argue — that trees and stone cannot be animated, and deceased ancestors are no longer conscious of what the living do, and the phenomena of nature are explicable by natural causes, — therefore the necessity for religion and for all those restraints which people impose upon themselves as the result of religious beliefs has disappeared. In the opinion of scientists there once existed a period of unenlightenment — the religious period. This was outlived by mankind long ago, but occasional atavistic symptoms remain. Then there came the metaphysical period, which also has been outlived. And now, we, the enlightened generations, live in the scientific period, — of positive science, — which replaces religion and leads mankind to a lofty degree of development which it could never have attained whilst it submitted to superstitious religious teaching.

At the beginning of 1901 the celebrated French scientist Berthelot uttered a speech (*Revue de Paris*, January, 1901), in which he communicated to his audience the idea that the age of religion had passed, and that it must now be replaced by science. I cite this speech because it is the first to my hand and because it was uttered in the capital of the cultured world by a universally recognized scientist. But the same idea has been expressed continually and everywhere from philosophical treatises down to newspaper articles.

Mons. Berthelot says in this speech that there were formerly two principles which moved mankind, Force and Religion. These motive powers have become unnecessary now, because their place has been taken by science. By science Mons. Berthelot evidently implies (as all men who believe in it do) a science which embraces the whole sphere of human knowledge, each branch classified according to the degree of its importance, and the whole harmoniously bound together. A science possessing such methods that all the data it discovers present one unquestionable truth. But such a science does not exist, as a matter of fact. What is called science to-day consists of a haphazard heap of information, united by nothing, often utterly unnecessary, and not only failing to present one unquestionable truth, but as often as not containing the grossest errors to-day put forward as truths, and to-morrow overthrown. It is evident, therefore, that the very thing which in Mons. Berthelot's opinion is to replace religion, does not exist. And therefore the assertion of Mons. Berthelot and those who agree with him, that science will replace religion, is entirely arbitrary, and is founded upon an unjustifiable belief in an Infallible Science, exactly resembling the belief in an Infallible Church.

And yet people who call themselves and are regarded as scientists are quite certain that already there exists a science which must and can replace religion, and even has replaced it.

" Religion has outlived its day ; to believe in anything except science is ignorance. Science will arrange all that is necessary, and one should be guided in life by science alone." So think and say both the scientists themselves and the crowd, which, although very far from being scientific, yet believes the scientists and together with them asserts that religion is an outlived superstition and that our life should be guided only by science, — that is, in reality, by nothing, because science, according to its own acknowledged definition as

the investigation of everything that exists, cannot furnish any guidance for man's life.

CHAPTER II

THE scientists of our times have decided that religion
is unnecessary and that science will replace or already has replaced it; and yet, now as before, no human
society or rational man ever has lived or can live without religion. (I say "rational" man, because an irrational man can live as an animal, without religion.) A
rational man cannot live without religion, because religion
alone gives the rational man the necessary guidance as
to what he should do, and what he should do first and
what next. A rational man cannot live without religion
precisely because reason is an element of his nature.
Every animal is guided in its actions — except those to
which it is attracted by the direct demands of its desires
— by consideration about the immediate results of its
actions. Having considered these results by the aid of
those means of comprehension which it possesses, the
animal conforms its actions to the results, and always
acts under the influence of these considerations in one
and the same way, without wavering. Thus, for instance, a bee flies in search of honey and brings it home
into its hive because in winter it will require the food it
has collected for itself and the young; and beyond these
considerations it knows nothing and is unable to know
anything. A bird acts in the same way when it makes
its nest, or migrates from the north to the south and *vice
versa*. And so also does every animal when it commits
any act, not from a direct immediate necessity, but under
the influence of considerations about expected results.

But it is not so with man. The difference between a
man and an animal consists in this, that the perceptive
faculties in the animal are limited by what we call
instinct, whereas reason is the essential perceptive fac-
ulty of man.

A bee collecting its food can have no doubts about

the rightness or wrongness of what it is doing. But a man gathering in the harvest cannot but reflect whether he is destroying for the future the growth of the wheat or fruit, and whether by thus gathering he is not depriving his neighbor of his food. He also cannot but think of the future of the children whom he feeds; and of many other things. The most important questions of conduct in life cannot be solved definitely by a rational man, precisely because of the multitude of results which he cannot help seeing. Every rational man feels, if he does not know, that in the most important affairs of life he cannot be guided either by the impulse of personal feelings or by considerations of the immediate results of his activity, because he sees too many different results, and often contradictory ones; results, that is, which with equal probability can be either beneficent or harmful, both to himself and to others.

There is a legend about an angel who descended to earth into a God-fearing family and killed a child in its cradle; when asked why he had done this, he replied that the child would have become a great malefactor and would have brought misery to its family.

But not only in the question, Which human life is useful, useless, or harmful? — not one of the most important questions of life can be solved, for a rational man, by considerations about immediate relations and results. A rational man cannot be content with the considerations which direct the actions of animals. Man may regard himself as an animal amongst animals, living from day to day; he may regard himself as a member of a family or of a society or of a nation living from century to century; he may, and even necessarily must (because his reason irresistibly attracts him to this), regard himself as a part of the whole Infinite Universe existing infinitely. And therefore a rational man is obliged to and always does do, in relation to the infinitely small circumstances of life which influence his actions, what in mathematics is called integration, that is, besides his relations to his immediate circumstances, he must establish his relation to the whole universe, infinite in time and space, and conceived as a whole. And such an establishment by man of his relation to that whole of which he feels himself a part and from which he obtains guidance for his actions, is precisely what was and is called Religion. And therefore religion always has been and cannot cease to be an indispensable and permanent condition of the life of a rational man and of rational humanity.

CHAPTER III

AND it was in this way that the men who were not bereft of the capacity of the higher (that is, the religious) consciousness, which distinguishes man from the animal, always understood religion. The oldest and most common definition of religion, from which the word itself is derived (*religio* — *religare*, to bind back), is that religion is a connection between man and God. "*Les obligations de l'homme envers Dieu, voilà la religion*" ("Man's obligations toward God ; that is religion "), says Vovenargue. A similar meaning is attached to religion by Schleiermacher and Fehrbach, who recognize as the foundation of religion man's consciousness of his dependence on God. "*La religion est une affaire entre chaque homme et Dieu.*"— Beile. ("Religion is a matter between every man and God.") "*La religion est le résultat des besoins de l'âme et des effects de l'intelligence.*" — B. Constant. ("Religion is the result of the needs of the soul and the effects of the reason.") "*Religion is a certain method by which man realizes his relation to the superhuman and mysterious powers from whom he regards himself dependent.*" — Goblet d'Alviella. "*Religion is the definition of man's life by the connection of the human with that mysterious spirit, the power of which over the universe and himself he recognizes and with which he feels himself united.*" — A. Reville.

So that the essence of religion was always and is still understood by men who are not bereft of the highest human capacity, as the establishment by man of his relation to the Infinite Being or Beings whose power he feels over himself. And however different this relation has been for different peoples at different times, it has always determined for man his destination in the world, from which naturally followed the guidance of his actions also. A Jew understood his relation to the Infinite as that of a member of a people chosen by God in preference to all other peoples, and who must therefore keep the Covenant concluded between God and this people. A Greek understood his relation as that of a being dependent upon the representatives of infinity, the gods, and who must therefore do what was pleasing to the gods. A Brahman understood his relation to the Infinite Brahma by considering himself a manifestation of this Brahma, and that it was his duty to strive to unite with this highest being, by the renunciation of life. A Buddhist understood and understands his relation to the Infinite as that of one who, passing from one form of life into another, inevitably suffers, and that as these sufferings proceed from passions and desires, therefore one should strive to destroy all passions and desires and so pass into Nirvana.

Every religion is an establishment by man of his relation to the Infinite Existence of which he feels himself a part, and from which relation he obtains the guidance for his conduct. And therefore any religion which does not establish the relation of man to the Infinite, as, for instance, Idolatry, or Magic, is not a religion, but only a corruption. And if a religion, although establishing a relation of man to God yet establishes it by assertions which disagree with reason and the modern knowledge of man so that man cannot believe such assertions, then this also is not religion, but an imitation. If a religion does not connect the life of man with the Infinite Existence, this also is not religion; and demands of faith in propositions from which no definite direction of man's actions follows, are also not religion.

True religion is the establishment by man of such a relation to the Infinite Life around him, as, while connect-

ing his life with this Infinitude and directing his conduct,
is also in agreement with his reason and with human
knowledge.

CHAPTER IV

THE modern scientists, notwithstanding that never
and at no time have people lived, nor do they now
live, without religion, say, like Molière's involuntary
doctor who asserted that the liver is on the left side:
"'We have changed all that,' and one can and should
live without religion." But religion remains as it always
was, the chief motive power, the heart of the life of
human societies, and without it, as without the heart,
there can be no rational life. There have been, and
there are, many different religions, because the expression of the relation of man to the Infinite, to God, or the
gods, is different at different times, according to the
different degrees of development of different nations;
but no society of men since men have become rational
beings could ever live and therefore never did live and
cannot live without religion.

It is true that there have been (and still occur) periods
in the life of nations when the existing religion was so
distorted and so far behind life that it no longer guided
man. But this cessation of the influence of religion,
which has occurred at certain moments with every religion, has been only temporary. Religion, like everything vital, has the capacity of being born, developing,
growing old, and dying, of reviving again, and reviving
always in a more perfect form than before. After the
period of the highest development of religion there
always follows a period of weakness and lifelessness,
after which again there generally follows a period of
regeneration and of the establishment of a religious
teaching more clear and rational than before. Such
periods of development, decline, and regeneration have
occurred in all religions: in the profound Brahman religion, in which the moment it began to grow old and to
crystallize in coarse, permanently established forms de-

viated from its fundamental conception, there appeared on the one hand the revival of Brahmanism itself, and on the other the lofty teaching of Buddhism, which advanced mankind's understanding of its relation to the Infinite. A similar decline occurred in the Greek and Roman religion, and here also, after the decline had reached its lowest point, Christianity appeared. The same occurred with Church Christianity, which degenerated in Byzantium into idolatry and polytheism, at which time, as a counterbalance to this perverted Christianity, there appeared on the one side Paulicianism, and on the other, in opposition to the teaching of Trinity and Maryolatry, the severe Mohammedanism, with its fundamental dogma of One God. The same thing happened also with the Papal Medieval Christianity, which called forth the Reformation. So that periods of the decline of religious influence upon the majority of men present a necessary condition of the life and development of all religious teachings. This proceeds from the fact that every religious teaching in its true meaning, however crude it may be, always establishes the relation of man to the Infinite, identical for all men. Every religion recognizes man as equally insignificant in relation to Infinity; — and therefore every religion always contains the idea of the equality of all men before that which it regards as God, whether that be lightning, the wind, a tree, an animal, a hero, a deceased or even a live king, as it was in Rome. So that the recognition of the equality of men is necessarily an essential feature of every religion. But since in reality never and nowhere has there existed, nor now exists, an equality between men, therefore the moment a new religion appeared, which always included the recognition of the equality of men, then immediately those to whom inequality was advantageous endeavored to conceal this essential feature, and distorted the teaching itself. And this was what occurred always and everywhere, when a new religion appeared.

And this occurred, in the majority of cases, not consciously, but merely because men to whom inequality was advantageous (those in power, and the wealthy), in order to feel themselves in the right in the face of the accepted teaching without altering their position, tried by every means to attribute to the new religious teaching a meaning which would allow inequality to be possible. And this distortion of the teaching, which allowed those in power over others to consider themselves in the right, being naturally transmitted to the masses, convinced them also that their submission to those in power was a demand of the religion they professed.

CHAPTER V

EVERY human activity is called forth by three influences: Feeling, Reason, and Suggestion (the suggestion which medical men call Hypnotism). Sometimes man acts only under the influence of feeling, and strives to attain his desires. Sometimes he acts under the influence of reason alone, which indicates to him his duties. Sometimes, and most often, man acts because he himself or other men have suggested to him a certain activity and he unconsciously submits to the suggestion. In normal conditions of life all three influences participate in man's activity. Feeling draws man toward a certain activity; reason verifies the agreement of this activity with the surrounding conditions, with the past, and with the anticipated future; and suggestion compels man to fulfil, without feeling, or thinking, the act elicited by feeling and approved by reason. If there were no feeling, man would undertake nothing; if there were no reason, man would simultaneously yield himself to many contradictory feelings, harmful to himself and others; if there were no capacity of submitting to one's own or other people's suggestion, man would have to experience that feeling which prompted him to a certain action, unceasingly, and continually to exert his reason in testing the expediency of his reason. And therefore all these three influences are indispensable to every human activity, however simple. If a man is moving

in a certain direction it is because his feeling has
prompted him to move from one place to another, his
reason has approved of this intention, has indicated the
means to realize it (in the given case, walking along a
certain road), and the muscles of his body obey. And
the man advances in the desired direction. While he
is advancing, his feeling and reason become free for
another activity, which could not occur if the capacity
of submitting to suggestion did not exist. So it is with
all human activities, and so also with the most important of all — the religious activity. Feeling calls forth
the necessity of establishing the relation of man to God ;
reason defines this relation ; and suggestion prompts
man to the activity which follows from this relation.
But it takes place thus only while religion has not yet
suffered distortion. As soon, however, as this distortion commences, suggestion becomes stronger and
stronger, and the activities of feeling and reason weaker
and weaker. As to the methods of suggestion, they are
everywhere and always the same. They consist in
profiting by those conditions of man when he is most
susceptible to suggestion (childhood, and during important events in life — deaths, births, marriages), to influence him by works of art: architecture, sculpture,
painting, music, dramatic performances, — and in this
state of susceptibility, similar to that attained over separate individuals by hypnotic sleep, to incite him to that
which is desired by the inciters.

This phenomenon is observable in all the old religious
teachings : in the lofty teaching of Brahmanism, degenerated into a gross worship of innumerable images
in various temples with singing and incense burning ;
and in the ancient Hebrew religion as preached by the
prophets, transformed into the worship of Jehovah in
an imposing temple with solemn hymns and processions ;
in transcendental Buddhism, degenerated, with its monas-
teries and images of Buddha, with its innumerable
stately rites, into Occult Lamaism ; and in Taoism, with
its magic and exorcism.

Always, and in all religious teachings, when they begin

to be distorted, their guardians, having brought men
into a state of weakened mental activity, use all their
efforts to instil into them what they think necessary.
And in all religions it was necessary to instil the same
three doctrines which serve as the foundation for all
the distortions to which all degenerating religions are
submitted.   Firstly, that a certain class of men exist
who alone can be the mediators between men and God
or gods; secondly, that miracles have occurred or are
occurring which prove and corroborate the truth of that
which is asserted by the mediators between men and
God; and thirdly, that there are certain words, repeated
verbally or written in books, which express the un-
changeable will of God or gods, and therefore are
sacred and infallible.   And as soon as these doctrines
are accepted under hypnotic influence, then all which is
asserted by the mediators between God and men is
accepted as sacred truth, and the chief aim of the distortion of religion is attained; — not only the concealment of the law of human equality, but also the
establishment and confirmation of the greatest inequality, the division of men into castes, into men and Yogi,
into Orthodox and heretics, saints and sinners.   This
has taken place and is taking place with Christianity:
complete inequality has been recognized, and men are
divided not only in the understanding of the teaching,
into clergy and laity, but also in relation to social position, into those who have power and those who must
submit to power; and this is recognized as established
by God Himself according to the teaching of Paul.

CHAPTER VI

THE inequality of men, not only as clergy and laity,
but also as rich and poor, master and slaves, has
been established by the Christian Church-Religion in as
definite and rigid a form as in other religions.   And yet
to judge by the data we have concerning the primitive
condition of Christianity, and by the teaching expressed

in the Gospels, it would seem that the chief methods of
distortion used in other religions had been foreseen, and
a distinct warning against them uttered. Against a
caste of priests it was distinctly said that no one can be
another's teacher (" Be not ye called Rabbi. . . . And
call no man your father. . . . Neither be ye called
masters"); against attributing a sacred meaning to
books it was said that it is the spirit which is important
and not the letter, and that men should not believe
human traditions, and that all the law and the prophets,
that is, all the books regarded as Holy Writ, are
summed up in this saying, that one should act toward
one's neighbors as one would wish them to act toward
oneself. If nothing is said against the miracles, and if
in the Gospel itself miracles are described as if performed by Jesus, nevertheless from the whole spirit of
the teaching it is evident that Jesus bases the truth of
his teaching not on miracles but on its own merits.
(" If any man willeth to do his will, he shall know of
the teaching, whether it be of God, or whether I speak
of myself.") But above all, the equality of men has
been proclaimed by Christianity no longer as a deduction from man's relation to the Infinite, but as the fundamental teaching of the brotherhood of men, all men
having been recognized as sons of God.

It would seem, therefore, to have been impossible to so
distort Christianity as to destroy the consciousness of
the equality of all men. But the human mind is ingenious, and it invented, perhaps unconsciously, or half
consciously, a new method or *truc*,[1] as the French say,
to render the Gospel warnings and the clear declaration
of the equality of men ineffectual. This " dodge " consisted in attributing infallibility not only to certain words
but also to a certain body of men called The Church,
which has the right to transmit this infallibility to other
men elected by it. A little addition to the Gospel was
also invented, — that Christ when leaving for heaven
transmitted to certain men the exclusive right not only
of teaching others the divine truth (according to the

[1] Trick, cunning, dodge. — TR.

letter of the Gospel, he transmitted also at the same time the power, not generally used, of being invulnerable to serpents, poisons, and fire), but also of making men saved or unsaved, and, above all, of transmitting this right to other men. And as soon as the idea of the Church was firmly established, then all the Gospel warnings for preventing the distortion of the religion became ineffectual. Reason was termed the source of error, and the Gospel was interpreted not as common sense demands, but as those who composed the Church desired.

And therefore all the three previous methods of distorting religions — Priesthood, Miracles, and the Infallibility of Writings — were also admitted into Christianity in their fullest power. The lawfulness of the existence of mediators between God and men was recognized, because the necessity and lawfulness of mediators was recognized by the Church; the reality of miracles was recognized because the Infallible Church witnessed to them; the Bible was recognized as sacred because the Church so recognized it.

And Christianity was distorted just as all the other religions were, but with this difference: that precisely because Christianity proclaimed with especial clearness its fundamental doctrine of the equality of men as the sons of God, it was necessary to distort the whole teaching with especial force in order to conceal this fundamental doctrine. And by the help of the idea of the Church, this was accomplished to an extent greater than in any other religion.

And as a result no religion ever proclaimed statements so obviously out of agreement with reason and contemporary human knowledge. Not to mention the absurdities of the Old Testament, such as the creation of light before the sun, the creation of the world six thousand years ago, the housing of all the species of animals in the ark, and various immoral abominations such as the direction to murder children and whole populations at the command of God; not to mention also that absurd sacrament, about which Vol·

taire even used to say that though many different religions had existed and still existed, never before had
there been one the principal religious act of which consisted of eating one's God — to pass these things by,
what can be more senseless than the assertions that the
mother of God was both a mother and a virgin — that
the sky opened and a voice was heard issuing from it —
that Jesus flew away into the skies and is now sitting
somewhere there on the right hand of the Father —
or that God is One and Three, and not three Gods like
Brahma, Vishnu, and Siva, but One, and at the same
time Three? And what can be more immoral than that
awful theology according to which God is cruel and re-
vengeful, punishes all men for the sin of Adam, and to
save them sends His Son to the earth knowing before-
hand that men will kill him and will be cursed for doing
so ; and that the salvation of men from sin consists in
being christened, or in believing that all this is actually
true, that the Son of God was killed by men for the
salvation of men, and that those who do not believe this
will be punished by God with eternal torments? So that
leaving aside the additions, as some regard them, to the
chief dogmas of this religion, such as the beliefs in the
various relics and *ikons*, of the Virgin Mary, of petition-
ary prayers directed to various saints according to their
specialities, — leaving aside also the Protestant doctrine
of predestination, — the foundations of this religion,
established by the Nicene Creed, and recognized by
every one, are so absurd and immoral, and are developed
to such a degree of contradiction to normal human feeling and reason, that men cannot believe them. Men
may with their lips repeat certain words, but they cannot believe that which has no sense. One may say
with one's lips : "I believe that the world was created
six thousand years ago ; " or, "I believe that Jesus flew
away into the skies and is sitting on the right hand of
the Father ; " or, "God is One, and also Three ; " — but
no one can believe it, because the words have no sense.
And therefore the men of our modern world who profess distorted Christianity, in reality believe in nothing.

And it is in this that the peculiarity of our time con·
sists.

CHAPTER VII

In our time men believe in nothing, and yet, owing to
the false definition of faith which they have drawn
from the Epistle to the Hebrews, incorrectly attributed
to Paul, they imagine that they have a faith. Faith,
according to this definition, is ὑπόστασις (the realization)
of things hoped for, and ἔλευχος (the certainty) of things
not seen. But besides the impossibility of faith being
the realization of things hoped for, faith being a mental
state, and the realization of things hoped for an external
event, — faith also is not the certainty of things unseen,
for this certainty, as stated in the comment farther on,
is founded on confidence in the witness of the truth, and
confidence and faith are two different conceptions.

Faith is not hope, and not confidence, but a separate
mental state. Faith is man's consciousness of a certain
position in the world which imposes on him the obligation to fulfil certain actions. A man acts according to
his faith, not, as it is said in the Catechism, because he
believes in the Unseen as much as in the seen; and not
because he hopes to receive his expectation; but only
because having defined his position in the Universe he
naturally acts in conformity with this position. So that
an agriculturist cultivates the land, and a sailor under-
takes a voyage, not because, as it is stated in the Catechism, they both believe in the Unseen, or hope to
receive a reward for their action (this hope does exist,
but it is not by it that they are directed), but because
they regard this activity as their calling. So also the
religious believer acts in a certain way, not because he
believes in the Unseen, or expects a reward for his activity, but because, having understood his position in
the Universe, he naturally acts in accordance with this
position. If a man has defined his position in society as
that of an unskilled or skilled laborer, or a government
official, or a merchant, he regards it as necessary to

work, and as an unskilled or skilled laborer, an official, or a merchant, he does his work. So also in general a man who defines his position in the Universe in one way or another, inevitably and naturally acts in accordance with this definition (sometimes even not a definition but only a vague consciousness). Thus, for example, a man who has defined his position as that of a member of a people chosen by God, who, in order to profit by God's protection, must obey the commands of this God, will so live as to obey these commands; and a second man who has defined his position as that of one who has passed and is passing through various forms of existence and from whose actions depend whether his future will be better or worse, will also be guided in life by this definition of his; and the conduct of a third man, who has defined his position as that of an accidental combination of atoms in which consciousness has become kindled for a time, but which will eventually perish forever, — will differ from the two former men.

The conduct of these men will be quite different because they have defined their position differently; that is, they have a different faith. Faith is the same as religion, only with this difference, that by the word *religion* we imply a certain phenomenon externally observed, whereas by *faith* we mean the same thing experienced by man within himself. Faith is man's conception of his relation to the Infinite Universe,[1] and the direction of his activity resulting from that conception. And therefore true faith is never irrational, or in disagreement with existing knowledge, and its feature cannot be supernaturalism and senselessness, as is sup posed and has been expressed by a Father of the Church, who said, "*Credo quia absurdum.*" On the contrary, the assertions of true faith, although they cannot be proved, not only never contain anything contrary to the reason and the knowledge of man, but always explain that which in life without these conceptions of true faith appears irrational and contradictory.

[1] The Russian word, translated here as "Infinite Universe," embraces the whole spiritual and material existence. — *Trans.*

Thus, for instance, the ancient Hebrew who believed in the existence of a Supreme, Eternal, Almighty Being, who created the Universe, the Earth, the Animals, Man, and so forth, and promised protection to His people if this people obeyed His law, — this man believed in nothing irrational or opposed to his knowledge, but on the contrary his faith explained to him many things in life which otherwise were inexplicable.

So also the Hindoo who believes that our souls have been in animals and that according to our good or bad life they will pass into higher or lower animals, explains to himself by this belief much which without it is incomprehensible.

So too with a man who regards life as an evil and the object of life as the attainment of peace by the annihilation of desires. He believes not in something irrational, but on the contrary in that which renders his life-conception more rational than it was without this belief.

So too with a true Christian, who believes that God is the spiritual father of all men and that man's highest welfare is attained when he recognizes his sonship to God and the brotherhood of all men.

All these beliefs, even though they may not be provable, are not irrational in themselves, but on the contrary supply a more rational meaning to the phenomena of life, which appear irrational and contradictory without them. And besides this all these beliefs defining the position of man in the universe necessarily demand certain actions corresponding to this position. And therefore if a religious teaching establishes senseless ideas which explain nothing, but only still more confuse the understanding of life, then this is not faith but a distortion of faith, which has already lost the features of true faith and which lays no obligations on men but rather becomes their tool.

One of the chief distinctions between true faith and its corruption, is that when it is corrupted man demands of God that in return for his sacrifices and prayers God should fulfil his desires, should be the servant of man. Whereas according to true faith man feels that God demands of him, a man, the fulfilment of *His* will, demands that man should serve Him.

And it is just this faith which is not only lacking in the men of our times, — they even do not know what it is, and imply by faith either the repetition with the lips of whatever is taught them as the essence of faith, or else the fulfilment of rites which according to the teaching of Church-Christianity contribute to their obtaining what they desire.

CHAPTER VIII

MEN to-day are without faith. One set, the educated well-to-do minority, have freed themselves from the influence of the Church and believe in nothing, regarding all faiths either as absurdities or as useful tools for keeping the masses under their power. Whereas the great destitute uneducated majority who with some few exceptions do indeed believe, being under hypnotic influence, imagine that what is suggested to them as faith is faith, but in reality it is not faith, as it not only fails to explain to man his position in the Universe but still more confuses him.

From this situation and from the mutual relation between the unbelieving and simulating minority and the hypnotized majority, is composed the life of our so-called Christian world.

And this life, both of the minority which holds in its hands the means of hypnotism, as well as of the majority which is hypnotized, is terrible, both because of the cruelty and immorality of the rulers and of the crushed and stupefied state of the great working masses. Never at any period of religious decline did the indifference to and forgetfulness of the principal feature of all religions, and especially of the Christian one, — the equality of man, — attain the degree it has reached in our day.

Besides the complete absence of religion, the main reason of the awful modern cruelty of man to man is also due to that refined complexity of life which con ceals from men the effects of their actions. Howevei cruel Attilas and Khenghiz Khans and their men may have been when they themselves killed face to face with their victims, the process of killing must have been much more unpleasant to them, and still more so the consequences of the killing, the cries of the relatives, the sight of the corpses; so that the consequences of their cruelty moderated it. But in our time we kill men through the medium of so complicated a transferring apparatus, and the consequences of our cruelty are so carefully removed and concealed from us, that there are no influences to moderate the cruelty, and the cruelty of one group of men toward others keeps increasing and increasing, and has at the present time attained limits which it never before reached.

If in our day any man — I do not say a Nero, a recognized villain, but any ordinary man — should wish to construct a pond of human blood for the purpose of enabling sick wealthy people under the advice of scientific medical men to bathe in, I think he would be able to arrange it without hindrance so long as he did so in the ordinary respectable way; that is, did not by force compel people to shed their blood, but placed them in a position where they could not live without shedding it; and, besides, if he invited the clergy, who would consecrate the new pond, just as they consecrate cannons, rifles, prisons, gallows, and men of science, who would invent the proofs of the necessity and lawfulness of such an institution, just as they have discovered the proofs of the necessity of wars and houses of ill-fame.

The essential principle of all religions, the equality of man, has been forgotten to such an extent, abandoned, and obstructed by various absurd dogmas, in the religion professed; whilst in science inequality in the form of the struggle of existence and the survival of the fittest has also been so completely recognized as the necessary phenomenon of life — that the destructior of millions of human lives for the convenience of those in power is regarded as a most ordinary and necessary phenome- non of life, and is continually being produced.

Men of our day cannot sufficiently plume themselves on those brilliant, unprecedented, colossal successes which have been won in the technical sphere during the nineteenth century.

There is no doubt that there has never been in history so great a material success — so great a control over the forces of nature — as that which has been attained in the nineteenth century. But there is also no doubt that never in history has there been such an example of immoral life, free from any forces that control the animal propensities of man, — as that lived by our Christian humanity, which is becoming more and more bestial.

The material success attained by the men of the nineteenth century is indeed great, but this success has been and is bought by an indifference to the most elementary demands of morality to which humanity has never before attained, even in the times of Khenghiz Khan, Attila, or Nero.

There is no dispute that ironclads, railways, bookprinting, tunnels, photographs, Röntgen rays, and so forth, are all very fine. They are all very fine, but human lives are also fine, incomparably fine, as Ruskin used to say, those human lives which are pitilessly ruined by the million to purchase ironclads, railroads, tunnels, which not only do not adorn but disfigure life. To this it is generally replied that appliances are already being invented, and in the future will be invented still more, by means of which human lives will not be ruined as they are now; — but this is not true. If men do not regard themselves as all brothers, and human life is not considered the most sacred object, which not only cannot be violated, but the maintenance of which should be regarded as man's first and most urgent duty, — that is, if men do not regard each other religiously, they will always for their own personal advantages ruin each other's lives. Not even a fool will consent to spend thousands when he can attain the same end by spending a hundred, with the addition of a few human lives which are in his power. In

Chicago approximately the same number of men are killed by the railways every year. And the owners of the railways quite naturally do not adopt those appliances which would reduce the number, calculating that the annual payment to the injured or their families is less than the interest on the cost of the appliances.

It may well be that those who ruin human lives for their own advantages will be shamed by public opinion and compelled to adopt the necessary appliances; but if men are not religious and do their deeds to please men and not to please God, then, having adopted appliances to save human lives in one place, they will profit in some other way by human lives, as the most advantageous material for increasing their wealth.

It is easy to conquer nature, to construct railways, steamboats, museums, and so forth, if one is not sparing of human lives. The Egyptian kings were proud of their pyramids, and we admire them enthusiastically, forgetting those millions of lives of slaves which were destroyed during their construction. And so we admire also palaces, as we see them in exhibitions, our iron-clads, our transoceanic cables, — forgetting what we pay for all this. We might be proud of these things if it were all done voluntarily by free men, and not by slaves.

The Christian nations have conquered and subdued the American Indians, Hindoos, Africans, are now conquering and subduing the Chinese, and they are proud of this. But these conquests and subjugations occur not because Christian nations are spiritually superior to those conquered, but on the contrary because spiritually they are incomparably inferior. Leaving Hindoos and Chinese aside, even the Zulus had and have obligatory religious rules of some kind which imposed certain actions and forbade others; whereas our Christian nations have none. Rome conquered the whole world just when it had become free from every religion. This, only in a still stronger degree, is now also taking place with the Christian nations. They are all in the same condition of the absence of religion, and therefore, notwithstanding their inner dis-sensions, they are all united as one federated band of robbers in which theft, loot, depravity, murder of indi-viduals and masses are accomplished not only without the least tremor of conscience but with the greatest self-satisfaction, as in China the other day. Some be-lieve in nothing, and are proud of it; others simulate belief in that which for their own advantage they instil into the people under the pretense of faith; others again — the great majority, the whole of the people — accept as faith that hypnotic suggestion to which they are subjected, and servilely submit to everything de-manded of them by the ruling suggestors who them-selves believe in nothing.

And these suggestors demand what was demanded by all the Neros who tried to fill up in some way their empty lives — the satisfaction of their insane luxury spreading out in all directions. And luxury is attained by naught else than the enslavery of man; the moment there is slavery luxury augments; the increase of lux-ury inevitably drags with it the increase of slavery, because only hungry, cold, want-driven people will all their lives do what is unnecessary for themselves but necessary for the amusement of their rulers.

CHAPTER IX

In the sixth chapter of the Book of Genesis there is a passage of deep meaning, in which the author says that God, before the Flood, having seen that that Spirit of His which He gave to men for His ser-vice was only used by them for the service of their flesh, — was so angry with them that He regretted their creation, and before their entire destruction de-cided to shorten the life of men to a hundred and twenty years. It is just this which according to the Biblical narrative angered God and caused Him to shorten the life of man, which has now occurred with the men of our Christian world.

Reason is that power in men which defines their relation to the Universe; and as the relation of all men to
the Universe is the same, the establishment of this relation, that is, religion, unites men. And the unity of
men affords them the highest physical and spiritual welfare accessible to them.

Complete unity in the most perfect, lofty reason, and
therefore complete welfare, is the ideal toward which
humanity is striving; and every religion which answers
the questions of the men of a given society both as to
what is the Universe, and what they are in this Universe,
unites men, and therefore brings them nearer to the
realization of complete welfare. But when reason,
abandoning its proper function of defining man's
relation to God and his corresponding activities, is
directed not only to the service of man's flesh, and not
only to cruel strife with men and other beings, but also
to the justification of their life, which is contrary both
to the nature and the destiny of man, then occur those
terrible calamities from which the majority of men are
now suffering and those conditions which appear to pre-
clude all possibility of a return to a rational and righteous
life.

Heathens mutually united by the crudest religious
teaching are much nearer the conception of the truth
than the pseudo-Christian nations of our time, who live
without religion, and amongst whom the foremost men
are persuaded and teach to others that religion is not
necessary, and that it is much better to live without any
religion.

Amongst heathens there may be found men who,
having become conscious of the contradictions between
their faith and their increasing knowledge and the demands of their reason, will work out or assimilate a new
religious teaching more in harmony with the new mental
state of their nation, — a religion which will be accepted
by their countrymen and fellow-believers. But the men
of our world, some of whom regard religion as an instrument for subjugation, others as nonsense, and others
again, — the great majority of the people, under the in-

fluence of a gross deceit, — believe they possess true religion, the men of our Christian world have become
impenetrable to the influence of any progressive movement toward truth.

Proud of their improvements for the life of the body,
and of their refined idle theories which not only justify
their life, but also demonstrate their superiority to all
nations of all past epochs, — they stagnate in their ignorance and immorality, in the full assurance that they stand
on a height to which humanity had never before attained, and that each step on the road of ignorance and
immorality lifts them up to a yet higher plane of enlightenment and progress.

CHAPTER X

It is natural to a man to establish conformity between his physical and his rational activities. A man can
have no peace until he has established this conformity
one way or another. But it can be established in two
ways. One way is when a man is persuaded by his
reason of the necessity or desirability of a certain action
or actions, and then acts according to this decision. The
other way is when a man acts under the influence of
his feelings, and then invents a mental explanation or
justification for his act.

The first method of conforming one's action with
one's reason is natural to those who profess some kind
of religion, and who know by its precepts what they
should and what they should not do. The second method
is natural chiefly to irreligious people, who do not possess any general principal for deciding the qualities of
their actions, and who therefore always establish the
harmony between reason and conduct, not by subordi-
nating conduct to reason, but, after having acted under
the influence of feeling, by using their reason to justify
their action.

A religious man, knowing what is good or bad in his
conduct, and that of other men, and why one thing is
good and another bad, will, if he sees a contradiction

between the demand of his reason and his actions, or those of other men, use all the efforts of his reason to discover a way to destroy these contradictions; that is, to learn to harmonize his actions with the demands of his reason in the best way   Whereas an irreligious man, having no guide to decide the merits of his actions other than the pleasure they afford him, surrendering to the impulse of his numerous and often antagonistic feelings, involuntarily falls into contradiction; and having so fallen endeavors to solve or conceal it by arguments more or less complicated and ingenious, but always untruthful.   And therefore, while the reasoning of religious people is always simple, uncomplicated, and truthful, the mental activity of irreligious people becomes especially subtle, complicated, and untruthful.

I will take the commonest example.   A man is addicted to depravity; that is, is unchaste, unfaithful to his wife, or else lives immorally being unmarried.   If he is a religious man he knows this is wrong, and the whole force of his reason is directed toward finding a way to free himself from his vice: avoiding association with adulterers, increasing his labors, arranging a rigorous life, not allowing himself to look on women as objects of lust, and so forth.   And this is all very simple and can be understood by every one.   But if the depraved man is irreligious, he immediately invents all sorts of reasons why it is very good to love women.   And here begin all kinds of most intricate, cunning, and refined considerations, about the affinity of souls, about beauty, about free love, etc., — which the more they are developed the more they obscure the question and conceal what is essential.

The same thing occurs with irreligious people in all spheres of action and thought.   With the object of concealing their inherent contradictions, they accumulate all sorts of elaborate and specious arguments, which by filling their minds with unnecessary frivolities divert their attention from the important and essential, and give them the possibility of becoming hardened in that deceit in which the men of our world live without noticing it.

"Men loved the darkness rather than the light, for their works were evil," it is said in the Gospels. "For every one that doeth ill hateth the light, and cometh not to the light lest his works should be reproved."

And therefore the men of our civilized world, having organized the most cruel, animal, immoral life, owing to the absence of religion, have also brought their involved, elaborate, useless mental activities, concealing the evil of this life, to that degree of unnecessary complication and intricacy that the majority have entirely lost all capacity of recognizing the distinction between good and evil, falsehood and truth.

To the men of our civilized world not one question exists which they can approach directly and simply: every question, economical, civic, political, diplomatic, scientific, to say nothing of philosophic and religious questions, are presented so falsely and artificially, and are therefore enveloped in so dense a shroud of intricate, unnecessary arguments, of elaborate distortions of ideas and words, of sophisms and disputations, that all discussions of such questions move in circles, and, like wheels without a connecting strap, which propel nothing, lead to no results, except the one object for which they were produced: the concealment from oneself and others of the evil in which men live and which they commit.

CHAPTER XI

In all the spheres of the so-called science of to-day there is one feature which renders ineffective all the efforts directed to the investigation of the various departments of knowledge. This feature is that all the investigations of contemporary science avoid the essential problem to which an answer is required, and study secondary matters, the investigation of which leads to nothing and becomes the more confused the longer it is continued.

And indeed this cannot be otherwise with a science

which selects the objects of its investigations accidentally
and not according to the demands of a religious conception of life, which would define what should be studied
and why, what first and what after. Thus, for instance,
in the at present fashionable sciences of sociology or
political economy, one would think there could be but
one question : What is the cause and purpose of some
people doing nothing and others working for them?
(If there is another question : Why people work *sepa-
rately, hindering each other, and not together, in
common, which would be more advantageous?—this question is included in the other. If there were no inequality
there would be no struggle.) One would imagine there
was only this one question, but science does not even
think of putting it and answering it, but instead it raises
its own distant discussions and then leads them so that
in no way can their deductions either solve or contribute
to the solution of the fundamental question. Arguments
are started about what was and is, and this past and present is considered as something as unalterable as the
movements of the stars. Abstract theories are invented
about values, capital, profit, interest, — and a complex
mental play, a hundred years old, ensues between dis-
puting men. Whereas in reality the question is solved
very simple and easily.

The solution is in this : As all men are brothers and
equal, each should act with others as he desires that
others should act with him ; and therefore the whole
kernel of the matter lies in the destruction of the false
religious law and the reëstablishment of the true law.
But the leaders of our Christian world not only decline
to accept this solution, — on the contrary they endeavor
to conceal the possibility of such a solution, and for this
purpose lend themselves to those idle theorizings which
they call science.

The same thing occurs in the sphere of jurisprudence.
One would imagine that the one essential question is,
Why do people exist who allow themselves to exercise
violence toward other men, to rob, imprison, execute
them, send them to wars, and much else ? The solution

is very simple if the question is considered from the only standpoint which is adequate — the religious standpoint. From the religious point of view man cannot and should not exercise violence toward his neighbor; and therefore to solve the question one thing is necessary: to destroy all the superstitions and sophisms which admit violence, and to instil into men the religious principles which clearly exclude the possibility of violence.

But the leaders not only refrain from this, but use all their mental subtlety to hide from men the possibility and necessity of this solution. They write a mountain of books about various rights — civil, criminal, police, ecclesiastical, financial, and so forth, and dilate and dispute on these themes, quite persuaded that they are doing not only a useful but a very important work. As to the question why amongst men who are in essence equal, some judge, coerce, plunder, and execute others, — to this they not only give no answer, they do not even recognize its existence. According to their doctrine it appears that these acts of violence are accomplished, not by men, but by some sort of abstraction called The State.

In the same way the scientists of our day avoid and pass by in silence all the essential questions and hide the inner contradictions in all spheres of knowledge.

In the sphere of historical knowledge there is only one question — How the workers, that is, 999 thousandths of all mankind, lived? To this question there is not even the semblance of an answer. The question does not even exist, but mountains of books are written by historians of one class about the stomach-aches of Louis XI., about the villainies of Elizabeth of England and Ivan the Terrible, and who were their ministers, and what verses and comedies were composed by the *litterateurs* for the amusement of these kings and their mistresses and ministers; while the historians of another class write about the importance of the land in which the peoples lived, what they ate, what they traded in, and what clothes they wore, — in general about everything which had no influence on the life of the people but was the result of their religion, which is regarded by the historians of this category as itself the result of the food and clothing used by the people.

And yet the answer to the question, how the workers formerly lived, can be given only by recognizing religion as the necessary condition of the life of the people. And therefore the answer is to be found in the study of the religions professed by the nations, which placed them in their several positions.

In the sphere of natural sciences one would think there was no particular necessity for obscuring the common sense of people, but here also, owing to the trend of thought which the science of our day has taken, instead of the most natural answers to the question, What is the description of this world of human beings, plants, and animals, and how is it subdivided? — only idle, obscure, and utterly useless chatter is circulated, chiefly directed against the Biblical story of the creation of the world, and about how organisms originated, which is really of no use to any one, and besides cannot be ascertained, as this origin, however we explain it, will always be concealed from us in the infinitude of time and space. And on these themes theories, refutations, and supplementary theories have been invented which form the subject of millions of books, and the unexpected deduction from which is only one: That the law of life to which man must submit is the struggle for existence. More than this, practical sciences like technology and medicine, in consequence of the absence of a leading religious principle, involuntarily diverge from a rational end and take a false direction. Thus all technology is directed, not to the end of alleviating the labor of the people, but to improvements necessary only for the wealthy classes, and which tend to separate still further the rich from the poor, the masters from the slaves. And if certain advantages from these inventions and improvements, some crumbs, fall to the lot of the masses, this is not at all because they have been apportioned, but only because they are of such a character that they cannot be kept back.

And so with medical science, which has in its false

direction reached that stage where it is accessible only
to the wealthy classes, whereas the masses, owing to
their mode of life and their poverty, and to the neglect
of the chief problems of the amelioration of the life of
the poor, can only profit by it in such proportions and
under such conditions that its help only demonstrates
more clearly the deviation of medical science from its
proper end.

But these deviations from, and the distortion of, the
essential problems is most astounding in what is called
Philosophy. One would think there is one problem
which philosophy ought to solve: What am I to do?
And if in the philosophies of Christian nations the
answers to this question have been unnecessarily associated with the greatest confusion, yet there were answers, in the teaching of Spinoza, of Kant in his "Kritik
of Practical Reason," of Schopenhauer, and especially of
Rousseau. But in later days, since the time of Hegel,
who recognized everything that is as rational, the question "What am I to do?" recedes into the background,
and philosophy directs the whole of its attention to the
investigation of that which is, and to conforming it to
a previously prepared theory. This is the first step
in the descent. The next step, which reduces human
thought yet lower, is the recognition of "struggle for
existence" as the fundamental law, merely because this
struggle is observable in animals and plants. According to this theory it is claimed that the destruction of
the weaker is a law which should not be opposed. Finally comes the third step, the mischievous attempts at
originality of a half-mad Nietzsche, which do not even
represent anything whole and connected, — the random
jottings of immoral thoughts founded on nothing, — but
which are recognized by advanced people as the last
word of philosophical science; and in answer to the
question "What am I to do?" one is told directly,
"Live for your own pleasure without attending to the
life of others."

If any one were to doubt that terrible stupefaction
and bestiality which has been attained by modern Chris-

tian humanity, then, leaving out of account the latest crimes, the Boer and Chinese wars, which are defended by the clergy and recognized as heroic feats by all in power, — this one extraordinary success of Nietzsche's writings may serve as an irrefutable proof. The disconnected writings of an agile but unintelligent and abnormal German, possessed of the mania of grandeur, appear, aiming at effect in the most trivial way. Neither in their ability nor their truth have these writings any real claim to the attention of the public. Such writings, not only in the time of Kant, Leibnitz, Hume, but even fifty years ago, would not only have failed to attract attention but could not even have appeared; whilst in our time, all so-called educated humanity is enchanted with the ravings of Mons. Nietzsche, refutes and interprets him, and his works are published in every language in innumerable copies.

Turgenieff has humorously said that reversed platitudes are often employed by incapable men to draw attention to themselves. For instance, every one knows that water is wet, but suddenly a man with a serious mien says that water is dry, alluding to ice, and such a statement, expressed with assurance, attracts attention.

Thus, also, the whole world knows that virtue consists in the subjugation of one's passions — in self-sacrifice. This is recognized not by Christianity alone, with which Nietzsche imagines he is fighting, — it is the eternal higher law which humanity has reached in Brahmanism, Buddhism, Confucianism, in the ancient Persian religion. And suddenly a man appears who declares that he has become persuaded that self-sacrifice, meekness, humility, love, are all vices which ruin mankind (he has in view Christianity, forgetting all other religions). One can understand that such an assertion staggers people at first. But having reflected a little and failed to find in the work any proof of this strange assertion, every rational man must thrust aside such a book, and only feel astonishment that in our time there is no absurdity too great to find a publisher. But with Nietzsche's books this is not the case. The majority of men, pseudo-

enlightened, examine the theory of the "Ober-Mensche"
seriously, and consider its author a great philosopher,
a successor to Descartes, Leibnitz, Kant.

And all this happens for this reason, that for the
majority of the pseudo-enlightened men of our day the
allusion to virtue and its principal basis, self-sacrifice,
love, which restrain and condemn their animal life, is
abhorrent, and it is pleasant to them to meet a doctrine
of cruelty asserting the justice of establishing one's
own happiness and greatness on the lives of the others
on whom we feed, even though expressed haphazardly,
illogically, disconnectedly.

CHAPTER XII

JESUS rebuked the Pharisees and Scribes for having
taken the keys of the Kingdom of Heaven, and neither
entered themselves nor allowed others to enter.

This is what is now being done by the scientific
Scribes of to-day : these men have taken the keys, not
of the Kingdom of Heaven, but of enlightenment, and
neither enter themselves nor admit others.   The augurs
— the Priesthood — by the means of every kind of deceit and hypnotism have persuaded men that Christianity is not a doctrine which preaches the equality of all
men and so destroys the entire modern heathen organization of life, but on the contrary that it supports it,
and dictates to men that they must distinguish some
from others, as stars are distinguished ; that they must
recognize that all power is from God, and willingly submit to it ; and in general persuades the oppressed that
their position is from God, and that they must bear it in
meekness and humility, and submit to those oppressors
who not only may not be meek and humble themselves,
but must, while correcting others, teach and punish, —
like Emperors, Kings, Popes, Bishops, and every class
of secular and spiritual rulers, — living meanwhile in a
splendor and luxury which it is the duty of their infe-
riors to supply.   It is, thanks to this false teaching,

which they support energetically, that those in power rule the people and force them to serve their idleness, luxury, and vices.

And the only men who are emancipated from the Church-hypnotism, and who alone might save the people from their oppression, and who say they do desire this, — the scientists, — instead of doing the things which might accomplish what they desire, do exactly the contrary, and imagine that they are thus serving the people.

One might think that the most superficial observation of that which above all preoccupies those who keep the people under their power would enable these men of science to understand what force moves and restrains nations in a certain position, and that they ought to direct all their attention to this force. But they not only fail to do this, — they regard it as utterly useless.

These men appear not to wish to see this, and they carefully, and often sincerely, do for the people the most varied things, but do not do that one thing which before all is necessary to the people. Their activity resembles that of a man who might endeavor to move a train by muscular efforts, — he need only mount the tender and do what he continually sees the engine driver do — turn the handle which admits the steam into the cylinder. This steam is the religious life-conception of men. And scientists need only observe with what jealousy all rulers reserve to themselves this motive force, through which they rule the nations, in order to understand to what their energies should be directed if they would liberate the people from their slavery.

What does the Turkish Sultan defend, and to what does he hold most closely? And why does the Russian Emperor, arriving at any town, go to kiss the local relics and *ikons* before he does anything else? And why, notwithstanding all the varnish of culture with which he covers himself, does the German Emperor, in all his speeches appropriately or inappropriately allude to God, to Christ, to the sanctity of religion and the oath, etc? Why, because they all know that their power is based

on the army, and the army, the possibility of the existence of the army, is based only on religion. And if the
wealthy are especially pious and pretend to be believers,
go to church and keep the Sabbath day, they do all this
chiefly because their instinct of self-preservation tells
them that their exceptionally advantageous position in
society is connected with the religion they profess.

These people often do not know in what way their
power is founded on the religious deceit, but through
the instinct of self-preservation they know where their
weak point lies, upon which their position is dependent,
and they protect this point before everything else.
These men will always permit, and have permitted within
certain limits, socialistic and even revolutionary propa-
ganda, but the religious foundations they will never
allow to be touched.

And therefore if the leaders of to-day, the Scientists,
Liberals, Socialists, Revolutionists, Anarchists, cannot
understand from psychology or history what it is which
moves nations, they might at least through this obvious
experience become convinced that the motive power lies,
not in material conditions, but only in religion.

But, strange to say, the scientists, the leaders of
to-day, whilst very excellently analyzing and understanding the conditions of the life of the nations, do not see
what so obviously strikes one in the face. If those who
act so leave the people in religious ignorance intentionally, in order to retain their advantageous position in
the minority, this is a terrible, an infamous deceit. Those
who so act are those very Pharisees whom more than
any one else, whom even alone amongst all men, Jesus
condemned — condemned because no monsters or mis-
creants have introduced and are introducing so much
evil into the life of mankind as they.

If, on the other hand, these men are sincere, then
the only explanation of this strange blindness is that,
as the masses are under the hypnotism of false religion,
so also these pseudo-enlightened people of to-day are
under the hypnotism of false science, which has decided
that the chief nerve by which humanity has always lived

and is living, is no longer necessary, and may be replaced by something else.

CHAPTER XIII

It is in this error or deceit of the Scribes — of educated men of our world — that the especial feature of our
period consists, and in this lies the cause of the calami-
tous state in which Christian humanity is living, and of
that animalism into which it is sinking deeper and
deeper.

Generally, the leading educated men of to-day assert
that those false religious beliefs which are held by the
masses are of no special importance, and that it is not
worth while to, nor is there any need of, contesting them
directly, as Hume, Voltaire, Rousseau, and others did.
Science, in their opinion, that is, that disconnected
casual information which they spread amongst the people, will attain this end by itself; that is, man, having
learnt how many millions of miles the earth is from the
sun, and what minerals the sun and stars contain, will
cease to believe in ecclesiastical doctrines.

In this sincere or insincere assertion or assumption
lies a great error or else a terrible piece of guile.
From earliest childhood, the age most receptive of
suggestion, at the very time when the educator cannot
be too careful about what he transmits, senseless and
immoral dogmas of so-called Christian religion, incompatible with reason or knowledge, are instilled into the
child. He is taught the dogma of the Trinity, un-
acceptable to common sense, the descent of one of
these three gods to earth to redeem the human race,
his resurrection and ascension to heaven; he is taught
to expect the second advent, and punishment with
eternal torments for unbelief in these dogmas; he is
taught to pray about his wants, and much else. And
when all these conceptions, opposed both to reason and
to modern knowledge, as well as to the human conscience, are ineffaceably printed on the receptive mind

of the child, he is left alone to discriminate as he can
among all those contradictions which follow from the
dogmas he has accepted and assimilated as the very
truth.   No one tells him how he can and should
reconcile these contradictions, and if theologians endeavor to reconcile them, their efforts only still further
confuse the matter.   And so by degrees the man becomes accustomed (and in this the theologians vigor-
ously support him) to the idea that one cannot trust in
reason and that therefore everything is possible in the
world, and that in man there is nothing by the aid of
which he can distinguish for himself good from evil and
falsehood from truth ; and that in what is most important for him — his conduct — he must be guided, not by
his reason, but by what other men tell him.   One can
understand what a terrible distortion must be produced
in the spiritual part of man by such an education,
maintained in maturity by all the means of hypnotic
suggestion which are continually being applied to the
people by the aid of the priesthood.

And if a man of strong spirit with great difficulty
and sufferings frees himself from the hypnotic influence
in which he was educated in childhood and confirmed in
maturity, then the distortion of his mind produced by
the persuasion that he must not trust his reason, cannot
pass away without leaving traces, just as in the physical
world the infection of an organism with a powerful
poison cannot pass without traces.   Having freed himself from the hypnotism of this deceit, such a man,
hating the lie from which he has just escaped, will
naturally adopt that theory of the leaders in which all
religion is regarded as one of the principal obstacles to
the advance of humanity along the way of progress.
And having adopted this view, such a man will become,
like his teachers, an unprincipled man ; that is, without
conscience, guided in life only by his lusts, and far from
condemning himself for this, will regard himself as on
the highest plane of mental development accessible to
humanity.

So it will be with the strong man.   Whereas the

weaker ones, although they may awake to doubt, will never altogether liberate themselves from that deceit in which they were educated, and accepting and inventing various ingeniously woven cloudy theories intended to justify the senselessness of the accepted dogmas, living in a region of doubts, mists, sophisms, and self-deceit, will only contribute to the blinding of the masses and to hindering their awakening.

And the masses, possessing neither the power nor the possibility of struggling with the hypnotic influence they are subjected to, will live and die, generation after generation, as they do now, bereft of the highest human welfare, — of a true religious understanding of life, — and will always be a passive tool in the hands of the classes which rule and deceive them.

And it is this terrible deceit that the scientific leading men say is not important and is not worth while fighting! The only explanation of such an assertion, if those who make it are sincere, is, that they are themselves under the hypnotism of false science. And, if they are not sincere, is, that to attack established beliefs is disadvantageous and often dangerous. One way or the other, at all events, the assertion that the profession of a false religion is harmless or merely unimportant, and that therefore one can spread enlightenment without destroying the religious deceit, is utterly untrue.

The salvation of mankind from their calamities lies only in their emancipation from that hypnotic influence in which they are held by their priests, as well as from that into which they are led by the scientists. Before one can pour anything into a vessel one must first empty it of what it already contains. So also it is necessary to free men from the deceit in which they are held in order that they may accept true religion, that is, a true relation to the source of all, — God, — corresponding to the development of humanity, and a guide for their actions deduced from this relation.

CHAPTER XIV

"But does a true religion really exist? All religions are infinitely different, and one has no right to call
any particular religion the true one merely because it
corresponds most nearly to our tastes," those will say
who examine religions in their externalities as some
sort of disease, from which they feel themselves free,
but from which others are still suffering. But this is
untrue: Religions are. different in their external forms,
but they are all the same in their fundamental principles.
And it is just these fundamental principles of all religions which represent that true religion which alone to-
day is natural to all men, and the acceptation of which
can alone save men from their calamities.

Humanity has existed for a long period, and just
as it has from generation to generation elaborated its
practical acquisitions, so also it could not help elabo-
rating those spiritual principles which have formed
the basis of its life, and the rules of conduct which follow from these principles. That blind men do not see
them is no proof that they do not exist.

Such a modern religion, common to all men, — not
some one particular religion with all its peculiarities and
distortions, but a religion consisting of those principles
which are the same in all the religions obtaining among
men and known to us, professed by more than nine-
tenths of the human race, — such a universal religion
does exist, and men have not yet become finally
brutalized only because the best men of all nations
adhere to this religion and profess it, even though
unconsciously, and it is only the inculcation of deceit
which is practised on men by the aid of the priests and
the scientists which hinders them from accepting it
consciously.

The principles of this true religion are so natural to
men that the moment they are communicated they are
accepted as something long familiar and self-evident.
For us this true religion is Christianity, in those of its

principles in which it coincides, not with the external
forms, but with the fundamental principles of Brahmanism, Confucianism, Taoism, Judaism, Buddhism, even
Mohammedanism. In the same way, for those who
profess Brahmanism, Confucianism, and so on, the
true religion will be the one the fundamental principles
of which coincide with those of all the other great religions. And these principles are very simple, comprehensible, and not numerous.

They assert that there is a God, the source of all;
that in man there is a particle of this divine element
which he can either diminish or increase by his life;
that to increase this element man must suppress his
passions and increase love in himself; and that the
practical means to attain this is to act with others as
one wishes others to act toward oneself. All these
principles are common to Brahmanism and Judaism and
Confucianism and Taoism and Buddhism and Christianity and Mohammedanism. (If Buddhism gives no definition of God it nevertheless recognizes that with which
man unites and into which he is immersed when he
reaches Nirvana. So that what man is united with
when immersed in Nirvana is the same essence which
is recognized as God in Christianity, Judaism, and
Mohammedanism.)

" But this is not religion," the men of our times who
are accustomed to accept what is supernatural, that is,
senseless, as the chief feature of religion, will say;
"this is anything you may like: philosophy, ethics,
reason, but not religion." Religion, according to their
conception, must be senseless and incomprehensible
(*credo quia absurdum*). And yet it was only out of
these very principles, or rather out of their being
taught as religious doctrine, that by a long process of
distortion all the absurdities about miracles and supernatural events which are regarded as the fundamental
features of religion were elaborated. To assert that
the supernatural and irrational elements represent the
essential features of religion, is like a man, while looking only at rotten apples, asserting that a repulsive

flavor and a pernicious effect on the digestion are the essential qualities of the apple as a fruit.

Religion must define the relation of man to the source of all, the destiny of man which follows from this relation, and the rules of conduct from this destiny. And the universal religion, the fundamental principles of which are identical in all faiths, entirely satisfies these demands. It defines the relation of man to God as that of a part to the whole; it deduces from this relation the function of man as the increase in himself of the divine element; and from this function it deduces practical rules from the principle of acting toward others as one wishes others to act toward oneself.

People often doubt, and I have myself at one time doubted, that such an abstract rule as the one that we should act toward others as we desire others to act toward oneself could be as obligatory a rule and guide in one's conduct as the more simple rules about fasting, prayer, communion, etc. But this doubt is irrefutably answered, if by nothing else, by the spiritual condition of the Russian peasant, who will rather die than spit the sacrament into the dust, although in obedience to the commands of men he is ready to kill his brothers.

Why should not the demands deduced from the rule of acting toward others as one wishes them to act toward oneself, — not to kill one's brothers, not to abuse men, not to commit adultery, not to revenge, not to profit by the need of one's brothers to satisfy one's fancies, and so on, — why should not these demands be instilled with the same strenuousness and become as obligatory and untransgressible as faith in the sanctity of the sacrament, *ikons*, and so on, for those whose faith is founded more on confidence than on a clear inner consciousness?

CHAPTER XV

THE truths of the universal religion of to-day are so simple, comprehensible, and near to the heart of every one that it would seem sufficient for all parents,

rulers, and teachers — instead of the outlived and senseless doctrines of Trinities, virgin mothers, redemptions,
Indras and Trimourtis, of Buddhas flying away into the
skies, of Mohammeds, in which they often do not themselves believe — to instil into children and adults those
clear, simple truths of the religion common to all men,
the metaphysical essence of which is that the Spirit of
God lives in man, and the practical rule of which is that
man should act toward others as he wishes others to act
toward himself, — for the whole life of mankind to
change of itself.

If instead of the faith that children are now taught
and adults are confirmed in, that God sent His Son
to redeem the sins of Adam, and to establish His Church
which must be obeyed, and the consequent rule that
one should pray and bring offerings at certain times
and at certain places, and refrain from a given food at
a given time and on certain days from work, — if
instead of this they were taught and confirmed in the
faith that God is a Spirit whose image lives in us, the
power of which we can increase by our conduct ; — if
only they were taught this and all that naturally follows
from these principles, in the same way that they are
taught at present those unnecessary legends, about impossible events and the rules of the senseless rituals
which follow from such tales, — then, instead of irrational strife and separation, very soon, without the help
of diplomatists, international law, peace congresses, political economists, and socialists of all sections, a peaceful,
friendly, happy life would come about for humanity,
directed by this sole religion.

But nothing of the sort is attempted : not only is the
deceit of false religion not destroyed and the true religion not preached, but on the contrary more and more
men farther and farther recede from the possibility of
accepting the truth.

The chief reason why people do not do what is so
natural, necessary, and possible, is that men of to-day,
owing to a prolonged irreligious life, have become so
accustomed to organize and establish their mode of liv-

ing by violence, — bayonets, bullets, prisons, gallows, — that they imagine such an order of life is not only nor- mal, but that no other is possible. Not only those to whom the existing order is advantageous think this, even those who suffer from it are so stupefied by the hyp- notic influence practised upon them that they also re- gard violence as the only means of securing good order in human society. And yet more than anything else this organization and establishment of social life by violence removes men from the possibility of under- standing the causes of their sufferings, and therefore from the possibility of true order; — like an incapable or ill-intentioned doctor when he drives inward a viru- lent eruption, thus not only deceiving the patient by his action, but increasing the disease itself and rendering a cure impossible.

To the rulers who have enslaved the masses and who think and say " After us, the Deluge," it appears very convenient, by the means of the army, the clergy, the police, and of the threats of bayonets, bullets, prisons, workhouses, gallows, to compel the enslaved people to continue to live in their stupefaction and slavery, and not to hinder the rulers from enjoying their position. And the rulers do this, and call it " right order," whereas nothing hinders true social order so much as this. In reality such an organization is not only not right order, but an organization of evil.

If the men of our world with the remnants of religious principles which still exist in the masses, had not con- tinually before their eyes the crimes of those who had taken upon themselves the duty of conserving social order and social morality, — by wars, executions, prisons, taxation, the sale of intoxicants and opium, — they would never have dreamed of carrying out one hundredth part of those evil deeds, deceits, acts of violence, murders, which they now carry out in the full persuasion that such deeds are good and natural.

The law of human life is of such a nature that the improvement of life, of the individual as well of society, is possible only by inward moral perfecting. Whereas

all the efforts of men to improve their life by external
influence and coercion serve as the most effective propa-
ganda and example of evil, and therefore fail not only
to improve life, but on the contrary increase the evil,
which, like a snowball, continually grows larger and
larger, and more and more removes people from the
only possibility of truly improving their life.

In proportion as the habit of violence and crimes
practised under the guise of law by the custodians of
order ana morality themselves becomes more and more
frequent and cruel, and is justified in greater measure
by the inculcation of falsehood uttered as religion,
people become more and more firmly established in the
idea that the law of their life is not love and mutual
service, but struggle and the devouring of each other.

And the more they become confirmed in this idea,
which lowers them to the plane of animals, the more
difficult is it for them to awaken from that hypnotic
influence to which they are subjected, and to accept as
the basis of life that true religion of our time common
to all humanity.

A vicious circle is established. The absence of religion renders an animal life founded on violence possible, and this animal life founded on violence renders
more and more impossible liberation from the hypnotic
influence and the assimilation of true religion. And
this is why people do not do what is natural, possible,
and necessary in our time: do not destroy the deceit of
the semblance of religion and do not accept and preach
the true religion.

CHAPTER XVI

Is any issue out of this enchanted circle possible, and
where is it?

It seems at first that the Governments, having taken
upon themselves the duty of guiding the life of nations
for the welfare of the nations, ought to lead men out of
the circle. So those who have endeavored to replace the

order of life founded on violence by a rational one founded on mutual service and love have always thought. So also thought Christian reformers, as well as the founders of the various theories of European Communism, and so also thought the famous Chinese reformer, Mi-Ti, who proposed to the Government to teach children in the schools not military sciences and exercies, and to give rewards to adults not for military exploits, but to teach children and adults the rules of respect and love, and to distribute prizes and encouragements for exploits of love.

And thus also many Russian religious reformers from the people have thought, whom I have known and of whom I now know many, from Sutaief to the old man who has already submitted a petition to the Emperor five times, begging him to command the canceling of the false religion and the preaching of true Christianity.

People naturally think that Governments who justify their existence by their care of national welfare must, in order to insure this welfare, desire to use that sole means which cannot in any way harm the people, but only produce the most fruitful results. But Governments have not only never and nowhere taken this duty upon themselves, but on the contrary have always and everywhere defended with the greatest jealousy the existing false and outlived religious teaching, and persecuted by every means those who have attempted to transmit to the people the foundations of true religion. And indeed it cannot be otherwise: for Governments to reveal the falsehood of the existing religion and to preach the true one would be like a man chopping the branch on which he is sitting.

But if Governments do not do this, it would seem that it certainly ought to be done by those men of science who, having freed themselves from the deceit of false religion, desire as they say to serve the people who have reared them. But these men, like the Governments, do not do this. Firstly, because they regard it as inexpedient to subject themselves to the unpleasant-

nesses and dangers of persecutions by the Governments
for revealing the deceit upheld by the Governments,
and which, according to the conviction of these men,
will disappear of itself; secondly, because, regarding all
religions as outlived errors, they have nothing to offer
the people in the place of the deceit which they might
overthrow.

There remain those great masses of unlearned people
under the hypnotic influence of the Church and Government deceit, and who therefore regard the semblance of religion instilled into them as the only true
religion, believing that there is not and cannot be any
other.   These masses are under the continual strenuous
influence of hypnotism; generation after generation is
born, lives, and dies in that stupefied state in which it is
held by the priesthood and Government; and if any
become freed from it, they inevitably drop into the
scientific school, which denies religion, and their influence becomes as useless and harmful as the influence
of their teachers.

So that for some it is disadvantageous, for others it is
impossible.

CHAPTER XVII

It looks as if there were no issue.

And indeed for irreligious people there is and can
be no issue from this position; people who belong
to the higher ruling classes, even if they pretend that
they are anxious about the welfare of the masses, will
never (nor can they, being guided by worldly motives)
seriously destroy that stupefaction and enslavement in
which these masses live, and which give the higher
classes the possibility of ruling over them.   In the
same way those also who belong to the enslaved, in
like manner being guided by worldly motives, cannot
desire to render worse their at present difficult position
by struggling with the higher classes for the purpose
of revealing the false teaching and preaching the true.

Neither have they any reason for doing so, and if they are intelligent men they never will do it.

But this is not so with religious people — those who, however depraved society may be, always by their lives preserve that sacred fire of religion without which human life could not exist. There are times (such is the present one) when these men are not seen, when, despised and humiliated by every one, they pass their lives obscurely, as with us in Russia, in exile, prisons, penal battalions, — but they exist, and on them depends the rational life of mankind. And it is these religious people, however few they may be, who alone can and will sever that enchanted circle in which men are riveted. These men can do this because all those disadvantages and dangers which prevent the worldly man from opposing the existing order of life, not only do not exist for the religious man, but increase his zeal in the struggle with falsehood, and in the profession by word and deed of that which he regards as divine truth. If he belongs to the ruling classes, he will not only not desire to conceal the truth out of regard to his advantageous position, but, on the contrary, having come to abhor these advantages, he will use all the powers of his soul to free himself from these advantages and to preach the truth, as he will no longer have any other object in life than that of serving God. If, on the other hand, he belongs to the enslaved, then, having likewise abandoned the desire common to people of his position, of bettering the conditions of his physical life, such a man will have no other object than the fulfilment of the will of God by revealing falsehood and professing the truth, and no sufferings or threats will any longer compel him to cease to live in accordance with that sole meaning which he has recognized in his life. Both the one and the other will act thus as naturally as the worldly man labors and undergoes privations for the possession of riches and for satisfying the ruler from whom he expects advantages. Every religious man acts thus because the human soul enlightened by religion no longer lives merely by the life of this world as irreligious people live, but lives by the eternal, infinite life, for which sufferings and death in this life are as insignificant as the corns on his hand and the fatigue of his limbs are insignificant to a laborer plowing a field.

It is these people who will sever the enchanted circle in which men are now riveted. However few they may be, however low their social position, however weak they may be in education and intellect, these men, as surely as fire ignites the dry prairie, will ignite the whole world, — all the hearts of men dried up from a long period of irreligious life and thirsting for renovation.

Religion is not a faith established once for all in supernatural events, supposed to have taken place at some time or other, or in the necessity of certain prayers and rites; neither is it, as the scientists think, the remains of the superstitions of ancient unenlightenment which in our time have no significance or adaptation to life: Religion is the relation of man to eternal life, to God, in accordance with reason and contemporary knowledge, which alone moves man forward toward the end for which he is intended.

"The human soul is a lamp of God," says a wise Hebrew proverb. Man is a weak, miserable animal until in his soul there burns the fire of God. But when this fire kindles (and it kindles only in a soul illumined by religion) man becomes the most powerful being in the world. And this cannot be otherwise, because then it is no longer *his* power which works in him, but the power of God.

So this is what religion is, and in what its essence consists.